The ISI Game Plan

Attention Authors

Manas Publications is fighting a war to tell the world that India can win the battle not only by the bullet but also by the pen. We are converting fighters into writers. There is no dearth of intellectuals in our country, however, their knowledge is confined to them only. No sincere effort has been made by any other publisher to give the right direction to their knowledge and the talent of every intellectual is lying hidden. An author always presents the raw material in the shape of a manuscript and it is the job of the publisher to convert it to a finished product. Manas has been continually motivating intellectuals and publishing their manuscripts for more than two decades and would like to publish your manuscript too. If you or your colleagues have a manuscript ready for publication or are working on it, contact us with a detailed synopsis and list of contents. Manas will also suggest you a suitable title for writing related to your area of expertise. Manas is known for its publishing quality. We take utmost care in publishing and also give wide publicity to the book and its author through our national and international distribution network.

The ISI Game Plan

A Novel by

Brig YPS Mohan, VSM

Manas Publications
New Delhi-110002 (INDIA)

MANAS PUBLICATIONS
(Publishers-Distributors-Importers-Exporters)
4402/5-A, Ansari Road (Opp. HDFC Bank)
Darya Ganj, New Delhi - 110 002 (India)
Phones: Off.: 011-23260783, 23265523,
Res.: 011-23842660
E-mail: manaspublications@gmail.com
manaspub6@gmail.com
www.manaspublications.in

2018

ISBN 978-81-7049-356-3

Rs. 495/-

Designed at
Manas Publications

Printed in India at
HS Offsets, Delhi
and published by Mrs Suman Lata for
Manas Publications, 4402/5-A,
Ansari Road (Opp HDFC Bank),
Darya Ganj, New Delhi - 110002 (INDIA)

For
Sushila,
Akanksha and
Abhinandan

Preface

The ISI Game Plan is a thriller based on factual fiction. I am aware that Indian writers in English have hardly ever attempted this genre. It is said that fools rush in where angles fear to tread. I am not rushing in but trudging in slowly, cautiously and anxiously into an arena that I have observed and admired only from the outside so far. It is the prerogative of the reader to decide whether or not I have succeeded in my venture as a writer of a thriller.

I share a belief with most of my countrymen that most of the terrorist attacks in India are sponsored by the Inter Services Intelligence of Pakistan. The ISI Game Plan is based on this belief. It appears that the ISI feels that it can achieve its objectives only by bleeding India. It does not realize that our democracy has made our country a strong and stable country. Overt and covert operations of the ISI only strengthen our resolve to stay united and emerge even stronger than before as has been proved by the Mumbai attacks of 26/11. How much do I wish that the ISI would one day realize the follies of their hate policies and start acting in a responsible manner!

I believe the people of Pakistan and their democratically elected governments always want peace to prevail in the Indian subcontinent. Unfortunately, that is not the case with the ISI. I hope the day is not far when the rogue elements in the ISI will be reigned in by the Government of Pakistan. I see a day, in not so distant future, when India and Pakistan will live like brothers and work together towards alleviation of poverty and illiteracy from the sub continent.

I wish to thank some of my friends and well wishers for their help and encouragement in helping me make my dream of writing a book come true. Notable among them are Maj Gen SK Sen, VSM (Retd); Maj Gen V Sadasivam, VSM, Shri VS Saxena and Brig G Bhuiyan for their help in revising the manuscript of this book. I also wish to thank my publishers for having reposed their trust in a budding writer.

YPS Mohan

Chapter 1

15 March

Islamabad

Lieutenant General Raheel Ginai, the Chief of the Inter-Services Intelligence (ISI) of Pakistan, was quite intrigued to receive the American request for an urgent one-on-one meeting with Gordon Mathews, Director of the United States National Security Council (NSC) to discuss Kashmir. The meeting was scheduled for today.

NSC is an important policy making body of the US government. It aims to protect the American interests in foreign countries. While the better known CIA, which has similar responsibilities, is an autonomous body, the little known NSC is a political cum intelligence organization working under the incumbent Secretary of State. Since the

Director of NSC has direct access to the Secretary of State, he wields fair bit of clout with the US government and with the foreign intelligence agencies.

Over the years, the ISI too has earned the reputation for being one of the most powerful intelligence agencies in the world. It is often described by its counterparts as a "State within a State". The media in Pakistan often calls it as "our invisible government" or as "our secret godfathers".

The ISI is generally proud of its accomplishments. But what pains it the most is the fact that despite all the operations that it has undertaken in India over the years, it has not succeeded in one of its main objectives, which is to help Pakistan wrest Kashmir from India. It was not surprising, therefore, that when the Americans approached Ginai for an urgent meeting to discuss Kashmir, he made it clear to them that he would be interested only if the Americans had something concrete to offer to Pakistan on the issue. In return, he was prepared to do anything for them, even help them in their endeavour to capture the Command Centre of Al Qaeda.

It is an open secret that the ever mobile Command Centre of Al Qaeda functions from somewhere in the hills on the Afghanistan-Pakistan border and even after trying for all these years, the Americans still have not been able to get any clue of its exact whereabouts. They are sure, however, that the ISI is not as clueless about the location and movements of Al Qaeda headquarters as they themselves are. It suits the ISI not to dispel this impression.

So when the Americans insisted on a one-on-one meeting with General Ginai, he allowed a sense of anticipation to overtake him.

"Sir, Mr. Gordon Mathews," announced Major Qureshi, the staff officer to the ISI chief, when he opened the door to usher in the US NSC Director into the chamber of his boss.

"Good morning, General Ginai!" said Gordon Mathews, as he walked briskly towards the chief's table. He was a tall and well built American, about fifty years of age, wearing a navy blue suit with a striped tie on a white shirt.

"Good morning, Mr. Mathews," responded the chief as he got up from his chair and extended his right hand to his guest. "Welcome to Pakistan!"

"Thank you," said Gordon Mathews as he shook hands with his host across the table.

"Please sit down."

"Thank you!"

"Thank you Qureshi!" the chief waived off his staff officer. "Please make sure that we are not disturbed by anyone."

"Roger sir," affirmed Major Qureshi as he walked out of the room and closed the door behind him.

"So Mr. Mathews! How are you?"

"Not too bad. What about you?"

"I can't wait to hear what brings you here today!"

"I like that. Straight to business, without wasting any time."

"I take it as a compliment. So please tell me what is so urgent that you want to discuss with me on Kashmir?"

Gordon Mathews took a deep breath. "I think, General," he said as he leaned forward, "we have a solution to the Kashmir problem."

"To us there is only one solution. Kashmir belongs to us. But it is under enemy occupation."

"And that occupation must be vacated."

"Absolutely!"

"Perhaps our help will be desirable in this regard."

"Not desirable. It is essential. I am aware of that."

"We are prepared to help you, provided ...."

"Provided?"

"Provided you help us get the Command Centre of Al Qaeda."

"Is Pakistan not doing enough already to get you Al Qaeda, Mr. Mathews?"

"I am not talking of Pakistan. I mean, the Government of Pakistan. I am talking of the help of the ISI."

"Aren't we under the Government of Pakistan?"

"Let us not get into that. You are an intelligent man and I am not dumb either."

There was a long silence.

"Anything else?" asked the ISI chief.

"Yes," Mathews replied. "You will have to make some concessions to the Indians and give some guarantees."

"What are those concessions?" asked Ginai. "And what are those guarantees?"

"Well, General Ginai, our proposal is a compromise between the stated position of India and the seven-point formula floated by General Pervez Musharraf in 2004. You will get Kashmir; virtually, the whole of the Kashmir Valley. But you will withdraw from the Karakoram range in upper Ladakh and from the areas adjoining Jammu below the Pir Panjal range. Jammu will remain with India and Azad Kashmir with you. The Karakoram range in Ladakh and the areas near Jammu below the Pir Panjal range will go to India. After all, the Indian leaders too have to show some territorial gains to their people in lieu of the Kashmir valley in the cause of lasting peace!"

The ISI chief pondered over the proposal for a long time. Gordon Mathews decided not to rush him into any hasty response.

"Have the Indians accepted your proposal?" asked the chief after he had analysed the pros and cons of the American proposal.

"We have not spoken to them on the subject yet", replied Gordon Mathews.

"Then what makes you so sure that they will accept your proposal?"

"For that, we will have to create certain conditions which should not be too difficult. But before I spell out these conditions, I would like to have your views on this proposal."

"Your proposal sounds good because for us, Kashmir essentially means Kashmir valley. All other areas are negotiable. But you have come to the wrong person. I do not have the mandate to decide on such issues. It is only the Government of Pakistan that can take such decisions."

"I know that. But the proposal can move forward only if it has the backing of the ISI and the Pak army. We know your worth. If you agree, only then the Secretary of State will take up the matter with your President, General!"

Ginai closed his eyes and pondered over the proposal in silence for some more time. "You mentioned some guarantees as well," he pointed out to his guest as he opened his eyes.

"Well", began Gordon Mathews, "the guarantees that we require are that you will stop support to all jihadi organizations fighting against the West and India. You will stop interfering in the internal affairs of India. They, in turn, will guarantee not to interfere in yours. You will help us persuade your army and your government in dismantling your nuclear program. You won't need it, in any case, after you get Kashmir. We do not want your weapons to fall into jihadi hands. And lastly, and most importantly, you will help us find Al Qaeda's headquarters in a month's time at the most, after you get India's acceptance on handing over Kashmir to Pakistan."

There was a period of long silence.

"You also said that some conditions have to be created for the Indians to accept this proposal," the chief pointed out.

"Yes. For that we need your help."

"What kind of help?"

"That is a difficult one", replied Gordon Mathews. "Well! Um..... Pakistan will have to invade Kashmir."

"Invade Kashmir?"

"Yes. Invade Kashmir."

"And Indians will be waiting for us on the LOC with garlands and sweets in their hands?"

"I have no doubt in my mind that the Indians will confront you with all the might of their armed forces."

"You want our men to get butchered at their hands? Mr. Mathews, I thought you were a reasonable man."

"No one will butcher anyone. General Ginai, you are missing my point. We want you to invade Kashmir to provoke India into declaring war against Pakistan. Once that is done, you will threaten India with your nukes, though, not actually use them. Indians too will be compelled to threaten you with their nukes. That will create a perfect ground for the United Nations to intervene. The Security Council will then pass a resolution to settle Kashmir dispute, once and for all, on the lines I have just explained to you. We shall bring full international pressure on India to accept the resolution. I am sure Indians will find it well nigh impossible not to accept it. Once Kashmir dispute is resolved, you will be required to fulfil your part of the deal. I hope it makes sense to you now!"

"It indeed does," the ISI chief admitted. The ISI chief had listened to Gordon Mathews with awe and admiration at the sheer audaciousness of the proposal. But deep down in his heart he knew that difficult problems could be solved only with crazy solutions. "I admire your planning," commented the chief, "but I still have my doubt if you can make the Indians accept this proposal. After all, their politicians never tire of proclaiming that Kashmir is Bharat ka atoot ang - an inseparable part of India?"

"You need not bother about that," assured Gordon Mathews. "This proposal will be fully backed by the United Nations.

This time there will be no veto in the Security Council on the Kashmir resolution. We'll ensure that. All major powers want an end to the Islamic jihad against the West. That is possible only if we get your support against Al Qaeda. We know you will support us only if we help you get Kashmir."

"OK, Mr. Mathews" said the chief. "Give me some time to think and discuss the details with my senior officers. I will get back to you at the earliest."

"Please do, General Ginai," said Gordon Mathews while leaving. "I hope we will hear from you some time soon?"

"I hope so too, Mr. Mathews!" said the ISI chief.

"But just one word of caution General Ginai, before I leave," said Gordon Mathews. "On Al Qaeda, we have run out of our patience. I have made you a reasonable proposal and this time we expect total cooperation from you. If we don't get Al Qaeda, don't blame us for doing an Iraq or Afghanistan in Pakistan."

Chapter 2

21 March

It was one of those days when the lead story in all the national dailies in New Delhi was the same. It was the report of the third major Cabinet reshuffle at the Centre since the formation of the government of Prime Minister Prabhat Rai. The reshuffle was announced, the previous night, on the eve of the third anniversary of his government. The reshuffle was seen as an indicator of the performance of various ministers. Those who did well in relatively less important ministries, were 'promoted' to the 'A' grade ministries, which included Home, Defence, Finance, Commerce and External Affairs. The incumbents of 'A' grade ministries who did not come up to the expectations of the Prime Minister, had to make way for the upcoming and promising ministers.

In the current reshuffle, while Finance Minister Vinayak Bagchi, Commerce Minister Birender Singh and Minister of External Affairs Zafar Khan had kept their places, the ones holding Home and Defence portfolios were shifted to less important ministries. Sukhraj Malik, who had run the Ministry of Railways efficiently over the last three years, was given the portfolio of Home and Raman Kumar, the successful Human Resource Development Minister over the same period, was elevated as the new Defence Minister. The media widely viewed the change in the portfolios of Malik and Kumar as richly deserved promotion for the two competent ministers. Their elevation assumed additional significance because now they also became members of the all important Cabinet Committee on Security (CCS). As per the declared policy of Prabhat Rai's government, the five ministers in charge of the 'A' grade ministries automatically became members of the CCS by virtue of the offices they held. CCS, which was headed by the Prime Minister himself, handled all the important decisions of the government relating to the security of the country.

At eight in the evening, Prime Minister Prabhat Rai went on the air to deliver his anniversary address to his compatriots on the health of the nation.

"My dear fellow countrymen," began the Prime Minister, reading from the prepared text. "It is a matter of great pride for me to address you on completion of three years of my party leading the National Progressive Alliance government at the Centre. During the last three years we have tried our very best to do all that was needed to be done to improve the lot of all sections of our society, particularly of the poorest of the poor. We have succeeded in most of our endeavours, as any impartial observer would testify. But I realize all too well that for all that we have been able to achieve, a lot more still needs to be done. The reforms that we have undertaken, in the fields of economy, education and social uplift of the weaker sections of our society, are now beginning to show their results. Yet, in order to take these reforms to their logical conclusion, I call upon the support of all such people who share with us our plans, our objectives, our policies and our dreams. We will continue with these reforms with renewed vigour in the days to come so that we can realize all our cherished dreams. The dreams, where the poor will have stars in their eyes not tears; they will have smiles on their faces, not fear; they will lead a life they would love to live."

The Prime Minister continued to speak in this lyrical manner for some time. He spoke about the economic programs, the social imperatives and the political reforms that his government intended to tackle in the coming year. He also spoke on the environment in some detail. Towards the end of his speech, he moved on to foreign affairs.

"In foreign affairs we shall continue to be guided by the principles of equal opportunities for all nations. We will continue to resist the imposition of one-sided judgments by strong nations on the weak. Self-interest, self-determination and self-reliance are as important to small nations as to major powers. Our number one priority in foreign affairs, however, would be our attempts to secure close ties and closer cooperation with our neighbouring countries. While the long time enemies in the rest of the world are making peace with each other, we are still plagued by mutual distrust and self doubt. The time has come when we must learn to trust one another, respect one another and live like brothers. We have so much in common with one another that by learning to live in harmony and peace, we have nothing to lose and everything to gain. I call upon the leaders in our neighbouring countries to hold the hand of friendship that we have extended to them so that together we can make progress; together we can realize our cherished dreams."

"Together my foot!" murmured the ISI Chief with contempt. He was monitoring the speech of the Indian Prime Minister on the TV in his office in Islamabad where he often sat late. "I know Mr. Rai, this is a conspiracy to finish my country. Otherwise where is the need to develop and test fire Rudra, your Medium Range Ballistic Missile, and buy a full squadron of Sukhoi-33 fighter aircraft from Russia which are capable of delivering nukes anywhere in Pakistan? All your bus journeys, all your train links and all your so-called Confidence Building Measures are a ploy to make us complacent. You want us to become complacent so that you can strike at us at the first available opportunity and blow us apart. But don't think that we are fools Mr. Rai! You will soon see what we are capable of doing."

The ISI chief got up from his chair and switched off the TV. The Indian Prime Minister had already finished his address to the nation.

General Raheel Ginai was extremely proud of the position that he held. He was fiercely nationalist and a devout Muslim. He was a workaholic and considered leisure a sign of moral degradation. His obsession for hard work and his informal lifestyle had won him great respect and admiration from his subordinates. To them, working for their chief and working for their country was one and the same thing. His subordinates believed that if there was one person in Pakistan who could devise a strategy to wrest Kashmir from India, it was General Ginai. For the politicians in Pakistan, Kashmir was the core issue. For the ISI, Kashmir was the only issue that mattered.

Being a Kashmiri himself, General Ginai nursed a burning desire to vacate the Indian "occupation" of Kashmir before he retired from service in about a year's time. The Indian Prime Minister's speech made him even more resolute than before to pursue Gordon Mathews's proposal on Kashmir with vigour.

General Ginai picked up the phone and dialed the number of his friend in the foreign intelligence agency whose name starts with a capital C.

Chapter 3

22 March

The last paper in the annual examination of the final year of Master's Degree in Mass Communication and Advertising was completed at 12 noon, barely 10 minutes earlier. There was a lot of excitement outside the examination hall in the Delhi University campus.

"I could not complete my last question yaar. But to hell with it! I am so happy that the damn exam is finally over."

"Over! Yes it is over, man! What a terrific feeling! No bugs, no jigs. We are free birds man! We are free birds now!"

"What does it mean yaar? Bugs! Jigs!"

"Hee ! Hee! Hee! You Harrys! You don't know anything man! Hee! Hee!"

"Bugs is books. Jigs is classes."

"That is Chinky English for you."

"Hee! Hee! Hee!"

"Well, folks! How do we celebrate the big day?"

"With booze. Easy!"

"Booze is for the beginners. Speed! Speed for me!"

"To hell with you and your speed."

"We must go beering yaar! It is indeed an occasion to be celebrated with beer."

"No such stuff for me."

"Go to your mama and ask for a bottle of milk, eh!"

"Thanks for your suggestion. But I would rather go to the canteen and have something to eat right now. Anybody joining me?"

"Beer, booze this side, please! Invitation to all to come to 180, Doctor Mukherjee Nagar."

"Who will foot the bill?"

"Enough raddi. A room full of old books. Raddiwala is on his way."

"Speed man, speed. Any takers?"

Soon they dispersed in small groups in various directions. One group went to the canteen, the other to the hostel and yet another to Doctor Mukherjee Nagar. The remaining students left in twos and threes to destinations of their choice. Sunita Mathur and Yogesh Naqvi formed one such twosome. They looked to be a made-for-each-other couple.

Yogesh Naqvi had a Hindu first name and a Muslim surname. His mother was a Hindu and his father, late Maior Saif Naqvi was a Shia Muslim. Yogesh was a handsome young man. He was 5'8" tall, had a slim but strong body, wheatish complexion, an attractive face, neatly trimmed hair and, as always, was meticulously dressed. He was a devoted student with a very good academic record.

Sunita Mathur was a Kayastha Hindu. She was a graceful young woman and she too was a brilliant student. She was about 5'4" in height, had fair complexion, long black hair, shining eyes, lovely face and a well proportioned figure. Yogesh and Sunita had been very close to each other during the two years of their college life. Both knew that they had developed a soft corner for each other but strangely enough, they kept their feelings to themselves.

Today they got together instinctively and started walking towards the Coffee House that was located on the other side of the campus.

"Two coffees, please," ordered Yogesh as the waiter removed the empty dosa plates from their table. The dosa, that the two had eaten, was good but neither Sunita nor he could relish it. Ever since they left their friends outside the examination hall and came to the Coffee House, some kind of tension appeared to have cropped up between the two of them. They knew that they had already let two years pass by without admitting their true feelings towards each other. Now that they would no longer be attending their classes together, one of them would have to take the initiative and then let events take their own course. Sunita was relieved when Yogesh, at last, appeared to have decided to take the lead.

"Sunita!"

"Yes, Yogesh!" she responded, her heart pleading with him to say those three words that would be music to her ears.

The waiter placed two cups of coffee on the table. They added sugar to their respective cups and stirred the coffee.

"I want you to meet my mother," said Yogesh.

Sunita had known that one day Yogesh would ask her to meet his mother. She had decided to tease him by insisting on knowing why he wanted her to meet his mother, before agreeing to it.

"When?" That was all that Sunita could utter when the moment came.

"You tell me." Yogesh replied.

"Why not today? We can go to your house and meet her today. In fact, I am dying to meet her."

"Why?"

"Because," Sunita replied, taking a deep breath and looking straight into his eyes, "I want to ask her why she has made her son such a coward. He loves a girl but cannot tell her that he loves her."

Her reply startled Yogesh. He blushed for a while and then gave a low, relaxed laugh. He looked up and saw her sitting calm, confident and composed. He loved her even more for that. He laughed again. This time he laughed aloud.

"Come," he said as he made the payment to the waiter. "Let us go to my house. I am sure Ma will be glad to meet the girl with whom her son is madly in love and with whom he is going to spend the rest of his life."

Sunita and Yogesh took the metro from Delhi University to reach Safdarjung, the station closest to RK Puram where Yogesh lived with his mother. They indulged in casual conversation on the way.

"Don't stare at me like that, Yogesh!"

"I am not staring at you."

"Then why don't you look at other girls too? There are many pretty faces in this coach."

"None is prettier than you."

"Why didn't you tell me before?"

"Why didn't you ask me before?"

"Yogesh, how long have you been in love with me?"

"From the very first day I saw you two years ago."

"And you wasted two years in expressing your love for me?'

"I was not sure."

"Sure of what?'

"Of your reaction. I was afraid that you might reject me. Sony, I did not want to be rejected".

"No one wants to be rejected."

"How long have you been in love with me?'

"I don't know!"

"Please Sony! This is not fair!"

"OK. Let me try to recall. Um... I think I fell in love with you when I found out that you were in love with me."

"But I never told you earlier that I was in love with you!"

"You didn't have to tell, silly. I just knew it."

"Then why didn't you tell me?"

"I was waiting for the right moment. And that moment came only today."

"Oh poor me! I wish this day had come two years ago!"

"Things happen only when they have to happen. Now stop chattering because Safdarjung Station has already come."

"So fast?"

"How do we go to RK Puram from here?"

"Bus number 615 will take us home my dear and Ma should be there by now."

Sunita knew all about Yogesh's mother. She was a widow and Yogesh was her only son. His father Major Saif Naqvi had been an officer in the Indian Army. He was killed fighting the insurgents in the northeast more than twenty years ago. Yogesh was barely a year old at that time and his mother hardly twenty-five. She had married Saif against the wishes of her parents. They had severed all ties with her when she announced her decision to marry a Muslim boy. The only member of her family who supported her decision was her brother Sanjay Sarang, who too was an army officer and a close friend of Saif. In fact it was through Sanjay that the two had first met. He was the only person present from the bride's side during their wedding.

After the untimely death of her husband, Yogesh's mother moved to Delhi. She took a job as a teacher in a government school and devoted her entire time, attention and energy to her son and her students. She had also become deeply religious. Yogesh was very much attached to his mother. Though she could not afford to give him the many luxuries during his childhood and adolescence that many of his classmates enjoyed, she did not let him feel deprived of the joys of childhood and boyhood either. When, after completing his degree in commerce two years earlier, he asked his mother to allow him to study for a Postgraduate Diploma in Mass Communication and Advertising, she readily agreed.

Sunita had joined her PG course after completing BA (Honours) in Economics. She had liked Yogesh from the very first day they had met in one of the early classes. His being a half Hindu and half Muslim, like the reigning Bollywood superstar Shahid Kapoor, was also a factor in Sunita being attracted to him.

Sunita and Yogesh always enjoyed each other's company. It was their upbringing that came in their way in expressing their love to each other. He, being the only son of his mother, felt a kind of obligation towards her and wanted to stand on his own feet before building a new relationship. Sunita was the daughter of caring parents who were like friends to her. She and her younger brother Sumit both had emotionally rich and contented childhood. Her father S.N. Mathur was a civil servant. He was a very well read person. Books were his first love. Her mother was a perfect foil for her thinking husband. She was his greatest critic. The husband and wife were deeply attached to each other. They did everything to make each other happy and gave full attention to their children

Sunita had learned the value of a disciplined life from her parents. Studies had been her first priority in school and college. She had decided early on that she would not allow herself to drift into temporary liaisons and think of a permanent relationship only after completing her studies.

"Ma, meet Sunita," said Yogesh, introducing her to his mother as soon as she opened the door. "She is my classmate. And, Sunita, meet Mrs. Naqvi, my mother. Call her Ma."

"Namaste, Ma," said Sunita with folded hands as she met his mother, a serene looking middle-aged woman, with partly grey hair, pale-white complexion and a sober expression on her face.

"Namaste, my child," said the woman with a smile on her face. "Please come in."

Yogesh and Sunita moved into the drawing room that was sparsely but aesthetically furnished.

"Sit down, Sunita, and you too, Yogesh," said.Mrs. Naqvi, pointing towards the sofa. She gave a long, loving glance to Sunita.

"Ma," called Yogesh as if asking his mother to stop staring at her. "Sunita has wanted to meet you for quite some time. So, today as the exam was over, I asked her to come with me to meet you."

"That was very nice of you," said his mother, "I am myself so glad to see her. But tell me first, how was your paper today?"

"It was Okay Ma. I think I did well."

"And what about you, Sunita?"

"I think I did well too."

"How did you do with your earlier papers?"

"Well, I am quite satisfied with my performance," replied Sunita. "But more importantly, I am happy that the exam is finally over. Perhaps we may not have to sit for another such exam ever in the future."

"You are right," Yogesh intervened to prolong the conversation. "However well you prepare, the examination makes you feel nervous. No more exams for us now. Only job interviews."

"I hope you won't have any problems there," said Mrs. Naqvi. "What would you have Sunita? Have you taken lunch?"

"Yes, Ma, we have had it," replied Sunita.

"We had dosa in the Coffee House," added Yogesh.

"What about you?" Sunita asked the lady. "I hope you were not waiting for Yogesh?"

"No, Sunita, I do not eat any lunch. I only take a late breakfast and an early dinner. A habit with me for more than twenty years now."

"How can you do that, Ma? I can't do without lunch even for a day!"

"When I was young I also used to be like you," said Mrs. Naqvi with a smile. "It is good to have strong appetite when you are young."

Sunita wanted to point out to her that twenty years earlier, when she decided to skip lunch; she must have been just about as young as Sunita was today. But she decided not to press the point any further.

"I'll make cold coffee," said Mrs. Naqvi. "I hope you like it, Sunita?"

"I love it."

Mrs. Naqvi got up from her seat and moved towards the kitchen. Suddenly she halted, turned back, looked at her son and asked, "Yogesh, why don't you go to the market and bring some cake and pastries?"

"I think there is no need, Ma," said Yogesh. "What about you Sunita?"

"Yes. No need really!" she replied.

"Yogesh, please do as I say," said his mother.

Yogesh could now make out that his mother wanted to spend some time with Sunita alone. He got up and left, smiling to himself. "OK, Ma, as you wish."

"Sunita," called Yogesh's mother.

"Yes, Ma."

"You mind if I ask you to join me in the kitchen?"

"Not at all. My pleasure!"

Sunita was impressed to see everything kept so well in the kitchen. She saw Mrs. Naqvi proceed methodically, collecting the items required to make cold coffee - the blender, the sugar and the coffee powder. She then took milk and ice from the refrigerator.

"Sunita," Mrs. Naqvi said, even as she continued to do her work. "I know my son well enough. I know that if he has brought you home to meet me, you must be someone special to him. Tell me honestly, how special are you to him?"

Sunita blushed, as she did not expect herself to be in a situation where she would have to answer that question to her would be mother-in-law in their first meeting.

"Don't feel shy, my dear," said Mrs. Naqvi reassuringly. "Tell me how special are you to him or he to you?"

"Well, we have known each other for the last two years and we like each other," replied Sunita, still blushing.

"Does it mean that you love each other?"

"Yes," said Sunita. This time a little more confidently.

"Does it also mean that you wish to marry?" asked Mrs. Naqvi, looking smilingly at her.

"Well, Ma, if you permit."

Mrs. Naqvi pressed the button and the machine began to whirr to blend the coffee. She allowed it to run for about two minutes and then pushed the stop button. She then turned back and took Sunita's face in her hands. She looked at her young, beautiful face and said, "God bless you, my child. I trust my son's judgement. I am sure that you are the right match for Yogesh and I can assure you that he too will be a worthy life partner for you."

Tears came to her eyes as she spoke. She lifted her hands from Sunita's face, turned and spoke again, "Give me that jug, please!"

She wiped her tears with the help of one corner of her sari. Sunita felt immensely close to her as she handed over the jug to her. She came very close to hugging her but refrained from actually doing it.

"We will wait for Yogesh to come and then serve it," said Mrs. Naqvi, as she put coffee into the jug. She cleaned the machine and carefully put each item back in its place. She then asked Sunita to follow her to the drawing room.

They sat on the sofa, facing each other. There was silence for a few moments before Mrs. Naqvi composed herself and spoke, "Sunita, please tell me something about your family."

"Sure, Ma" she replied. "My father is in government service. His name is Mr S.N. Mathur. Presently he is posted as Chief Postmaster General of Delhi. My mother is a housewife. I have a brother, Sumit, who is about five years younger than me. He has just finished his school finals. He and I have both done our schooling in Central Schools at various places in the country as my father has a transferable job. I did my BA (Honours) in Economics from KM College and then joined this PG Course in Mass-Comm and Advertising." She paused to think what more to say.

"Do your parents know about you and Yogesh?" asked Mrs. Naqvi.

"Yogesh has been to our house on a few occasions and has met my family," replied Sunita. "But they only know that he is a good friend of mine. In fact, Ma, I am feeling a bit embarrassed to tell you that it is only today for the first time that we have declared our feelings towards each other. We knew that we were fond of each other but somehow we could never manage to express ourselves to each other earlier. Perhaps we both wanted to complete our studies first."

Mrs. Naqvi smiled and said, "That is a remarkably high self-restraint for young people to show these days!"

"Hardly that, Ma," said Sunita. "We haven't wasted even a day once the final exam is over. To be honest, I am surprised at the speed at which the events are taking place. At this speed we might even get married before the month is over!"

"Why not?" said Mrs. Naqvi in an excited voice. "Why not, Sunita, why not?"

Just then Yogesh returned with cake and pastries. "Yogesh," said his mother, as she took the polyethylene bag containing the cake and pastries from him. "I have learnt from Sunita all that I wanted to learn about you and her. All I wish to say is that I am extremely happy. I want to meet her parents at the earliest so that I can bring her home without wasting any time."

Yogesh felt relieved that Sunita had done the job of informing his mother about them. He was glad that his mother gave her consent so easily, though he had not expected her to do so otherwise. He was not, however, sure of the reaction of Sunita's parents. "But, Ma, we have yet to speak to Sunita's parents about it," Yogesh pointed out as he took the mug of coffee from his mother.

"That can be arranged today," said Sunita, "Papa returns home from his office around 6 PM. You can come, both of you, anytime after that."

"I think, Yogesh, you go with Sunita today," said Mrs. Naqvi. "I'll meet them sometime next week after letting them know of the purpose of my visit."

"As you please, Ma," replied Yogesh.

Sunita's mobile phone rang just when Yogesh and she were about to leave. It was her mother on the line.

"Yes, Mom!"

"Sunita, where are you?"

"Mom, I am with a friend. I am coming home soon."

"Are you with Yogesh?"

"How did you know, mom?"

"I am your mother, Sunita! I know all about your feelings for Yogesh."

"Mom, you are too bad!"

"That means my reading is correct. Are you with him?

"Mom, actually I am at Yogesh's house. I came to see his mother today. But I am leaving now. In fact, Yogesh too is coming with me."

"He is most welcome. Come soon!"

Yogesh, who had overheard the conversation, asked, "I hope your mother is not upset?"

"Upset? She sounded quite pleased to know that I am with you."

"Does it mean it is green signal from your side too?'

"It looks like that."

"Oh, Sony! I feel so relieved and I am so happy. I love you!'

"I love you too, Yogesh!"

Chapter 4

25 March

Raman Kumar, the new Defence Minister, was having a chat with his three service chiefs, General Surinder Pal, Air Chief Marshal Chatterji and Admiral Namboodri. This was his first meeting with the three of them after taking over as the Defence Minister two days earlier. The meeting was an informal chat with his service chiefs.The briefings were kept for a later date. The purpose of the meeting was simply to let the new Defence Minister know the three service chiefs and get a feel of the war preparedness of the country's armed forces.

"Sir," spoke the General, "you will be glad to know that after developing Nag, Prithvi and Agni we have now succeeded in developing Rudra, which is a Medium Range

Ballistic Missile, capable of carrying nuclear warheads to anywhere in our neighbouring countries."

"That is good news," commented the Defence Minister. "When is it being test fired?"

"Sir, I spoke to the DRDO Chief the other day. Together we have tentatively fixed the date for its test fire on the 11th of May, subject to your approval and availability."

"Of course I will be available. But why me? This is a great step in the country's defence preparedness. We will invite the Prime Minister to see the test. The test will be conducted in Orissa, I believe?"

"Yes sir. In Chandipur-at-sea, off the coast of Orissa."

"11th of May, you said?"

"Yes sir".

"OK. I'll speak to the Prime Minister about it. Let us see if he can spare time, though, I see no reason why he cannot."

The three chiefs had read and heard a great deal about the dynamism of Raman Kumar that he had shown as the HRD Minister. But none of them had known him personally before. Their first impressions of the man were positive. They felt quite comfortable with him.

"How is the morale of our personnel?" the minister asked, addressing no one in particular.

"Oh it is very high," the Air Chief Marshal declared proudly.

"Our boys are quite motivated," the Admiral asserted forcefully.

"Same is true for the army," the General announced reassuringly.

"What about the officers?" The minister probed. "I believe there is some frustration among the superseded officers!"

"That is bound to be there sir," commented Air Chief. "Our organizations are based on a pyramid type structure and have to be so to ensure a unified command. In such a structure not everybody can make it to the top levels. After all, you can't promote everybody to the next rank. Some supersession is inevitable."

"He's right," added the Army Chief. "As you know, we have automatic promotions only up to the rank of Lieutenant Colonel. Thereafter it is all by selection. It is the survival of the fittest. Those who are left behind do feel bitter. But that can't be helped. There is no solution to this problem."

"If there is a problem, it must have a solution," said the Defence Minister.

The three service chiefs remained silent for some time.

"Sir," it was the Naval Chief who broke the silence. "We have taken some steps in the recent past to address this problem but have achieved only partial success. I think the time has come to examine this problem afresh from all angles. For that, one needs time."

"I agree with you," said the minister. "You form a study group of some brilliant officers from the three services. Let them prepare a report covering all aspects of this issue. Let us see what we can do to find a solution to your problem."

The minister got up from his chair and shook hands with his service chiefs as he bid goodbye to them. Then he lifted the phone, pressed the buzzer and spoke to his Personal Secretary. "Mehta, I need an appointment with the Prime Minister in the first week of April in connection with the test fire of Rudra. Please note it down in your diary and speak to the PMO about it."

Just when Raman Kumar was having his first meeting with the three service chiefs, Sukhraj Malik had called a meeting of three senior officers of his ministry to get a first hand information on the law and order situation in the country. The three officers were Ramachandran, the Home Secretary, Arif Ghauri, the Director General of Central Reserve Police Force, and Amrit Lall, the Director of Special Protection Group (SPG). The Home Secretary briefed him on the sociopolitical climate in the sensitive states and gave an update of the special reports received from these states. The DG Central Police gave an outline of the deployment of para military forces in various states and its adequacy or the lack of it. Lall gave a briefing on the role of the SPG that was responsible for the VVIP security in India.

"Which are the agencies that provide personnel for the SPG?" asked the Home Minister.

"Sir, they are selected, after a series of vigorous tests, from the army, the Central Reserve Police Force and other para military forces," replied Lall.

"Do they all undergo the same basic training?" queried the minister.

"Yes sir," Lall confirmed. "They have to undergo a tough commando training."

"And the best must be on duty with the President and the Prime Minister?" asked the minister.

"Er! Yes sir," replied Lall.

"In fact it is the army chaps who are given this duty," interjected Arif Ghauri. "The police commandos are earmarked for other VVIPs." The touch of sarcasm was clear in his voice.

"Nowadays the training and deployment of the SPG is under the overall control of the army," said Lall. "They believe that the army commandos are more competent than police commandos."

"What happens if some police commandos perform better than the army fellows during the training?" asked the Minister.

"It is their bad luck," commented Ghauri. Lall kept quiet.

"I do not understand why we cannot do away with this labelling business," said Malik. "Why is it that it is the label on a person that determines his suitability? Why not his performance? You set some clearly defined standards and whosoever meets those standards should be picked up for the top job!"

Arif Ghauri allowed a smile to come on his face. He was happy to know the mind of his new minister. None of the three officers however made any other comment.

"All right gentlemen," said the minister. "I will speak to the Defence Minister about it. Let me see what we can do. I want Director SPG to hold on for some more time. I want to discuss with him some issues relating to the security of our Prime Minister. You two may go."

Ramachandran and Ghauri took leave of the minister. Lall continued to sit as desired by his boss.

"Mr. Lall," the minister began as soon as the other two officers left his room. "I believe your tenure as Head of the SPG is coming to an end next month?"

"Yes sir," said Amrit Lall.

"I hope you had a happy tenure?"

"Very satisfying sir! Very satisfying indeed."

"Whom do you recommend to be your successor?" enquired the minister.

"Sir, I would recommend the name of my Deputy, S S Dhillon, without any reservation. He is a highly competent professional and is fully qualified to hold this sensitive appointment."

"I am sure he is," said the minister. "I will keep your recommendation in mind while making the final decision. Now Mr. Lall, I want from you a brief outline of the security cover that you give to the VVIPs, particularly to the Prime Minister when he is on tour."

"Right sir," said Lall and began to explain the security plan as desired by his minister.

In the North Block, Finance Minister Vinayak Bagchi was being briefed by his Personal Secretary, Sudhir Nanda.

"Sir, on the twenty-eighth, you have to attend a meeting of CCS."

"What is the agenda?'

"There is presentation from Mr. Suraj Chopra, the National Security Advisor, on some Chinese proposal."

"What else?"

"On the first of April, you are in Mumbai to address a meeting of the Federation of Chambers of Commerce in India."

"On All Fools day?"

"Yes sir!"

"What an appropriate occasion!"

"Sir the draft speech is ready. I have put it up to you for your approval."

"Anything else?"

"Rest is routine sir. But there are some pending files that need your approval."

"Fine. I'll clear all the files before I leave office today. Thank you!"

"Thank you sir!"

Commerce Minister Birender Singh was quite happy to retain his portfolio. He was having his morning tête-à-tête with K Muniappa, his Personal Secretary.

"Muniappa, our new exim policy finally appears to be showing results!"

"It was bound to show sir. It is the most comprehensive Exim policy that India has ever formulated."

"I am quite happy to see 18% growth in exports over the last year."

"Yes sir. The growth rate has been remarkable!"

"What pleases me most is the fact that the growth has been achieved, not by the traditional exports like InfoTech and pharmaceuticals. It is the agro-based products that have led this growth."

"It is indeed very good news for the rural economy."

"That is in keeping with the NPA manifesto."

"At this rate we'll soon catch up with China in our rate of economic growth."

"Why only catch up Muniappa, we'll beat them to second place. All we need is a good monsoon this year."

Foreign Minister Zafar Khan was discussing the Iraq-US imbroglio with his Foreign Secretary, Kunal Sen.

"Sen, there is not going to be any peace unless the Americans leave Iraq."

"But they can't afford to do that. They did not remove Saddam Hussain to hand over Iraq to the jihadis."

"I agree. But the longer they stay there, the stronger the support that Al Qaeda will get from the Muslims, the world over."

"It is ironic indeed. The Americans invaded Iraq to finish Al Qaeda; it is this invasion which is proving to be the lifeline of Al Qaeda now."

"You think we have a role in Iraq?"

"Are you referring to sending our troops there?"

"No, not that. What I meant was, if we could think of some honourable way out for the Americans from Iraq."

"Why should we do that sir? The Americans have never really helped us in our fight against cross border terrorism. Let them fight their own war just as they want us to fight our war ourselves."

"They can't do it on their own, Sen. They have not been able to capture Al Qaeda Command Centre all these years despite knowing fully well that it is located somewhere in the hills on the Afghan-Pak border."

"Sooner or later they will realize that they have been backing the wrong horse. The ISI is simply not going to deliver it to them."

"The sooner they realize it, the better it is for us."

Chapter 5

27 March

Yogesh had been going to Sunita's house daily since the day of their final paper. Her parents were quite happy that Sunita and Yogesh had decided to tie the nuptial knot. They had liked Yogesh since the day Sunita had first brought him home. They had no objection to his being a half Muslim and half Hindu. 'We kayasths too consider ourselves to be half Hindu and half Muslim because our religion is Hinduism but our customs are Islamic,' Sunita's father had commented. The consent of Sunita's parents was a foregone conclusion. Rather than waiting for Mrs. Naqvi to come to their house, it was they who first went to her house. 'We are the girl's parents and it is our duty to approach the boy's parents with the wedding proposal,' they had reasoned.

"I agree with your mother, Yogesh!" said Sunita's father. "Since you have decided to marry, and we all support you on that, there is no point in delaying the wedding. As it is, among Muslims and kayasths, it is an established custom to marry early. Come an auspicious day and the marriage can be solemnized."

"How about on baisakhi?" suggested Sunita's mother. "It is an important festival and we cannot ask for a more auspicious day than baisakhi for the wedding. Moreover, it falls on the 13th of April which is two weeks away. That would give us enough time to make preparations for the wedding."

"That sounds fine," said Yogesh, trying hard to hide his elation. "I think Ma will have no objection to it. In fact she would be thrilled!"

"Let it be on baisakhi then," said Sunita's father. "We will come to meet your mother tomorrow evening to finalise the date. I hope she doesn't have any other engagement?"

"I don't think so," said Yogesh as he got up to take leave. "Ma is a very private person and mostly stays home after returning from her school. Please come tomorrow. We will wait for you. Right O' then. I will better take leave now. It is getting rather late. Good night Sunita and good night everybody!"

"Good night Yogesh!" said the happy family.

Chapter 6

28 March

It was the first meeting of the newly reconstituted Cabinet Committee on Security (CCS). The meeting was chaired by the Prime Minister. Apart from Suraj Chopra, the National Security Advisor, the meeting was attended by the five Cabinet Ministers who were the members of the CCS. They were Defence Minister Raman Kumar, Home Minister Sukhraj Malik, Finance Minister Vinayak Bagchi, Commerce Minister Birender Singh and Foreign Minister Zafar Khan. All the members were in a sombre mood. They had just been briefed by the National Security Advisor on the grand plans of China to divert river waters from the Tibetan Plateau to its Northern Provinces, which, if implemented, would have serious consequences on the ecology, economy and national security of India.

China has been somewhat of an enigma for the Indian policy makers. Despite their best efforts to befriend China, Indians have never succeeded in winning the trust of the Chinese. When the communists took over the mainland China in 1949, India was among the first countries to recognize the new government in Beijing. When the Chinese occupied Tibet, India acquiesced in to the new reality without murmur. Jawaharlal Nehru signed Panchsheel with Zhou En Lai with the hope that the five principles of friendship on which Panchsheel was based, would indeed lead to a lofty brotherhood between India and China. 'Hindi-Cheeni Bhai Bhai' was the slogan he gave to the Sino-Indian brotherhood. But the ink on the Panchsheel agreement had hardly dried when the Chinese army invaded India across the Himalayas, leaving Nehru totally devastated and shattered.

The 1962 Sino-Indian war did not, however, stop Indians from espousing the cause of the Communist China to be admitted to the United Nations at the expense of Taiwan. Over the years, successive governments in New Delhi have tried unsuccessfully to build bridges with Beijing but China has remained steadfast in its refusal to settle boundary dispute with India in a peaceful manner and its support to Pakistan, India's fiercest opponent in the world affairs. The biggest jolt that India received was when China thwarted her attempts to gain a permanent seat in the UN Security Council with veto power when it was revamped a few years ago. This rebuttal and the great economic development that India had achieved over the past two decades, made Indian policy makers realize that India would have to learn to stand up to the bullying by China to win their respect. Accordingly, India started pursuing a more assertive foreign policy in her relations with China. This change in attitude indeed seemed to work now. China had begun to consult India on important issues, something, which was unimaginable earlier.

Only last week China sent a proposal to the Indian government to form a Joint Consultative Machinery (JCM) to study the issues relating to their proposed construction of dams on major rivers originating from Tibet. All the major rivers of North India have their origins in Tibet. These rivers are the lifeline of India, Pakistan and Bangladesh. But the growing desertification in Northern Provinces of China has forced the Chinese government to consider a grand plan of diverting some part of the waters of Tibetan rivers to those provinces. It is a well known fact that it is an impossible task to construct any dam on the Tibetan Platéau by conventional means. China will have to resort to the nuclear devices to divert these river waters to the Yellow River in North China. The diversion of scarce waters and the flow of nuclear waste down the Himalayas will lead to lot of hue and cry from India and is likely to escalate into a major international crisis for the Chinese. It is for this reason that China has decided to seek India's help and co-operation. It is to discuss this proposal of the Chinese that Prime Minister Prabhat Rai has called today's meeting of the CCS.

"Well friends!" began the Prime Minister, after the National Security Advisor finished his thirty-minute long presentation, covering all aspects of the Chinese proposal. "You have been briefed by Mr. Chopra on a matter that has major implications for us on the political, ecological and economic fronts. We have to analyse the whole issue in depth and arrive at a decision on what kind of response we send to the Chinese. Would any one of you like to offer any comment?"

"Rai Sahib," it was Sukhraj Malik who took the lead. "I am of the firm view that we cannot trust the Chinese on any matter. They have taken us for a ride far too many times in the past. We should not allow them to do so this time as well. Their request is just an eyewash to tell the world that they indeed consulted India before starting on their river-diversion project. For all we know, they might have already made up their mind on what they are going to do. But we must bring pressure on them in the beginning itself so that they do not embark upon this ambitious but foolish project that is bound to lead to ecological disaster, not only in India, but in the whole of South East Asia. We must take countries like Burma, Thailand, Vietnam, Cambodia and

Malaysia into confidence, apart from the SAARC countries, particularly, Pakistan, Nepal and Bangladesh."

"Malikji is right," said Birender Singh. "We must not allow this plan to take off at any cost. If the dams on major rivers in Tibet come up, we will be totally at the mercy of the Chinese. They will hold back water during the dry months when we need it most and release excess water during the monsoons when their reservoirs will overflow but our rivers too will be full already. Either way, it will be disaster for India."

"Our economy is heavily dependent on these rivers," said Vinayak Bagchi. "Imagine Sutlej and Brahmaputra being dry during winter and over flooded during the monsoon months. It will become a never ending cycle of famine and floods in our country. Our economy will be ruined."

"To me, the most worrisome aspect of the construction of dams in Tibet is the nuclear fallout," said Raman Kumar. "Our rivers will get contaminated, our fields will get contaminated and our flora and fauna will get contaminated. We cannot bear with such consequences!"

"Sir this is indeed time to revive the SAARC spirit," chipped in Zafar Khan. "If we can get Pakistan, Nepal and Bangladesh on board, we can bring added pressure on China to desist from implementing their grand plans. China might have unwittingly given us an opportunity to bring SAARC countries together. Let us make the best of this opportunity."

The discussion continued for about an hour. To buy more time, it was decided to ask the Chinese on what kind of guarantees they were willing to offer to India if India accepted their proposal.

"All right gentlemen," said the Prime Minister, bringing the meeting to a close. "The National Security Advisor will prepare draft minutes of this meeting and circulate to you all before putting them on record. Though all of you know the rules, yet, I see no harm in reiterating that our discussion here is to be kept absolutely confidential. Goodbye and good night!"

Chapter 7

03 April

"For Flights of Fancy, Fly with Kingfisher", screamed the punch line in the page long advertisement on one of India's fastest expanding airlines in the morning paper as Yogesh opened it. A nostalgic feeling went through him when he saw the prominently displayed punch line. He remembered one of the tag lines that his group had given to Fancy brand of ready-to-cook food, as a part of the project work during the second year of the PG course.

Foods of Fancy from the Fancy Foods!

Sunita, he and three other students of his class were members of that group which had prepared the ad. He recalled that he and Sunita shared a common interest in advertising. They had both enjoyed the subject of Marketing in their PG course, and Advertising was their favourite topic. It was only natural that they had decided to join some Advertising Agency after their marriage on the 13th of April.

The thought of his coming marriage with Sunita made him feel romantic. He kept the newspaper aside and started day-dreaming about her. The more he thought of her, the more deeply he felt he was in love with her. The secret desire to possess her that he had cherished for two years was now showing in all its intensity. He was sure that Sunita was as passionately in love with him as he was with her. It clearly showed the way she looked at him, the way she talked, walked, dressed and behaved.

During the university days they had not declared their love to each other. Now that they had been able to do so, they could not get an opportunity to enjoy their romance. Their romance was restricted to their long phone chats or exchange of SMS messages. Though Yogesh had been going to Sunita's house almost daily over the last ten days, yet, he had met her only when one or the other member of her family was also at home. It was not that her parents had any objection to their going out together. Only he could not muster enough courage to ask them to let him take her out.

Enough was enough, Yogesh thought. He must take Sunita out on a date at least once before marriage. He picked up the phone and dialled her number. It was Sumit who answered the call.

"Hello Sumit, Yogesh here."

"Hi!" said Sumit. "Wait a minute please!" Saying so he called Sunita to take the phone. Yogesh appreciated that Sumit had called Sunita even before he could ask for her.

"Yes Yogesh!" came Sunita's voice. "How come? So early?" She sounded surprised as well as pleased.

"Hi Sony! I was wondering if I could take you for an outing today."

"What?" exclaimed an incredulous Sunita.

"I said, I would like to take you for a date today," replied Yogesh. "We'll see noon show at the newest multiplex in the city, PVR Chanakya, have lunch at Nirula's, spend some time in the Lodi Garden and go to Connaught Place or wherever you like." Yogesh reeled off the day's program.

"That sounds fine but I will have to ask mama," said Sunita.

"Please do it for me, now," pleaded Yogesh.

"O.K. Hold on for a sec." Yogesh heard Sunita tell her mother about his proposed programme. She then turned back to the phone and said, "Yogesh, mama says no problem. What time will you come here?"

"I'll reach your house at 10:30. Be ready."

"I'll be ready, but how will you come? I mean, shall I ask Papa for his car?"

"Not required. I am coming on the motorbike. I will borrow it from Rishabh."

"See you, then!"

"See you."

Yogesh reached Sunita's place five minutes before time. He was thrilled to see her wearing blue jeans and a light yellow cotton top. She looked very sexy in that dress. He recalled that it was not often that she wore jeans. 'Perhaps she does not know how great she looks in jeans,' he thought. One of his favourite fantasies had been to ride a motorcycle with Sunita on the pillion, sitting with her legs on the two sides of the seat, holding him firmly with her arms and pressing her breasts against his back. He felt excited and had to hold the helmet in front of his trousers to hide the visible erection. He hastily bid goodbye to Sunita's mother and found himself rushing out of the house when they left her place. He started the motorcycle, sat on it and asked Sunita to take her seat. His heart pounded with excitement at the thought of two lovely legs rubbing against his buttocks and two bouncy bosoms pressing against his back. He covered his face with the dark sun visor attached to the helmet so that his face might not betray the state of his mind.

"Yes please," said Sunita as she sat on the motorcycle. Yogesh felt surprised as the expected did not happen. He looked back and saw Sunita comfortably sitting about six inches behind him. He was about to ask her to move closer to him but refrained from doing so when he saw Sunita's mother waiving her hand affectionately at them from the main door of the house. He released the clutch and off they went on their first real date.

"Why don't you sit properly?" asked Yogesh when they had covered about a kilometer.

"What?" Sunita could not hear him as the motorcycle was in speed. She expected Yogesh to slow down so that they could have an easy conversation but he swerved the motorcycle to the left of the road and brought it to a complete halt. He lifted the sun visor of the helmet and turned his face towards Sunita.

"I said why don't you sit like the other girls do?"

"Other girls?"

"Haven't you ever seen boys and girls on the mobikes in the campus? How lovingly they cling to each other!"

"Oh I see. Well, OK!" Sunita moved forward.

"Move further my dear!"

"Alright, if that is what makes you happy," said Sunita as she moved further forward.

"That is like a good girl. Now hold me tight."

"Come on Yogesh don't be funny. I am quite comfortable."

"But I am not."

"Alright," said Sunita as she put her arms around Yogesh's waist.

Yogesh wanted her to move even closer but decided not to press her further for the time being. He restarted the motorcycle and they were soon racing down towards Chanakya Puri. The tingling sensation that he felt every time Sunita's frontage rubbed against his back, made him feel horny. He was finding it difficult to control his breathing. Years of abstinence were having their toll. After about ten minutes of ride, when he could not contain his excitement any more, he once again swerved his motorcycle to the left of the road and brought it to a complete halt.

"What is it now?" asked a surprised Sunita.

"Sony, may I suggest some change in the day's programme?"

"What change?"

"Let us skip the movie."

"And do what?"

"Ma has gone to school and won't be home before 2 P.M. We will go to my place and spend some time in each other's company."

Sunita now understood the reason for Yogesh's strange behaviour. She stared at him for a moment and then burst out laughing.

"What is there to laugh?" asked Yogesh.

"I will come to your house but not today," replied Sunita smilingly. "For that you will have to wait for about ten days more. Remember! Thirteenth is only ten days away."

"That is different," said Yogesh. "Please Sony! You don't know how I feel. Please, for my sake. Let us go and spend sometime together at my house. You know, how much madly I am in love with you?"

"I am equally madly in love with you," replied Sunita. "But that does not mean that we allow our desires to take over our judgement. We have lived by certain values and must not forget them in a moment of weakness. Now be a good boy and start the motorcycle. We will stick to the original programme."

"But we are engaged to be married and that too within ten days! Where is the question of forgetting our values?" said Yogesh, almost pleading with her.

"Ten days means it is all the more important that we should show self-discipline and do only what is right for us."

"Please Sony!"

"No Yogesh, no,"

"Please!"

"That is enough Yogesh," said Sunita indignantly as she got down from the motorcycle. "I am not interested in your programme any more. You be on your own and I am going back home." She turned back and started walking down the road.

The snub had the desired effect. Yogesh felt utterly stupid and all his excitement vanished in no time. He soon composed himself and called Sunita back. But she continued to walk, pretending not to hear him. Yogesh quickly got down from the motorcycle and pulled it on its stand. He ran towards Sunita and was able to catch up with her about twenty meters away.

"Please stop Sunita!" he pleaded with her.

"No, I won't" she replied emphatically but halted her steps, nonetheless. "You are becoming impossible, you know?"

"I know," said Yogesh with a sigh, "and....and I am sorry. Now please don't leave me like that!"

"Give me your word first that you will not budge from the original programme," demanded Sunita.

"You have my word for it," assured Yogesh. "Now please get back. Please! People are watching us."

"OK," she relented.

They walked back to the motorcycle and resumed their date. They reached PVR Chanakya about ten minutes before the start of the noon show. 'Gone With the Wind' was having a return for about the fifth time in New Delhi and attracted a large crowds every time it was screened, despite its easy availability on VCDs and DVDs. Yogesh and Sunita had not seen it before. They bought balcony tickets and found the hall more than two-thirds full when they entered it. The cool air from the air conditioner filled the hall. The dim lights and the cosy seats made for a comfortable three hours viewing. Soon the lights were switched off and it was time for the commercials. The movie started about ten minutes later. Yogesh had many funny ideas about what he was going to do while watching the movie but had to drop them all after the snub he received earlier on. They soon found themselves in the company of Rhett Butler and Scarlet O'Hara and began to enjoy the movie.

The movie was over in three and a half hours. Sunita and Yogesh were particularly impressed by the quality of the film.

"Excellent!" Sunita praised the movie as they came out of the hall.

"Yeah!" commented Yogesh. "Only Americans can produce such quality films. And can you believe, they made this movie in 1939. Look at the colour, the photography, the grandeur and the scale at which it was made!"

"Just compare it with the trash that has been coming out of our Bollywood at least till a few years ago," said Sunita.

Having exchanged their critical comments they hurried towards Nirula's, the extremely popular fast food restaurant on the basement of Chanakya. But they were disappointed to see an exceptionally heavy rush inside.

"We'll have to wait," said Yogesh.

"Even then we may not get a seat," said Sunita.

"It will have to be a standing lunch, in all probability."

"That is not my idea of having a good time."

Yogesh looked at Sunita and said with a shy smile, "If you don't mind, can I suggest one minor change in the day's programme?"

"What?" she asked smilingly.

"Let us go to Connaught Place. We will have our lunch in some good restaurant there."

"Change approved."

"Thanks your majesty!"

They had a leisurely ride through the outer ring of the Connaught Place and chose Standard Restaurant in the Regal Building for having their lunch.

"Here we are," said Yogesh. "We can have a relaxed lunch now."

"Smart change," said Sunita approvingly." But I hope you have enough dough with you? Otherwise I am ready to split the bill."

Yogesh burst out laughing. "Thanks for your offer but I won't need your help. Courtesy ma, I am adequately prepared for my first date."

"My first date too!"

The tension between the two had completely evaporated by now. They ordered orange juice for both, to be followed by a meal of Butter Chicken, Mushroom Peas, Dal Makhani and Naan.

"Tell me Yogesh," Sunita asked when they had fully settled down, "what made you plan this date today?"

"An ad in the paper," replied Yogesh.

"Which ad?"

"It was an ad on Kingfisher Airlines. Something like 'For Flights of Fancy, Fly with Kingfisher Airlines'. It reminded me of our project work in the second term on Fancy Foods. That reminded me of you. The more I thought about you, the more desperate I felt to have a date with you."

"How interesting!" gushed Sunita. "I am happy about our choice of profession if for no other reason than for the one that whenever you will prepare some new campaign, you will think about me."

"Ha! Ha! Ha!" Yogesh laughed. "But I don't think I'll have to think about you when we get our jobs. After all we will be working together, won't we?"

"You think it is possible for both of us to get a job in the same agency?"

"Why not?" assured Yogesh. "In fact when I contacted Megatech and Renaissance which are two of the top Advertising Agencies, both appeared to be more interested in our working as a team rather than separately."

"That should be real fun!" exclaimed Sunita.

Food was excellent and the setting just right. They thoroughly enjoyed their meal.

They left the restaurant well after 3 P.M. and headed for the nearby ice-cream stall. Sunita was particularly fond of ice-cream. Yogesh did not have much liking for it but gave her company, nonetheless. Thereafter they went to the underground air-conditioned market on the Central Metro Station and just moved around for a while. Evening was fast approaching when they came out of the Metro Station market and it became quite pleasant outside as well.

"Shall we go to Lodhi Garden now?" asked Yogesh.

"Sure," said Sunita. "But remember I have to get back home before sunset."

"No problem, dear, no problem," said Yogesh lovingly.

At Lodhi Garden, Sunita removed her shoes and held them in her hands as she walked on the carpet of grass. Yogesh enjoyed watching her. He was finding her irresistible but could not dare make any move because of the rebuff that he had received in the morning. They saw many couples sitting or lying on the lawns. Some of them were conscious of the passers-by. Others were oblivious of the world around them. They soon found a bush behind which there was thick shade.

"Lovers' nest," whispered Sunita.

"What?" asked Yogesh.

"I said lovely place," replied Sunita. "Let us sit here for some time." He was delighted that the proposal had come from her.

"Come," was all that Yogesh said as they sat down. She looked lovingly at him and he felt good.

"Why don't you lie down?" Sunita asked.

"Lie down! Why?"

"Just like that. I want to keep your head in my lap."

"Any time" said Yogesh. He lay down on his back and placed his head in her lap. Her touch, the look in her eyes and the smell of her body were having an intoxicating effect on him. He closed his eyes as he could not look into her eyes any longer. She started caressing his hair and seemed to enjoy doing what she was doing. After some time Yogesh opened his eyes and found Sunita still looking lovingly at him.

"Sony!"

"Hum!"

"You know, you are beeuu.....tiful!"

"Thanks," she replied. "Yogesh!"

"Yes!"

"I am sorry I was a bit rude to you in the morning. I did not mean to be."

"I think I deserved it. I acted silly."

"But you acted very nice after that. I am so proud of you!"

"Thanks. You make me feel good."

"I think you deserve some reward for your conduct."

"Really?"

"Yes."

Sunita looked around. There were no intruders. She again looked at Yogesh who continued to stare at her, not knowing what exactly she had in her mind. Slowly she lowered her face towards his face and quietly placed her lips on his lips. This had an electrifying effect on Yogesh. He put his arms around her back and pulled her firmly towards himself. They were locked in a deep passionate kiss for some time.

"I love you Yogesh," said Sunita as she parted her lips from his.

"I love you too, my sweet!" said Yogesh.

They got up and left the lovers' nest. They walked hand in hand for a short distance in complete silence.

"Sony! Thank you for making my day," it was Yogesh who broke the silence.

"It is thanks to you Yogesh. But tell me honestly. Haven't you had any girlfriend before?"

"None. I swear!"

"It is strange really. You are smart, intelligent and handsome. How come no girl ever got interested in you?"

"Actually there was a girl in P.G.D.A.V. College, my classmate. She was interested in me. But I hated her"

"Why?"

"She was too fast for me! She would have a new boy friend every new season. She did not have good reputation. But she was very pretty otherwise."

"What was her name?"

"Neena. Neena Singh."

They stopped when they came across a beautiful rose garden in one corner of the park. The rose garden had a large variety of roses in different colours. They were in full bloom and presented a very colourful sight.

"Lovely flowers!" said Sunita. "See, how many colours they have! White, pink, purple, yellow, blue, but none to beat the original red. Red rose is my favourite. See how majestic the red roses are?"

"Red is O.K." said Yogesh. "But to me black is beautiful. I would like to have black roses."

"Black roses? You must be joking!"

"No, I am serious. I like black roses. These are rare but the rarity adds to their mystique."

"We'll see them when we have time," said Sunita. "But right now it is time for me to get back home. Let us go."

They left Lodhi Garden and reached Sunita's place slightly after 6 P.M. Her mother was happy to see her daughter being so happy.

Yogesh was about to take leave from Sunita when her father returned from office.

"Good evening!" Yogesh greeted his would be father-in-law. He could not bring himself to address him as papa yet. May be after the wedding, he had told himself.

"Good evening, Yogesh!" Mathur returned the greeting. "Nice to see you. When did you come?"

"I came in the morning. In fact I am leaving now."

"Can you hold on for some time? I wish to discuss something with you and Sunita."

"Sure."

"I'll change and will be with you in a minute." Mathur hurried into his bed room.

Yogesh looked inquisitively at Sunita, trying to find out what the old man had in his mind. But she was as clueless as he was. Mathur returned to the room in about five minutes.

"Well Yogesh, Sunita!" he spoke to them as he settled down. "Tell me something about your future plans. I mean, what have you decided to do for your living?"

They looked at each other and in a mere glance it was decided that Yogesh would answer the query.

"We plan to join some well established Advertising Agency," replied Yogesh. "In fact I have already contacted a couple of agencies and their response has been positive."

"Advertising Agency!" Sunita's father repeated "That sounds good. Sunita had mentioned to me that you both shared a common interest in advertising. I think it is an excellent line to follow. But why don't you start your own agency? Why work for others?"

"But papa!" Sunita decided to join the discussion. "For that, one requires lot of money, and lot of experience. We have neither of the two."

Her father gave her a long look and then said, "Experience my child, can be a two-edged sword. At times it helps you to make the right decisions but at times it also works as a dampener on your enterprising spirit. It makes you too cautious and conservative. Lack of experience is many times a boon. You think fresh, act fresh and there is greater possibility of your succeeding. So don't bother too much about the experience or, rather, the lack of it." Having said so, he turned instinctively towards Sunita's mother, as if asking for her appreciation. She gave a smile, conveying the same. "As far as money is concerned, that can be arranged. By the way, how much money would you require for a start?"

Yogesh made some mental calculations and said, "To begin with we will need about one million of our own capital."

"One million!" repeated the old man. "Means ten lakhs of rupees. That is indeed a big amount. Let us see how this amount can be raised. But you must start your own Advertising Agency. "

"But no dowry please!" said Yogesh emphatically.

"Oh no!" said Sunita's father. "Dowry is meant for a comfortable living, not for doing business."

Yogesh left their house after some time, still wondering why the old man said that the money to start their company could be arranged. The idea of starting their own company was exciting but he knew that they will have to save some money first before dreaming of taking any such

Chapter 8

04 April

Islamabad

The ISI chief was waiting for his guest who was the second important foreign guest that General Ginai was going to receive in a fortnight. The guest was the Director of the foregin intelligence agency whose name starts with a capital C.

The General felt good about the enormous power that the ISI had begun to wield in Pakistan. It boosted his ego when foreign dignitaries called on him. It was an acknowledgement of the clout that the ISI enjoyed these days. But the clout did not come easy. General Ginai remembered vividly how hard the ISI had to work for it.

When Pakistan was born in 1947, it had only one central intelligence agency - the Intelligence Bureau (IB). The agency was an offspring of the pre-partition IB of India. The ISI was created in 1948, mainly as a result of the unsatisfactory performance of the IB during the 1947-48 J & K Operations. Officers of all the three Services of Pakistan - the Army, the Air Force and the Navy - were drawn to man the ISI. Its main role was to collect, analyse and assess external intelligence, military and non-military, with its main focus being on India. Its main goal was to help Pakistan wrest Kashmir from India. But short-sightedness and political expediency of the Pakistani rulers soon added more teeth to the functioning of the ISI, which enabled it to abrogate some extra constitutional powers to itself.

By 1950, the work of the ISI was distributed among two divisions- the Internal Political Division and the Covert Action Division. Initially the Internal Political Division was given the mandate by President Ayub Khan to collect intelligence in East Pakistan, Pakistan Occupied Kashmir (POK) and Northern areas like Gilgit and Baltistan. Prime Minister Zulfiqar Ali Bhutto authorized it to work on Baluchi nationalists. President Zia-ul-Haq used the ISI to spy on Sindhi nationalist elements. He also ordered it to deal with the Shia organisations after the Iranian revolution in 1979.

While the Internal Political Division was getting deeper into the internal politics of Pakistan, the Covert Action Division was busy planning and executing various operations against India. At first, it started giving support to the insurgents in the North East, using East Pakistan as the base. In sixties it started assisting Sikh Home Rule movement of London based Charan Singh Panchhi and later it went all out to support Khalistan movement of Jagjit Singh Chauhan. Its support to the Sikh militants in Punjab in 1980s and J & K militants in 1990s is too well known.

The remarkable success of the ISI in these covert actions has given it immense clout among the centres of power in its own country. It uses this clout to interfere aggressively in the internal politics of Pakistan. Some people suspect that it was the ISI that got both sons of Zulfiqar Ali Bhutto, as well as his daughter Benazir Bhutto, assassinated. People also believe that it was the ISI that ensured the dismissal of Benazir Bhutto and Nawaz Sharif from the Prime Ministership of Pakistan, not once, but twice each when they tried to take control of the agency and curtail its powers.

By the end of the Twentieth century, the ISI had indeed become a "State within a State".

One thing that goes in favour of the ISI is the fierce loyalty of its rank and file to the organization. They distrust the politicians. The only person, who exercises some control over it, is the Chief of the Army Staff (COAS) of Pakistan. The ISI shares a symbiotic relationship with the COAS. They both need and use each other to protect their interests.

General Ginai was quite close to the present COAS. He was confident of winning his support to the ISI on the Gordon Mathews proposal. But he was not so sure if the proposal would get the full backing of all the permanent members of the UN Security Council.

The thoughts of the chief were interrupted when his guest was ushered in by his staff officer.

"Good morning brother," said the guest to the ISI chief, discarding all formality and official pretence.

"Good morning to you as well brother," responded Ginai with equal warmth and offered him seat across the table.

"So how are we?" asked the guest.

"With friends like you, Pakistan has no worries in the world."

"We have always considered Pakistan to be our all-weather friend!"

"And we trust you completely. We too shall never let you down."

"I am sure of that!"

"So, what brings you here my brother from your busy schedule?"

"What brings me here? Well, it is my desire to be of some use to you at this point in time."

"Your help is always welcome!"

"First of all, please tell me, what is the progress on the Kashmir proposal?"

"Well!" said the chief with a sigh. "As I had written to you earlier, the proposal is indeed very exciting. I am working out the details of its implementation. I have discussed the matter with the army chief. He thinks it is workable. But we are not sure of the response of our government. I believe the Secretary of State has broached the topic with the Prime Minister but he is not very enthusiastic. So if at all we go ahead with this proposal, our army will have to do it without the backing of our government. To tell you honestly, I am not sure how far we should go with this proposal. In fact I too have some reservations whether or not the Indians will accept their part of the deal."

"They will accept, if you make use of the help that I am going to extend to you today."

"Really?"

"Yes."

"Tell me how?"

"You will have to launch an operation." The guest then proceeded to give a brief outline of the proposed operation.

General Ginai's disbelief turned into astonishment as he heard out his VIP guest. The mind blowing information that the guest gave to the ISI chief had him excited all ends up.

"I know it is a difficult operation," the guest concluded his brief. "But going by your track record, you should not have any problems in executing it. And this man in New Delhi will help you in this operation," said the guest as he gave a name to the chief.

"I can't believe it!" exclaimed General Ginai.

"You better do brother," the guest assured smilingly.

"If you deliver this man to me," said the ISI chief in an animated voice, "I have no doubt about the success of this operation."

"Take him as delivered," assured the guest.

"Oh that is so kind of you my brother. I am so grateful to you. In fact the whole of Pakistan will forever remain grateful."

"Anything for friends," said the guest.

"By the way, what name do we give to this operation?" asked the chief.

"Anything," replied his guest. He glanced around the table and saw a vase full of beautiful red roses. He took out one rose and offered it to General Ginai. "We may call it Operation Red Rose, if you like."

Chapter 9

05 April

It was quite late in the evening but Bikshap Reddy, the Director of the Research and Analysis Wing (RAW) - India's premier agency for gathering intelligence - was still pondering over the contents of the disturbing piece of information that he had received a day earlier from one of his agents in Washington. He picked up the paper on which the message had been transcribed and read it for the umpteenth time. The message was short and unambiguous.

"CODE BLACK SHEEP (STOP) WATCH OUT (STOP) SOMEONE CLOSE TO TOP LEVELS OF INDIAN GOVERNMENT HAVING ACCESS TO CCS DELIBERATIONS IS CIA MOLE (STOP) COPY OF MINUTES OF LAST CCS MEETING LEAKED ALREADY AND BEINC

SENT BY COURIER AS EVIDENCE (STOP) DETAILS WILL FOLLOW WHEN AVAILABLE (STOP)"

Copy of the minutes of the last meeting of the CCS that had taken place barely a week earlier, had arrived by the courier today. It indeed appeared to be authentic, confirming the report of the RAW operative in Washington.

The existence of the CIA mole in New Delhi did not come as a surprise to the RAW Director. He knew it well that it was virtually impossible for any country to be free of the enemy agents. But the CIA, with enormous funds at its disposal, had its agents even in friendly countries. It understood the power of information and used it to its advantage in all bilateral relationships. RAW had limited budget for espionage but still managed to have contacts in the countries that mattered to India, particularly Pakistan. Agents from various countries were occasionally caught and exposed, causing minor embarrassment to the concerned Government. But despite that it was a game in which all countries indulged.

What agitated the RAW Director the most was the information that this time the CIA was able to plant a mole at the top levels of the Government of India who had access to the CCS deliberations. It was far more damaging than the Ravinder Singh episode when Singh, a top functionary of the RAW, got exposed as a CIA agent in 2004. All sensitive decisions pertaining to the security of the country were taken by the government in the CCS meeting. It was of paramount importance, therefore, for the sake of the security of the country, that the highly classified information that was available only to the members of the CCS or at the most to their personal staff, was kept top secret. If the CIA could have access to this information, it could pass it on to the ISI with whom it shared a now-on-now-off relationship. This would enable the ISI to remain two steps ahead of RAW in planning its activities and operations.

Reddy wasted no time in passing on the report to S.K. Sharma, Director of the Intelligence Bureau (IB), because it was the IB that dealt with the foreign spies working in India. Sharma was as shocked to read the report as Reddy. Being a thorough professional, he got on the job in the right earnest to identify the CIA mole at the earliest and expose him before he could cause any irreparable damage to the interests of the country. He felt grateful to the RAW which had made his task of identifying the CIA mole easier by pinpointing his position as having access to the CCS deliberations. He called for the dossiers of all members of the CCS and persons close to them. He studied each dossier in detail.

Prime Minister Prabhat Rai came from a family of the landlords. His forefathers had served the British in various capacities with distinction. His grandfather had been conferred the title of 'Rai Bahadur' by the British for his loyal services to the British Empire. His father served as a Judicial Magistrate. But he did not want his son to become a government servant. The country had become independent when Prabhat Rai was born. His father felt that the politicians had a much more important role to play in independent India than the government servants. When Prabhat Rai completed his schooling, his father advised him to specialize in law to become a successful politician. He groomed him into politics when he joined the Law College. He told him that it always helped to be born into a well-to-do family in a feudal society like India. If he carried himself well, he would easily become a popular leader. He taught him the manners and the etiquette that would announce his pedigree to the world without his saying a word about it.

Prabhat Rai learnt this art well. He was very careful about his speech. He would carefully select each word and phrase that he spoke and then deliver it with a finesse to produce a telling effect on his listeners. He spoke softly but firmly and his words often had a mesmerizing effect on his listeners. His qualities helped him emerge, as a popular student leader.

After college, he took up politics as a full time profession. Bigger successes soon followed. He became a member of the State Legislature at the young age of 27. He became a State Minister when he was in his early thirties. He was a national level leader even before he was 45. Now in his 50s he had become the prime minister of India. Ironically, while others gave full credit to him and his credentials for his steady rise in politics, he himself felt highly obliged to his spiritual guru Swami Suryananda.

One of the interesting features of the Indian political scene during the last few decades has been the presence of the self proclaimed god men in the higher echelons of power. Many politicians befriend swamis, tantriks and yogis. These god men move freely in the corridors of power. It is widely known that the politicians have immense faith in the 'supernatural' powers of their gurus. They often observe fasts, say prayers and sometimes perform special rituals called yagnas at their bidding to bring in propitious days for themselves. Some people think that over-dependence of the Indian politicians on these god men shows their insecurities and lack of self-confidence. But the phenomenon is common and cuts across party lines.

Swami Suryananda was one such high profile god man who had significant following among the country's politicians. He was well educated and was a college lecturer before taking up teaching of yoga and his own brand of Hindu philosophy as a full time profession. He was able to win large following within a short time. Most of his disciples were the rich and the well-to-do. One of the things that he enjoyed most was to be seen among his politician disciples but he chose his disciples with care. One such carefully chosen disciple was Prabhat Rai.

Initially, Prabhat Rai did not have much faith in Swami Suryananda or other god men. Vaunting ambition, however, soon took over and when the Swami promised to utilise his spiritual powers to ensure his rapid rise in politics, Rai could not resist the temptation of seeking his help. The Swami often made Rai perform yagnas from time to time. As Rai started moving up in politics, he found himself invariably consulting his guru before taking any major decision regarding his association with different lobbies and power centres in his party. It so happened that the advice given by the Swami always proved to be correct and that strengthened Rai's faith in the Swami even further. He started following the instructions given by him quite religiously. He felt that it was his guru's spiritual powers that had helped him become the Prime Minister of India in face of the stiff challenge put up by his one time rival, now Home Minister, Sukhraj Malik.

Besides Swami Suryananda, another person who enjoyed Prabhat Rai's complete trust was T. Joseph, his Personal Secretary. Joseph's was a typical rags-to-riches story. He had joined Rai's office as a stenographer when the latter was first elected as a Member of the State Legislature. His fortune was linked to the fortune of his master. It took a real upswing when Rai became the Prime Minister of India. Joseph became one of the most powerful men in New Delhi. Though he made a conscious effort to maintain a low profile, yet, he could not stop people envy him because of the strides he had made in his career.

Vinayak Bagchi's dossier showed that he was an economist by profession. He had served the World Bank and the International Monetary Fund (IMF) for more than two decades and had made quite a name for himself there. Prabhat Rai held him in very high esteem. When he became the prime minister of India, he invited the economist to join his ministry as Finance Minister to give further boost to the economic reforms that were already underway. Bagchi felt delighted to get an opportunity to serve his country. He gave up his lucrative job at the IMF and became India's Finance Minister. During the last three years, he had indeed lived up to his reputation. Because of the sound economic policies introduced by him, India had become a fast developing and thriving economy. Of course, he felt extremely grateful to his worthy predecessors like Dr Manmohan Singh, who later rose to become the Prime Minister of India and P Chidambaram, who had introduced the concept of dream budgets.

Bagchi's Personal Secretary, Sudhir Nanda, was a young I.A.S. officer. Nanda was a quiet, upright and hardworking bureaucrat with no known vices.

Zafar Khan, the Foreign Minister, was a career diplomat. He was an officer in the Indian Foreign Service for about thirty-five years before joining politics. A suave, sophisticated and soft-spoken man, he was everything that a foreign minister should be. He hardly ever lost his temper and handled the media with consummate skill. It was impossible for the media, anywhere in the world, to provoke him to say something that was not in tune with India's declared foreign policy. He had an excellent command over English language but spoke only as much as the situation demanded; nothing more and nothing less.

Zafar Khan was known to keep all the classified information only to himself. He would even go to the extent of typing out all top-secret documents himself and never parted with the keys of his office cabinet in which he kept these documents.

Birender Singh was a hard taskmaster and not many people liked to work with him. He changed his personal staff quite frequently. His only son was settled in USA and had no interest in India, something that had resulted in strained relations between the father and the son. Nobody knew whether the strain in their relationship was genuine or was merely a charade being put up by the two to keep suspicions at bay.

Home Minister Sukhraj Malik's dossier revealed that he was of about the same age as his Prime Minister. He had emerged on the political scene as a young and popular leader of farmers many years ago. He had got his education in the rural schools and colleges. After completing his graduation in Political Science, he decided to look after his large family farm and become a full time farmer. He soon began to feel that despite India being a predominantly agrarian economy, the farmers got a raw deal from the government. He felt that the industrialists and the traders exploited the farmers in connivance with the politicians and the bureaucrats. He concluded that unless the farmer - the kisan - had a say in the affairs of the government, his lot could not be improved. Accordingly, he started organising various kisan movements to demand more remunerative prices for the farm produce; low charges for the farm inputs like water, electricity and fertilisers; and waiving off of loans given by the public sector banks to the small farmers. These issues soon caught the imagination of the farming community in his home state. They rallied behind young Malik and accepted him as their undisputed leader. He pressed his demands harder with each passing season. This consolidated his position among the farmers of all classes.

Malik used his popularity among the farmers to realize his political ambitions. Initially he entered politics with the sole desire of improving the lot of his fellow farmers. But once he moved to the state legislature, his views about the problems of the country underwent a change. He came to realize that the economy of the country was the mixture of various sectors and these sectors were so much inter-dependant that no particular group could progress in isolation from the other sectors. This was the beginning of the grooming of a worthy national leader in him. This, coupled with his powerful personality, helped him move up rapidly in national politics. He first joined hands with Prabhat Rai to establish a power centre in his party. Both remained friends for a few years but then drifted apart as they foresaw that their paths would soon cross as only one of them could occupy the top seat in their party's government, if it ever came to power. However, they maintained a healthy respect for each.

When Prabhat Rai and Sukhraj Malik chose to go their separate ways, they became kingpins of two different power centres in their party. When their party led coalition of National Progressive Alliance (NPA) was voted to power three years ago, they both contested the leadership of the party. In a keenly contested election, Prabhat Rai defeated Sukhraj Malik by a margin of only fourteen votes. When Rai became the Prime Minister, he inducted Malik into his Cabinet as Minister for Railways. Malik initially felt slighted for not being made a member of the CCS, but he soon brushed his frustrations aside and began attending to his job in a devoted manner. Over the past three years he literally put the Indian Railways on a fast track. The time had come when the prime minister could no longer ignore Malik's claim to one of the 'A' grade ministries and rightly elevated him to be the Home Minister.

In many ways Prabhat Rai and Sukhraj Malik were a study in contrast. Rai was urbane, cool and calculating. Malik was rustic, rough, aggressive and often abrasive. He was fluent in Hindi but lacked command over English and this pained him. He often felt outraged at the fact that even after more than sixty years of India gaining independence from the British, Hindi still had not occupied the pride of place in the country. Malik longed to exercise good command over English so that he could meet the likes of Prabhat Rai on their own turf. He had only one daughter, Sarla, on whom he doted. He sent her to the best of English medium schools and when she married six years ago, she and her husband Balwant Naik became his most trustworthy aides. He often took lessons in spoken English from his daughter and son-in-law. This helped him to an extent but he still did not feel confident enough to speak extempore in English.

Sarla and Balwant were a highly ambitious couple. They managed all affairs of Sukhraj Malik and enjoyed the power they wielded. Some reports suggested that had it not been for the domineering couple, Malik would have been the prime minister of India. But Malik, like most fathers, was blind to the faults of his wards. He had immense faith in their capabilities and they were his only advisors.

Raman Kumar had an interesting dossier. He was a pioneer as well as a product of the literacy wave sweeping across the country. He had pronounced leftist leanings and was a firebrand student leader when he was in college. But on a visit to China in his younger days, he was so impressed by the economic reforms that were taking place in China that he became a champion of the free market on his return to India. He joined the ruling party but unlike other Indian politicians for whom politics was the be all and the end all of everything in life, he also devoted lot of time to social causes.

Right from his student days Raman Kumar was obsessed with bringing about revolutionary changes in the system of education in the country. He was of the view that the thrust of the new education policy should be towards raising the levels of adult and female literacy. He believed that other important measures, like the population control, communal harmony, national integration and self-employment would automatically follow once high levels of adult and female literacy were achieved. With the help of the voluntary services provided by college students, office workers, well-meaning citizens, he was able to start a literacy movement all over the country.

His suggestions received wide media coverage. Some newspapers even suggested that he was the right person for the job of heading HRD Ministry, which had got involved in one controversy after another in the previous governments.

Prime Minister Prabhat Rai was always on the look out for competent people to help him run the government. He was impressed with the achievements of Raman Kumar as a hard working politician and an active social worker. When Prabhat Rai became the Prime Minister of India three years earlier, he invited Raman Kumar to join his Council of Ministers as Human Resources Development Minister and implement his ideas as a part of the Central Government. He was only thirty-five at that time.

Raman Kumar introduced bold changes in the system of education in India and went about his job in a highly efficient manner. With his go-getter's attitude, he also became darling of the media.

One of his avid supporters was his own nephew, Nikhilesh. He had given up his research work in the field of Political Science at Jawaharlal Nehru University to join his uncle as his Political Advisor, a post specially sanctioned by the prime minister at the insistence of Raman Kumar. The uncle and nephew made a fabulous team. Both were known to be honest and hard working with leftist political leanings.

At the end of his study of the dossiers, S.K. Sharma jotted down the names of the possible suspects in his diary. These names were:

- Anand Mishra
- K Muniappa
- Sudhir Nanda
- Nikhilesh
- T Joseph
- Sarla
- Balwant
- Swami Surynanda

Sharma was tempted to include the names of at least two ministers in the list of the possible suspects. But on second thought, he decided to concentrate his efforts on observing the conduct of the aides of the ministers for the time being.

Chapter 10

06 April

Anand Mishra, the Personal Secretary to the Foreign Minister Zafar Khan, often had pangs of guilt about the life he was leading. He felt low. He felt miserable. But he could not do anything about it. He had broken the trust and the trust is like glass. Once broken, one cannot put the pieces back together to make it whole again. Even if one tried to glue the pieces together, the scars always remained. He was condemned to live the life that he had chosen to live.

K. Muniappa, Personal Secretary to Commerce Minister Birender Singh, reached the hotel. He was received by the man, who had come to see him earlier in the day,

"Welcome Mr. Muniappa!"

"Thank you!"

"Like to have some drink?"

"No thanks. I don't drink."

Muniappa looked around.

"You are looking for the girl?"

Muniappa smiled.

"You see that girl, over there, standing all by herself?"

"The one in black trousers?"

"That is right."

"Is she the one?"

"Yes Mr. Muniappa. She is the one."

"She looks great!"

"I am happy, you like her."

"Can we go to the room now?"

"Why not? Here is the key. Room number 420. It is booked in my name."

"Thanks!"

"But before you leave Mr. Muniappa, just one small request."

"Don't worry my friend. You can collect the papers from me tomorrow."

Muniappa walked up to the girl. She followed him to room number 420.

Sudhir Nanda, the Personal Secretary to the Finance Minister Vinayak Bagchi, was feeling depressed. Many times in the past he wanted to break free. But he just could not do it. He knew that he was caught in a web of his own making. He had made a good reputation for himself in his service. He had to protect it. He decided to continue to bear with the agony and the anguish that the situation inflicted upon him for as long as he could. He would break free when he could not bear with the situation any longer.

Nikhilesh, the Political Advisor to the new Defence Minister Raman Kumar, was with his latest girlfriend.

"Nikhilesh, when will you marry me?"

"I don't know honey. In fact I am not even sure if I should ever marry."

"Why?"

"In my life there is time only for one thing. And that is my work. Uncle gives me so much of work that I hardly get any time for anything or any one else. That is why, at times, I cannot meet you for weeks at a stretch."

"But I love you Nikhilesh!"

"I love you too my dear! But marriage is a distant proposition at the moment."

"But you must promise me that if ever you marry, you'll marry only me. I will wait for you!"

"That is a gentleman's promise dear. Trust me!"

Swami Suryananda walked into the chamber of T Joseph, Personal Secretary to Prime Minister Prabhat Rai.

"Namaskar Swamiji!"

"Namaskar Joseph! How are you?"

"I am fine Swamiji."

"Joseph, the big day is not very far now. We are just about a month away from the eleventh of May"

"I know Swamiji. I will tie everything at my end."

"Good. I just came to remind you that Amrit Lall, the Director of the SPG, will be handing over charge to S.S. Dhillon by the end of this month."

"Not to worry. I can handle Dhillon."

"Sure?"

"Absolutely!"

"Great! Goodbye Joseph."

"Bye Swamiji."

Joseph knew what he had to do next. He picked up the phone and dialled a number.

It was half an hour past midnight. Sarla and Balwant, the daughter and son-in-law of the Home Minister Sukhraj Malik, were returning in their car from the Farm House party of their friend. Balwant was driving the car and Sarla was sitting with him in the front seat. Both were absorbed in their thoughts.

"Balwant," called Sarla as they were approaching a red light.

"Hum!'

"Sometimes I wonder whether what we are doing is right!"

"Me too!"

"I think we should not have got involved in it."

"But it was your suggestion. You said that it would be quite a thrill."

"I agree that it was I who got you into it. But I was a fool. I should not have done it."

"There is no point in regretting now Sarla. Let us get on with it as long as it lasts."

"But suppose somebody comes to know of it?"

"It will finish us. There will be lot of adverse publicity."

"More than us Balwant, it will finish dad."

"I agree."

"Let us withdraw from it Balwant. Even now it may not be too late."

"Whatever you say Sarla. I am with you."

Raman Kumar was not surprised to find Swami Suryananda sitting with the Prime Minister as he entered the room.

"Good evening, sir," he wished the Prime Minister.

"Good evening Kumar," said the Prime Minister, returning the greeting with a smile. "Have you met Swami Suryanandaji? Swamiji, he is Mr. Raman Kumar, our new Defence Minister."

"Who doesn't know your brilliant Defence Minister?" said the Swami in reply.

"And who doesn't know the popular Swamiji? Namaste!" Raman Kumar spoke as he bowed to the Swami.

"God bless you," said the Swami, blessing Raman Kumar by raising both hands.

"I hope I am not intruding into your private conversation?" asked Raman Kumar.

"There is nothing to hide from you Kumar," replied the Prime Minister. "You know that I trust you."

"That is so kind of you sir," replied Raman Kumar.

"So Kumar," the Prime Minister spoke, "I believe you wish to discuss some official matter regarding our missile program with me?"

"That is right sir."

"What is it?"

"Sir you will be glad to know that our Defence scientists have succeeded in developing Rudra, our Medium Range and nuclear capable Ballistic Missile, which has a range of up to 1,500 kilometers."

"Very good. Our scientists deserve hearty congratulations."

"Yes sir!" Raman Kumar concurred. "Rudra is now ready for test-fire. As this is a big occasion in the indigenization and modernization of our defence program, I would request you to kindly spare some time to personally witness the test-fire."

"Sure! When is it being arranged?"

"On the eleventh of May, off the coast of Orissa, subject to your approval and availability."

Prabhat Rai remembered that on the eleventh of May he had to be in Haridwar to perform the last of his eleven yagnas. He looked inquisitively at Swami Surynanda. He was surprised to see him engaged in deep meditation with eyes closed.

"I hope the date does not clash with any other program of yours?" asked the Defence Minister, somewhat taken aback by the reaction of the Prime Minister.

The Prime Minister spoke after a pause, "I am afraid it does. Can't we postpone the date?"

"I think we can," replied the Defence Minister. "Any problem?"

"No problem really," replied the Prime Minister. "The only thing is that I am committed to an engagement on the eleventh of May that I cannot change. So the change will have to be with the date of test-fire of Rudra, if my presence is absolutely essential. Otherwise you go ahead with the test fire."

"No sir," replied the Defence Minister. "How can that be? We will postpone the test by a few days. But you must grace the occasion personally so that our defence scientists feel proud of their achievement."

"Alright," replied the Prime Minister. "Like to have a cup of tea?"

"Thank you sir! I would like to take leave of you now."

"Hold on Mr. Kumar!" Swami Suryananda called in a deep and sonorous voice as he opened his eyes. "We need to talk."

Prabhat Rai was as surprised as Raman Kumar at the interjection of the Swami.

"What is it Swamiji that you need to talk to Kumar?" asked the Prime Minister.

"Prabhat," the Swami drew a deep breath. "From the moment he walked in today I am getting a strong feeling that somehow his fate is linked to our yagnas. I don't know what it is. May be his life is in danger too! May be he too needs to perform some yagnas!"

"What yagnas Swamiji?" asked Raman Kumar in surprise.

Prabhat Rai and Swami Surynanda exchanged a knowing glance.

"Trust me Prabhat, we have to tell him," the Swami told his disciple.

"I trust you completely Swamiji," said Prabhat Rai reassuringly. "And I also trust Kumar. You may tell him whatever you like. I have no problem."

Swami Suryananda told Raman Kumar about his having gone into a spell of deep meditation a year earlier. After a week long meditation he had told Prabhat Rai that he foresaw a grave threat to his life in the coming year. To keep away the harmful planetary influences, he urged him to undertake a chain of eleven mini yagnas. The yagnas were to be performed under the guidance of the Swami. These were to be held once a month at about 03:00 AM on eleven consecutive no-moon nights at eleven selected holy places in India. Each yagna was to be followed by a holy dip in the adjoining river, pond or sea. Rai, the faithful disciple, agreed to undertake these yagnas as advised by his guru. He decided to keep these yagnas secret to avoid any adverse publicity. Over the last nine months, nine yagnas had already been held at nine holy places in India starting with Allahabad in July the previous year and continuing through Varanasi, Puri, Dwarka, Ujjain, Nasik, Parshuram Kund, Tirupati and Gangasagar. Only two more yagnas were left now. The next was due in April and the last one in May. These were to be held at Rameswaram and Haridwar respectively.

Not many people knew about these yagnas. Apart from Prabhat Rai and the Swami, only T Joseph, the Personal Secretary to the Prime Minister and his long time political aide, knew the details of the yagnas. To ensure adequate security for the Prime Minister at the time of holding of yagnas Joseph would call Amrit Lall, the Director, SPG, a few days before the scheduled date of each yagna and inform him of its time and place of the yagna. Between the two of them, Joseph and Lall had managed to keep the yagnas away from the probing eyes of the journalists. The Prime Minister would ostensibly go on official tour to the selected destination each month and quietly slip away at night to perform the yagna at the holy spot along with Swami Suryananda.

"I don't know why it is coming to me," Swami Suryananda continued. "But Mr. Kumar, I am getting a feeling that your life too is in some danger and your fate is linked to that of the Prime Minister in this whole affair. I urge you to do some yagnas with me."

"Swamiji, thank you very much for your concern and for your offer," said Raman Kumar in a calm and confident manner. "I have profound regards for you and your beliefs, especially, keeping in view the fact that my respected Prime Minister has so much faith in your powers. But I am an agnostic by faith and an educationist by training. As a matter of principle, I have to be a rationalist. As such I can't associate myself with any yagnas or any such practices. However, it will do no harm if you say some prayers for me."

"That I'll certainly do," assured the Swami. "But you please take care of yourself. Also, feel free to contact me if you change your mind any time."

"Thanks a lot Swamiji," said Raman Kumar. "I am sure that God is with us. Your yagnas will definitely succeed in keeping all our enemies at bay."

Chapter 11

07 April

Islamabad

The perceived enemies were the six men who sat, three on each side of the table, in the conference room of the ISI building, the headquarters of the Inter-Services Intelligence of Pakistan. They were the heads of the six sections, S-1 to S-6 that comprised the ISI. The six sections had been raised to replace the two divisions when the increased workload of the ISI could not be managed by the divisions.

The ISI functioned strictly on a professional basis where 'need to know' was the most important guiding principle. Accordingly, the chief normally conferred with each sectional head separately as each one of them had been given full autonomy in the sphere of his work. They met together only when it was decided that the issue at hand was important enough in which joint involvement of all the heads was absolutely essential. The six men, knew that their chief was up to one of his big operations that necessitated the meeting.

"Salamai-le-kum," wished the General as he entered the conference room from the side door that connected it with his chamber.

"Val-ek-ul-salam," responded the six men as they stood up to greet their chief who hurried towards his seat at the head of the table.

"Please sit down," said the chief as he took his seat. They also took their seats and turned towards the chief with a look of expectancy in their eyes.

"Well, friends!" began the chief, as usual, without wasting any time. "I have called you for this meeting to inform you that from now on there is going to be a major change in our policy towards Big Brother". The reference was to India. A wave of excitement passed through the room. "As you are aware, we have felt terribly constrained during the last few years with respect to our activities in India. I think the golden era of ISI operations in India ended with the passing away of our beloved President, General Zia-ul-Haq. May God bless his soul!"

"Amen!" they whispered.

"To put things in the right perspective," said the chief, "let me begin from the beginning. During the regime of President Zia-ul-Haq I worked in S-3 which, as you know, deals with gathering of intelligence in the enemy territory. The President had given us just one line directive. 'Liberation of Kashmir and dismemberment of Big Brother to be achieved by the turn of the century, whatever be the cost'. Thereafter he gave us a free hand to resort to any tactics we considered fit to achieve our goal. Accordingly, we drew up a plan and started its implementation in right earnest. God is our witness; we achieved unbelievably high success during those early years. In fact, the success of our operations in India during the mid-eighties was so overwhelming that the then chief had assured the President that the dismemberment of the Indian Union would be achieved by 1995, five years ahead of the target date. God knows, we would most certainly have achieved that goal had the Indians not succeeded in assassinating our beloved President."

Though they did not have any evidence to establish the involvement of RAW, many Pakistanis believed that the mid-air crash of the aeroplane in which General Zia-ul-Haq was killed, was caused by a bomb planted by the Indian Intelligence Agency. RAW had hotly denied the allegation.

"His assassination was a big blow to all Pakistanis, especially, to us in the ISI." General Ginai paused for a few moments, took a sip of water from the glass lying before him and resumed. "We, probably, could have still managed to pursue our objective of destabilising the Big Brother but none of our leaders who followed our beloved President, had his zeal or his vision. As a result, we were left with no other option except to take some bold decisions on our own, without consulting the Government. We launched Operation Kargil with the help of our army. As expected, we soon had the Indians by the scruff of their neck. Unfortunately, part of our strategy went wrong. Instead of claiming that Kargil heights had been captured by our army, we tried to pass it off as a mujahideen operation - which meant that we could not participate in the operations openly. But it was not so much the wrong strategy that did us in, we had not taken into account the role that the Indian media was going to play in the Kargil operation. I am certain that left to itself, the Indian Army did not have it in them to bear with the number of casualties that we inflicted upon them. But the glorification of the dead Indian soldiers by the Indian media lifted the morale of the Indian Army to an unprecedented level. In their will to die for their country, the Indian soldiers even surpassed the mujahideen. They came by the hundreds and died by the hundreds. As we all know, it is very difficult to fight a man who is not afraid of dying. We were done in by their fervour. In a way, it was Barkha Dutt and her ilk who defeated us in Kargil and not the Indian Army.

"After the Kargil debacle we got back into doing what we do best. We started training mujahideen in a big way and drew plans to strike at Big Brother at an opportune time. But just then 9/11 happened. Al Qaeda, along with Taliban, that had been our protégé all through. But they surprised us by keeping us all in the dark about their ill advised mission of 9/11 which turned the whole world against us."

The sectional heads of the ISI, who had been listening to the monologue of their chief totally engrossed, were jolted by the very mention of Al Qaeda in his diatribe against India.

"The pressure on Pakistan to fight Al Qaeda was too much to handle," the chief continued his discourse. "General Pervez Musharraff had to give in to the Americans. In a moment of weakness he decided to throw our lot with the West. The President was quite keen to hand over the top leaders of Al Qaeda to the Americans. We, in the ISI, managed to protect them as we knew that one day Pakistan could use them as a bargaining chip with the Americans. But for that a lot depends on our present government. Our current civilian President is a capable man but he too is peace loving. He wants to give peace a fair chance before giving us a free hand to carry on with our activities with respect to the Big Brother. Things became particularly grim for us after the President met the Indian Prime Minister Prabhat Rai at the SAARC summit at Thimpu last year. He says that he finds Rai to be the sort of person with whom one could do business. Our President always reminds me of Benazir Sahiba and he talks peace just like her. 'Move with caution' he said and 'move with caution' has been our policy ever since."

"Why not bump him off too?" suggested S-5.

"No my friend," replied the chief. "We have enough blood of our own leaders on our hands. I do not feel like adding any more. Moreover the President has a certain place in the world community. We might need him. He says that he finds it much easier to deal with a straightforward person like Prabhat Rai. He may be right if Rai is really as straightforward as our prime minister believes him to be. But this does not mean that we allow Big Brother to become so strong and powerful that our own existence gets threatened! Rai may be a good man but he is not going to last forever. What would happen if one of those fanatic Hindus assumes power when Big Brother is too powerful for us to handle? Remember, Narendra Modi has been knocking at the door of the Indian Prime Ministership for quite some time now. He has been able to project himself as a vikaas purush, the harbinger of progress.

"As for their power and progress, just see what great economic transformation they have achieved during the last decade or so. They are an IT superpower and they have become the most favoured destination for many countries for business outsourcing. Their foreign exchange reserves have crossed three hundred billion dollars. Their trade deficit has been almost entirely wiped out. Their economy is booming and unemployment has come down to acceptable levels. True, we have also made good progress during this period of relative calm but we must remember that Pakistan is a small country compared to India and at this rate, will forever remain small. In fact, if we do not act soon enough, our friends in the RAW are not going to sit and relax. They are not dumb. They also have plans to destroy Pakistan and going by what they are doing in Sindh and Baluchistan, we all must be truly worried. For us, it is a question of our survival and it is a race against time. If Pakistan has to survive, Big Brother must be disintegrated. Unfortunately, our politicians do not fully understand the seriousness of the situation. So we have to act on our own. And I assure you, this time our President will not interfere in our activities."

"Chief," interrupted S-1. "Has the President given green signal to reverse the 'Be Cautious' policy now?"

"Well!" the chief spoke after a pause. "The answer is no. That is why I said we will have to act on our own now. So all our planning on Big Brother must be kept strictly confidential. No politician or bureaucrat - be it the President, the Prime Minister, Defence Minister, Home or Foreign Minister or some top notch government secretary- none of them should ever come to know of our planned operations in India. We will inform them of our operations only when these have been successfully executed and they would be left with no other option except to support us and accept our operations as fait accompli. So we must act and act fast. Presently, we have got a very valuable contact close to the top levels of the Indian government who has entrenched himself so well in the present set up that he even has access to the decisions taken by their Cabinet Committee on Security which is the highest decision making body of the Indian government on matters of security. If we can't succeed in our mission now, we never will. And it is time that we encash our blank cheque called Al Qaeda."

There was a pin drop silence in the room for some time. The chief waited for someone to ask the obvious next question. He was relieved when S-4 came forward to do the bit.

"Has the time come for us to hand over Al Qaeda leaders to the Americans?" asked S-4.

"Yes," replied the chief. "The Americans have dug themselves into a deep hole in Iraq and Afghanistan. On top of that they are getting reports by the dozen on Al Qaeda planning 9/11 type of operations in the USA, Russia and other Western countries some time very soon. What the jihadis did to Hotels Taj and Oberoi in Mumbai in November 2008 is not lost upon anyone. The Americans have realized that they have to smash Al Qaeda Command Centre, once and for all, to have any chance of victory over the jihadis. They have also realized that they cannot do it on their own. They need us. But I have made it absolutely clear to them that you get me Kashmir, I'll get you Al Qaeda."

"So what do they say now?" asked S-1.

"A few days ago," the chief continued, "I received an honoured guest from that friendly agency whose name starts with a capital C, as all of you know. He has given me a proposal to launch an operation in India. He has given it the name Operation Red Rose which I like."

The chief then proceeded to give his officers an outline of Operation Red Rose.

"Right now," said the chief as he finished explaining the gist of Operation Red Rose, "I want each of one of you to think over this planned operation and see how we can make it succeed, how we can make use of this valuable contact in New Delhi to get a favourable decision from the Indians. Please come up with a workable draft plan within a week's time. We shall discuss your plans in the next meeting and pick up the best one for implementation. Any questions?"

"Just one question chief," asked S-5. "What operational levels can we include in the draft plan?"

"Good question," commented the chief. "You are free to include all levels of operations in your plan, even level five. In fact level five should be the preferred level. Enough of Kargils, Kandhars and Mumbais. It is time for some direct action. "

Everybody knew that level five included assassination of some top political dignitary in India.

Chapter 12

12 April

S.K. Sharma, the Director of IB, entered the Prime Minister's residential office. Despite a hectic day's work, Prabhat Rai looked calm and relaxed.

"Welcome Mr. Sharma and have a seat," said the Prime Minister as he shook hands with the visiting officer.

"Thank you sir," said Sharma as he sat in the chair.

"There must be something very important Mr. Sharma that you wished to discuss only with me and no one else?"

"Yes sir. I think it is very important."

"Not very serious, I presume?"

"I am afraid sir, it is serious. Let me explain. I will tell you in brief and be to the point."

"Take your time."

"Thank you sir! Sir, you may find it difficult to believe but as per our agent in Washington, there is someone close to the top levels of our government who is a CIA mole."

"That can't be true!" exclaimed Prabhat Rai.

"It would be true sir, if you just verify the authenticity of this document."

"What is this?"

"Sir this a copy of the minutes of the last CCS meeting held on the twenty-eighth of the last month. I am not supposed to have a copy of this top secret document but I got it from the Director of RAW who got it from his agent in Washington."

"Don't tell me that Mr. Sharma!"

"Sir, just have a look at it. If it is a fake document, none will be more relieved than me."

The Prime Minister did as requested. The IB Director observed the changed expression on the face of the Prime Minister that said it all.

"This copy is indeed authentic Mr. Sharma," despaired Prabhat Rai.

"That means sir, the report from RAW is true indeed," said Sharma in a quiet tone. "There is a CIA mole in our Government. He is someone who has access to the CCS deliberations. Unfortunately, RAW has not been able to establish his identity. So I have a job at my hand. Sir, you will agree with me that we cannot take chances with the country's security. I request you to kindly grant me permission to put some well connected persons in our government under surveillance."

"Mr. Sharma, I hope you understand the implications of what you are saying?"

"I really understand sir. But under the present circumstances, we have to take some hard decisions."

"Alright Mr. Sharma," said the Prime Minister after a long pause. "You have my permission. But who are the people whom you wish to shadow?"

"Sir, I will start with the people who may have some access to the CCS decisions."

"You mean, you suspect my ministers too?"

"Not ministers sir! I am sorry if I gave you such an impression. But I have to watch their staff and people close to them. If there is a CIA mole here, he has to be one of the aides of the top ministers."

"Why hasn't RAW got full details of the CIA mole's identity from their source in Washington, if indeed there is a mole here?" inquired the Prime Minister.

"They are trying to get that," replied Sharma. "But I want to get on with my job here as well."

"Okay Mr. Sharma," said the Prime Minister. "Please go ahead with your work and keep me informed of the progress you make."

"Sure sir," said the IB Director. "I'll take leave of you now. Good night!"

"Good night, Mr. Sharma!"

Prabhat Rai pondered over the whole issue for some time after the IB chief had left. He tried to anticipate the fallout of the expose of the CIA mole on his government as and when it became public. The administrator in him told him to keep the whole matter confidential so that IB could catch the traitor soon. But the politician in him told him to warn his colleagues of the perils of the expose and hope that whosoever was responsible for the leakage of CCS minutes to the CIA, would be able to retrace his steps from the potentially irretrievable situation. He let the politician prevail upon the administrator.

At about 11.30 PM Sukhraj Malik entered the residential office of the Prime Minister, not knowing why he had been called at that late hour. He was surprised to see other members of the CCS already sitting there and engaged in some casual conversation. They received him warmly. Sukhraj Malik found out that they were as ignorant of the purpose of the emergency meeting as he was.

"Good evening gentlemen!" said the Prime Minister Prabhat Rai as he joined the five wise men.

"Good evening sir!" the ministers extended their wishes as they got up to greet him.

"Please sit down," said the Prime Minister and they all occupied their seats. "So how is the new CCS doing?"

"Going great guns!" said Birender Singh smilingly.

"Good," commented the Prime Minister. Then he became quiet, somewhat pensive. The ministers, particularly Birender Singh, were taken aback by the Prime Minister's cold response. They knew that they had not been called to discuss the performance of the CCS. There was something else that appeared to be bothering the Prime Minister.

"Gentlemen," the Prime Minister spoke after some time. "I have called the five of you to share my anxiety with you over something very important. Mr S.K.Sharma, the Director of the Intelligence Bureau, came to see me this evening. He told me that he had received information from Washington, courtesy RAW, that there is a CIA mole working in the inner circles of our government."

"I can't believe it," shouted Birender Singh.

"How can that be?" asked Sukhraj Malik.

"This is really shocking!" commented Raman Kumar.

Zafar Khan and Vinayak Bagchi were equally shocked but remained silent.

"I did not believe it either when I first heard it," said the Prime Minister. "But RAW has given incontrovertible evidence in support of their claim. Sharma gave me a copy of the top secret minutes of the last CCS meeting which, I believe, are already doing the rounds of the intelligence agencies, the world over."

"That is indeed shocking sir," said Suraj Chopra, the National Security Advisor. "I gave copies of the minutes only to the members of the CCS."

"No one doubts that Suraj," said the Prime Minister. "But we have our personal staff that we trust completely. It is obvious that someone is misusing that trust."

"So what do we do now?" asked Sukhraj Malik.

"Malikji, this is a matter on which we cannot take any chances," replied Prabhat Rai. "I have authorized the IB Director to carry out full scale investigations and I need the unqualified support of the CCS for this decision. A collective decision is a must to face any adverse publicity that might result out of this affair. I hope I have the full support of each one of you?"

"Of course you have," said Zafar Khan. "No question about that." Others nodded in agreement.

"Good," said the Prime Minister. "Now please extend full co-operation to the IB and do not feel intimidated if you find them spying in your backyards. Please do not try to shield anyone. Who knows the CIA agent, if any, might be close to either of you or to me for that matter. We must trust IB to do a competent job. At the same time, let us hope and pray that it is only an empty alarm and the situation will blow over soon by itself. That is all I had to share with you. Since it is already late, we might as well call it a day. Good night everybody!"

Good night!" said the five bewildered men and left the Prime Minister's residence, one by one.

Chapter 13

13 April

Finally the big day for Sunita and Yogesh arrived when they were to become man and wife. They had decided to solemnize their marriage during the day time. Not many people had been invited and there was hardly any pomp and show at the Community Hall where the marriage had been arranged. Many of the invitees were classmates of Sunita and Yogesh. They were quite surprised at the speed with which the marriage had been arranged. They did not believe Sunita and Yogesh when they told them that their affair started only after the last paper of their final examination was over. They suspected that the two of them had concealed their romance from them and complimented them for keeping it a secret for such a long time.

Among the other guests there were a number of relatives from Sunita's side, her father's friends and colleagues and some of their neighbours.

From the side of Yogesh there was only one relative. He arrived when the marriage was being solemnized. "I am Sanjay Sarang, Colonel Sanjay Sarang from the Indian Army," he introduced himself to Sunita's parents. "I am Yogesh's uncle, his mother's elder brother."

"Where are you posted these days Colonel?" asked Sunita's father, as they shook hands.

"At Roorkee, in Haridwar District," replied Colonel Sarang.

"I know the place," said Sunita's father. "A small but lovely town. I have passed through Roorkee a number of times but never stayed there."

"Come over now," said the colonel. "Stay with me and see the army way of life."

"Sure!" said the Chief Postmaster General.

Tears came to the eyes of Colonel Sarang when he saw his sister. She put her arms around her brother and began to cry. Though they had maintained regular contact, it was not often that they got to see each other. Colonel Sarang always felt pangs of hurt and helplessness whenever he met his sister. Her husband, Major Saif Naqvi, would have been his age if he were alive. The death of his dear friend and brother-in-law had such an effect on him that he could never prepare himself to marry. He remained a bachelor all his life. Another person who arrived when the marriage ceremony was being held was Shafi Rehman, a friend of Yogesh from school days. They had joined the college also together but Shafi dropped out in the second year. From the school days his first love was theatre, not studies. While in college, he got an offer to work for a theatre group and he thought it more prudent to leave college and join theatre, a decision that he never regretted. He was not making much money but he was doing something which he thoroughly enjoyed.

The marriage ceremony was followed by lunch and presentation of wedding gifts by the guests to the newly weds. The friends of Sunita and Yogesh gave a joint gift in the form of booking of a special room in Hotel Hyatt Regency for their wedding night. "On the condition that you would describe the full details to us tomorrow morning so that we can all learn from your experiences," they joked.

Sunita's parents gave them virtually everything that was required by the young couple to make a comfortable living - a television set, an air conditioner, one refrigerator, some furniture, other household items and a motorcycle.

Yogesh felt a sense of outrage on seeing the dowry. But he had to give in to the reasoning put forward by Sunita's father. He had said, "Dowry is a curse if it is demanded as a price for accepting one's daughter's hand but if it is given by the girl's parents on their own accord and without taxing themselves, it is a useful custom. Dowry should be taken as a loan from one generation to the next. We have done our duty and when your turn comes, you do yours. The chain should continue."

The merry making continued till late in the afternoon. Finally the time came for the bride to take leave from her family. She left with Yogesh, sad to leave a home behind but with dreams of finding an equally happy home ahead.

Sunita was received by her mother-in-law at her house in the traditional manner, by pouring oil at the two sides of the main door of her house. They had an early dinner and Sunita and Yogesh left for the Hotel Hyatt Regency at just past 8 P.M.

The room at the hotel had been specially done up for the occasion. Dim lights emanated from the four corners of the room. Card-board cut-outs were hanging from the ceiling, displaying messages wishing Sunita and Yogesh a happy married life. They were grateful to their friends for arranging such a wonderful wedding gift.

They sat on the sofa to have some chat. Sunita took out one orange and peeled off its skin. They relished the orange and talked about their parents and friends for some time. Then Yogesh got up from the sofa. He opened the suitcase and brought out two pairs of gold bangles and offered them to Sunita. "Here is my wedding night gift for you," he said. She put on the bangles, one pair on each hand. He took out one blue nylon negligee as well and gave it to her. "I would like you to change into this," he said.

Sunita opened her vanity bag and took out a gleaming silver watch. "And I would like you to wear this," she said.

They hugged and kissed and felt very happy.

"I want to have a shower," said Sunita. "What about you?"

"Me too!"

"Then you go first."

"Why not go together?"

"Don't be naughty, you go," said Sunita and gently pushed him towards the bathroom.

Yogesh had shower and came out in his nightgown. "Your turn," he said.

Sunita also took shower. She was wearing the new blue negligee presented by Yogesh, when she came out of the bath room. She had sprayed an extremely musky perfume over her body. The perfume filled the room and proved to be a heady stuff. Yogesh's heart began to beat fast and he felt very excited. They stood about three feet apart and continued to look at each other for some time without saying a word.

"Darling!" Yogesh murmured after what appeared to be an eternity. "Please take off your negligee."

"You take off your gown first," she replied. Even in the dim light of the room he could see her cheeks turn red.

"Alright," he said. He could understand her hesitation to undress as he himself had a similar feeling while taking off his gown and the underwear. She followed him, throwing her negligee on the floor. She was not wearing any undergarments.

It was for the first time that Yogesh had seen a woman in all her nakedness. He was enthralled by what he saw. Her lovely face with seductive looks in her bright black eyes, her long black hair flowing on her shoulders and back, her fair complexion, the tautness of her skin and the roundness of her curves had him absolutely transfixed. Her presence and the apt surroundings had a kind of effect on him that he had never experienced before. He was finding it difficult to breathe. He felt giddy and had to shake his head to take control of himself. Slowly he moved towards her as she continued to look at him with lustful eyes. He took her hands in his and pulled her closer. They began to kiss passionately. While still locked in the kiss they moved to the waiting bed and amid a mixture of pain and pleasure, they consummated their marriage.

Chapter 14

14 April

Sukhraj Malik was in an agitated mood when his daughter Sarla and son-in-law Balwant entered his room. They had arrived in New Delhi in the evening after spending a week in Malik's constituency.

"What is the matter dad?" asked Sarla. "You appear to be upset?"

"I have reason to be upset Sarla," said Malik.

"Why? What happened?" asked Balwant.

"Just when we thought our government was doing extremely well, we have got this bad news," replied his father-in-law. "The Prime Minister had called the members of CCS to an informal meeting three days ago. He told us that as per our intelligence agency RAW, there is a CIA agent in the inner circles of our government who is supplying sensitive information to the Americans."

"Impossible!" blurted Sarla.

"Why impossible?" interjected Balwant. "I always suspected that holy man to be a foreign agent and now I have been proven right. It must be that lousy Swami, Suryananda. He is extremely close to Prabhat Rai. I am sure Rai confides everything in him. The Swami has contacts with many people abroad. I do not know what these foreigners see in our god men! The Swami has to be the CIA man."

"Don't jump to conclusions so quickly," Sarla cautioned her husband. "There should be some evidence against him before branding him as the enemy agent."

"His foreign contacts are the evidence," claimed Balwant. "Imagine, the spiritual guru of our Honourable Prime Minister, as the CIA man. Dad, we must not let go of this golden opportunity to settle old scores with Prabhat Rai. If we can prove the Swami to be the CIA mole, which in all probability he is, Prabhat Rai will fall flat on his face. In such a scenario, you won't have any other contender for the prime minister's chair."

"Dad, what Balwant says really makes sense," said Sarla. "We must expose the Swami, if he is what Balwant suspects him to be."

"I know Sarla," said Sukhraj Malik. "But we must have some clinching proof of his involvement in the spy affair before we can lay our hands on him. Otherwise the allegation may do us more harm than good."

"Don't worry about that dad," Balwant assured his father-in-law. "We will be careful in handling the whole affair. Let our intelligence people carry on with their investigations and we'll carry on with our own. God willing, that time may not be far when you will be the prime minister of India."

"How is it possible?" countered Nikhilesh when his uncle Raman Kumar told him about the existence of the CIA mole in the Indian Government. "It cannot be true!"

"It must be true," said Raman Kumar in reply. "RAW Director has received this information right from within the CIA and passed it on to the IB."

"How shocking indeed!"

"Sometimes I feel I should quit politics," said Raman Kumar. "It is such a dirty game. I was so happy doing my social work. I had made such a name for myself there. But now, here I am in the cesspool of politics. I have given my best to this government but how can you continue in a government where you can't hold any secrets? Can a government function with the knowledge that there is an enemy agent in its midst?"

"But what about the IB?" inquired Nikhilesh. "What are they up to? Do they have any suspects?"

"Must be having some," replied Raman Kumar. "They are doing their job and I am sure they will find out the guy soon. But that might result in the fall of our government under the weight of this hell of a scandal. I wish I had continued with my social work in the field. It was so satisfying. No scandals, no tensions."

"I think you and I have no reason to worry," said Nikhilesh. "We have nothing to do with the CIA. Let the worry be with the person who works for the CIA."

"Swamiji, we must find out the CIA man," Prabhat Rai told Swami Suryananda. "I am really worried."

"There is nothing to worry in it," said the Swami matter-of-factly.

"But it is a serious matter Swamiji!"

"Yes, it is serious," the Swami was still unruffled. "But running a government is always a serious matter. These things do happen in governments. Now-a-days there are no secrets between any two governments - be it the USA, UK, France, Russia or any other country. They have full information about the inside activities of one another. Traditional values are no more sacrosanct in today's world. Patriotism is an empty slogan. Money is the reigning god. If you have money you can easily purchase people. In fact, it is a buyers' market. There are so many people up for sale everywhere. So if the enemy has planted a mole here, there is no reason to get alarmed. They have done their job. Our intelligence people will do their job. But the work of the government goes on and must go on despite these setbacks. These are but an essential part of today's governance, a necessary evil you may say."

"Still, it is disturbing," said Prabhat Rai. "It is disturbing in the sense that you do not know whom to trust and whom not to trust."

"That is why ignorance is said to be bliss," the Swami continued with his sermon. "When you and others did not know about the existence of the CIA mole, you were quite happy with the way things were. Now that the matter has come out in the open, everybody is disturbed. Such things should not be allowed to come to the level of the prime minister or his senior ministers. Our people in RAW, in IB, the army and the police should deal with them at their own level."

"They are investigating the matter. I am sure; they will be able to identify the person soon."

"But will that make people happy?" asked the Swami. "The exposure might cause more harm than good. The mole might turn out to be a man whom one always trusted completely. The knowledge can have a damaging effect on the personality of the person who reposed the trust."

"But Swamiji, that does not mean people should be allowed to continue to carry on with their dangerous activities?"

"Not at all! Such people must be caught. But catching them should not become our only goal. There are men on the job and they should be left to sort it out themselves. We should concentrate on our mission which is to ensure that no harm comes to you as a result of the coming together of some unfavourable planets in your horoscope."

"I have nothing to fear so long as I have your blessings."

"Blessings are of the Almighty," the Swami declared. "My job is merely to remove all obstacles that come in your way."

"You have always succeeded in doing that."

"God willing, we will succeed this time also. After all we have successfully performed ten yagnas already!"

"Yes Swamiji. Now it is a matter of only one more yagna at Haridwar on the eleventh of May."

"Yes. Think of some way of being there. 'Operation Clean Up of the Holy Ganges' could be a good alibi."

"Yes Swamiji, Operation Clean Up or Tehri Dam. The Dam controversy is still going on."

"Make sure to side with the environmentalists. That would be in tune with your last annual address to the nation."

"Of course, Swamiji," said Rai.

The unorthodox reasoning of the Swami about the spy affair left Prabhat Rai a bit disturbed. He did not know why? But he felt good when he remembered that there won't be any more yagnas after Haridwar.

In the evening, Prabhat Rai discussed the same point with Joseph, his Personal Secretary and long time political aide. "You see, I find this information very depressing. I have worked very hard during my three decades of public life to build a clean image. I thought, when I leave the political scene, I would be leaving a fair reputation behind. This spy business, however, might cast its murky shadow over my reputation. No scandal has ever touched me during my political career. If this one comes out in the open and the man turns out to be somebody close to us, it would be quite a blow to my name."

"But sir, this could be a case of disinformation also," said Joseph. "Perhaps someone is playing a destabilising game, pinning one group in our government against the other and sowing the seeds of mistrust among our senior ministers".

"Could be, but unlikely," said the Prime Minister after pondering over what Joseph said. "I know the IB Director well. Sharma is a thorough professional and would come to me only after discounting all such possibilities."

"So how is IB going about it now?"

"The usual procedure; telephone tapping, mail censoring and keeping a watch on the suspects. IB Director has those powers, you know! And he must have already finalised the list of suspects".

Joseph wondered what the list would be like. He was anxious to know whether or not his name also figured in the list. He used his influence to find out from the Telecom authorities whether his phones were tapped or not. He was not happy when he came to know that his phones were also being tapped.

"How would you react if you are told that there is a CIA agent working in our government?" Vinayak Bagchi put the question, quite unexpectedly, to Sudhir Nanda, his Personal Secretary. Then he began to observe the changes in his face expression.

The question caught Nanda unawares. He looked blank, giving the impression that he had not been able to fully comprehend the question. "Please say it again sir!" he requested his minister.

"Never mind" said Bagchi with a smile. "I was just joking." He had already got his answer. Nanda was not a suspect as far as Vinayak Bagchi was concerned.

"Sir, here is the official record of the keys of your office cabinet." Anand Mishra was telling his minister, Zafar Khan. "As ordered by you, I have called for this register from the Central Issue Office. This cabinet has been supplied with only two keys and both these keys are held in your personal custody. You may rest assured that no other person has access to the documents kept in the cabinet."

"Thanks," said Zafar Khan as he returned the register to Anand Mishra. He was satisfied with the knowledge that no information could ever leak from his office.

"Muniappa I am a proud old man," Commerce Minister Birender Singh was discussing his personal life with his Personal Secretary. After the demise of his wife two years ago, Muniappa had been the only person before whom he laid bare his sorrows. "I can't go and beg of my son that I need him for emotional support. Ranjit is my only son and he is supposed to understand my needs."

"I think, sir, his business interests in the USA do not allow him to come and stay in India," said Muniappa.

"Where is the need to do business in the USA?" queried Birender Singh. "We have enough land of our own here to which he is the only heir. He can come and live here as the son of Birender Singh without doing any work!"

"Perhaps that is precisely what appears to be bothering him," said Muniappa. "He wants to prove that he is much more than the son of his father. He wants to show his individuality."

"Let him live with his individuality and his dollars," said Birender Singh, trying to bring firmness in his voice. "I'll learn to live without him."

Chapter 15

15 April

An extremely happy Sunita and Yogesh visited her parents' house to see them before going to Kasauli for a week long honeymoon. Her parents were happy to see them happily married.

"I have something important to discuss with you two before you leave for Kasauli," said Sunita's father.

"What is it papa?" asked Yogesh, addressing his father-in-law the same way as his wife, as per the Indian custom. He had a strange feeling when he addressed a man as 'papa' for the first time in his life. He had often pined for someone whom he could call 'papa'.

"This is about your future plans," replied Sunita's father. Sunita and Yogesh looked at each other in surprise. They had forgotten everything except the pleasures of the marriage. They had thought that the fun would never end. But her father brought them back to the world of reality.

"It is too early to think about that papa," said Sunita. "Our results will be out in about a month or so. Then we will see how to go about scouting for a job."

"New job, eh!" said her father. "But I thought you were going to start your own Advertising Agency?"

"Yes, we would love to, but where is the money?" asked Sunita in reply.

"Wait a minute," said the old man. He got up from his chair and went to his bedroom. He returned after a minute, holding a small plastic cover in his hand. "What about this?" he asked as he gave the cover to Sunita.

"What is it papa?" Sunita asked in surprise.

"See for yourself!" her father replied, smiling to himself.

Sunita opened the cover. It contained some papers. She pulled the papers and had a look at them. "Infosys?" she muttered.

"Infosys what?" asked Yogesh, surprised at the mention of one of the most successful software companies in India.

"Share certificates," she replied. "These are share certificates in my name from Infosys."

They were all silent for a while as her father continued to smile to himself. He looked towards Sunita's mother who gave him an appreciative glance.

"Papa I don't understand!" said Sunita, unable to comprehend anything. "I never invested any money in Infosys or any other company.

"You did not, but we did it for you, with your money!" he replied.

"My money? How?"

"You know how many shares you have in your hands?" asked Sunita's father, ignoring her question.

"Let me see." She began to browse through the papers.

"Seven hundred and twenty," her father volunteered the information.

"Seven hundred and twenty Infosys shares in my name?" asked an incredulous Sunita.

"You know the worth of one Infosys share today?" asked her father.

"I think it is three thousand plus," Yogesh chipped in.

"Three thousand and twentythree, to be precise, was yesterday's closing rate," said Sunita's father.

"Three thousand and twentythree?" exclaimed Sunita. "Papa, you mean, these documents that I am holding, are worth more than two million rupees?"

"That is absolutely correct my dear," said her father. "And please remember! This is your money, every penny of it."

"How can that be?" asked Sunita. "It must have cost you a fortune to acquire these seven hundred and twenty shares. I never had that kind of money with me."

"It did not cost me anything," the father replied.

Yogesh and Sunita were still as puzzled as before. They pleaded with the old man to unravel the mystery.

"There is no mystery really," he spoke with a smile. "Only prudence and luck. Sunita, the story goes back about twenty years. My father bought one hundred Infosys shares in a public issue. He gave these shares to you as gift on your first birthday. We were not sure how Infosys shares would fare in the long run. But under the dynamic leadership of Narayan Murthy and Nandan Nilekeni, the company made a phenomenal progress. Its shares scaled such heights as were never seen before in the Indian stock markets. However, I did not dispose off even a single share. On the contrary, I reinvested all the dividend earnings in Infosys itself and accepted all the bonus shares on your behalf. These have now multiplied to seven hundred and twenty shares worth over twenty lakh rupees. But essentially it remains a small investment of your grandfather's money which he gifted to you."

"Incredible!" exclaimed Sunita. "Thanks papa, thanks mom and thanks grandpa, wherever you are, up there," said Sunita, looking up to the sky. Then she got up and planted a kiss on the forehead of each of her parents. "You two have been wonderful parents. I wish everybody has parents like you. I am especially grateful to you for keeping the investment a secret from me all these years. Otherwise I might not have got the same joy as I am having now. Now we really have enough money with which Yogesh and I can start our own Advertising Agency."

Yogesh was too overwhelmed by the sudden turn of the events. For a moment he felt small. He thought that he would be living off his wife's money. But he soon consoled himself that he did not have any idea of how much money she had when he had proposed to her. He had loved her as a person and did not want to have anything other than her love for him. But what an upswing his fortune had taken! Till only a month ago, he was a lonely person living with a lonely mother. Within a month he had the woman he loved with all the passion in the world; he had all the necessities of a good life and now his wife had enough money with which they could start their own Ad Agency.

"By the way," said Sunita's father, "I know the proprietor of World Trade Towers and had casually asked him the other day if he could rent out some space for your office in the building. He has some space available right now. Would you be interested in it?"

"Why not?" replied Yogesh. "World Trade Towers is a well known shopping-cum-office complex and is ideally located near Connaught Place, the major business centre of Delhi."

"Then I'll have a word with him in a day or two," replied Sunita's father.

"When would you like to start your new venture?" inquired Sunita's mother.

"At the earliest," said Sunita.

"What about the shares?" asked her father.

"I think we can sell fifty of them straightaway," replied Sunita. "We'll need some cash."

"Fifty will be enough for the time being," added Yogesh.

"Right," said Sunita's father. "You go to Kasauli and I will tie up with the broker and the proprietor of World Trade Towers in your absence."

"I still cannot believe all this is happening," said Sunita. "I think Yogesh has proved to be really lucky for me."

"It is the other way round," said Yogesh. "It is you who have proved to be lucky for me."

"You are both lucky for each other," said Sunita's mother. "Remember, God is always kind and merciful to good and kind people. Be good and kind to each other and to others. God will give you more. You have made an excellent beginning to your married life and keep it that way."

The happy young couple sought the blessings of the happy old couple and left for Kasauli to celebrate their week long honeymoon.

Chapter 16

17 April

The Director of RAW was ready with his brief to the CCS. The three service chiefs were special invitees to today's meeting. All the members of the CCS were already present in the mini conference room, attached to the Prime Minister's chamber, when the Prime Minister walked in. They all stood up.

"Please sit down," said the Prime Minister, as he walked to his seat at the head of the conference table. They all resumed their seats.

"Gentlemen," began the Prime Minister, "I have called this meeting to share more bad news with you which might have serious consequences on the security of our country. This is the second bad news that Mr. Reddy has brought to us in less than a month. The omens are not good for our government. We need to do some serious thinking. Last time it was from Washington. This time Mr. Reddy has been able to gather some disturbing information from his sources in Islamabad. I'll request him to share that information with you all."

'Thank you sir," said Bikshap Reddy. "Gentlemen, as you know, it is not very easy to get any information out of the ISI. They generally have an impregnable wall around them which our boys have been able to breach only occasionally. Therefore, solid and reliable information is hard to come by from Islamabad. But recently, we have had some success in securing some information which appears to be disturbing."

"What is it Mr. Reddy?" asked Sukhraj Malik.

"Sir, it appears that the ISI is up to its dirty old tricks again. It seems that they are planning to launch a Kargil type misadventure in India once again."

"You mean they are preparing for another war?" asked Raman Kumar.

"May be or may be not," replied Reddy. "We have not got the details yet. But what they are planning to launch in our country, is an operation which they call Operation Red Rose."

"Operation Red Rose?" this time it was Zafar Khan. "What is that supposed to be?"

"As I said earlier, sir," replied Reddy, "the details are not known yet. But one thing is for sure. The main objective of that operation is Kashmir and when it comes to Kashmir, Pakistanis lose all sense of balance. They are quite capable of taking totally irrational and unexpected actions. An invasion of Kashmir, therefore, cannot be ruled out."

"They must have gone insane," commented Birender Singh. "They know that we both are nuclear powers. It might lead to catastrophic consequences for both countries if things go out of control!"

"What are the orders for us," asked General Surinder Pal, the army chief, matter-of-factly, on behalf of all three service chiefs. "Shall we mobilise our forces?"

"That may be a bit premature General," said the Prime Minister. "Mobilisation of forces without knowing the full details of the so-called Operation Red Rose may create an international furore. We'll not be in a position to explain to the satisfaction of other countries. It might cause us avoidable diplomatic embarrassment. But what you should do is, keep the forces on full alert. Review your war plans, check your logistics and be fully prepared to engage them, if the need arose."

The three chiefs nodded in agreement.

"But sir," interjected Zafar Khan. "You must speak to the Prime Minister or the President of Pakistan about it. It is quite possible that just as they did at the time of Kargil, this whole operation is being planned only by the ISI and the Pakistani army. The Government of Pakistan may be totally in the dark about it."

"You are right Zafar," said the Prime Minister. "I too am of the opinion that the Prime Minister of Pakistan is not a party to any action that can lead to escalation of hostilities between our two countries. I think I know him well. He appears to be an honourable man and, like me, he too is keen to have a peaceful resolution to the Kashmir problem. So I must speak to him to caution him of any misadventure on the part of his army. I will do that as soon as it is possible."

"Anything else sir?" Vinayak Bagchi addressed the Prime Minister.

"Only one thing gentlemen." responded the Prime Minister. "I have already spoken to all of you about the need to treat discussions in the CCS as top secret. I urge you once again not to discuss anything with anyone who is not authorised to know what is discussed here. This includes your family members, your aides and your personal staff. I do not want a repeat of the last CCS meeting. I hope I have made myself abundantly clear to all of you."

They nodded in agreement.

"All right then," said the Prime Minister." The meeting is closed."

Chapter 17

21 April

Sunita and Yogesh returned to New Delhi after spending a week at Kasauli. Their honeymoon was a rewarding experience for both. What started as a means of physical gratification, turned into a deep emotional bond between two individuals. For the first couple of days they did nothing but make love. And the two days of constant lovemaking left them completely exhausted. Thereafter what they enjoyed most was each other's presence, the closeness, the touch or simply lying together in the bed. They felt highly gratified. They realised that the lives of a man and a woman were complete only when each gave oneself completely to the other. The pleasure of giving was greater than the pleasure of receiving.

Sunita's father took them to the World Trade Towers to show them the moderately spacious room that was to be their office. He had successfully negotiated the deal in their absence. They liked the room which was located on the seventh floor of the building. The building housed a shopping plaza in its basement and on the ground floor. The upper floors had all been rented out to offices of various companies. As the shopping centre was restricted to only two floors, the presence of the customers did not cause any hindrance to the working of offices on the upper floors. On the contrary, it added to the glamour of owning an office in the World Trade Towers. Whenever the executives needed a change of scene, they could simply catch a lift to the ground floor and walk around, have a cup of tea or drink a glass of beer.

Sunita and Yogesh liked the deal. They calculated that they would require about 8-10 days to do the necessary furnishings. What they required in the beginning was some office furniture, telephone, a couple of PCs, a photocopier and some aluminium or glass partition to divide the room into three or four cubicles. They did not feel the need to hire any staff in the beginning other than one artist who could work either part time or full time with them if he was found to be not too expensive. They had planned to prepare some sample ads for some business firms and show these to their managements to win new contracts.

"Have you selected a name for your agency?" asked Sunita's father.

"Yes papa," replied Sunita. "We decided on the name when we were at Kasauli."

"What is it?"

"Sonyog," replied Yogesh.

"Sonyog!" repeated Sunita's father. "'Sony' from Sunita and 'Yog' from Yogesh. Excellent! Let us pray that 'Sonyog' would be a roaring success!"

Chapter 18

25 April

Islamabad

"Yes partner, what is so urgent?" asked the ISI Chief as soon as he saw S-3 enter his office. S-3 had just sought an urgent meeting with him.

"Sir," replied S-3, "I have some great news for you. What our friends have delivered to us in New Delhi is twenty-four carat gold. The man is strategically located and what is more important to us is that he is willing to go more than a mile to cooperate with us."

"That is fantastic," said a visibly happy chief. "I was waiting only for this day. I knew that a day would come when Allah would give us an opportunity like this. God save the Indians now that we have got our foothold in their government. But partner, please for God's sake, keep this information top secret. I don't want to take any chances now. One slip and Operation Red Rose is kaput."

"I'll ensure the confidentiality, sir," assured S-3.

"I appreciate that," replied the Chief. "I believe the Cipher Officer, who deciphered this message, will be the only one here, other than you and me, to know this information?"

"That is right sir," replied S-3.

"He should also be suitably instructed. Right now our main attention, however, should be towards maintaining contact with this source in New Delhi. We should not lose him at any cost. To deal with him we will step up the security classification of communication with him to Top-A, which means that from now on, his communication will be available to only one person in the ISI and that is me. Even you will not be privy to that communication. You know the rules!"

"Not to worry sir!" said S-3.

"Good," the chief continued. "I am an old fashioned man. I do not trust the electronic media for passing top secret information with all the spyware floating around on the internet and telephone networks. Tomorrow I will give you one sealed cover which should be got delivered to our contact in New Delhi at the earliest. The cover will contain instructions for him to launch Operation Red Rose. The instructions will go as a coded message. All coded communication from our contact will be handed over to me and I will personally decipher the same. Please tell our boys in New Delhi not to contact our source on telephone for some time. The RAW or the IB must have tapped telephones of all important persons. I haven't yet forgotten the embarrassment that we had to endure when those buggers recorded the full telephonic conversation of General Musharraf with our Chief of General Staff when he spoke to him over phone from Beijing during the Kargil Operations. I do not want a repetition. It would be much safer to exchange written information through trusted couriers and the couriers should be changed for every exchange so that nobody sees our agent meet the same man a second time. The exchange should take place in crowded public places, like shopping malls, theatres or hotel lobbies. To make sure that the communication does not fall into the wrong hands, the identity of the couriers should be established first. This can be done through the time-tested technique of use of passwords. I will write to our source the pair of passwords to be used. You send the same to our boys in New Delhi."

The chief noted down the pair of passwords on a piece of paper, folded it and handed it over to S-3. He collected the piece of paper and took leave of his chief. While walking to the door he unfolded the paper and casually glanced at the passwords. These were:

Contact -"Rose is Red."

ISI Man - "Black is Beautiful."

Chapter 19

30 April

'Havan' ceremony was just over at the new office of Sonyog. This was followed by its formal inauguration. The inauguration was performed by Mrs. Naqvi, Yogesh's mother, by breaking a coconut as per the Hindu custom. Though her husband was a Muslim, he had insisted that his wife need not change her religion simply because she married a Muslim. He had told her to convert only if she genuinely started believing in the principles of Islam. But before she could make up her mind about conversion, he died and she continued to follow her original religion.

The old lady was overwhelmed by the attention she received. She had forgotten how to live in limelight after having lived a lonely and secluded life all these years. But she was glad that her son and daughter-in-law had chosen a career that was likely to keep them in limelight most of the time. It was essential to build a person's self-esteem, she had realized.

After the inauguration, they all went to the World Trade Towers' Conference Hall on the second floor where a reception had been arranged. A number of eminent people had arrived to attend the reception. Yogesh and Sunita had used all their contacts and those of their friends, to give wide publicity to the launch of Sonyog. The morning papers carried the advertisement that they themselves had designed. It was an ad on their Advertising Agency. 'A New Advertising Agency Comes to Town', it read and went on to highlight its ambitions and its dreams.

Snacks, sweets, tea and cold drinks were served to the invitees. There was lot of conviviality all around. Sunita and Yogesh were discussing a minor point among themselves when a good-looking woman approached them.

"Hello! I am Natasha," she introduced herself as she extended her hand towards Sunita.

"Hello! I am Sunita."

"Hi! I am Yogesh."

They shook hands with her and wondered how to proceed further. Natasha made their task easier by volunteering information about her.

"I have been sent here by Anil Seth, the Marketing Director of Megatech," said Natasha. The reference to the top Advertising Agency of Delhi surprised Sunita and Yogesh. Megatech had run a successful publicity campaign of the ruling party in the last elections. They were not aware that the Marketing Director of Megatech would show any interest in their agency. They had sent the invitation card merely as a courtesy towards the market leader.

"In fact I work for Megatech," Natasha continued. "I am an artist, you know!" She looked every inch an artist. She appeared to be in her early thirties, had a slim figure, fair skin, carefully unkempt hair, deep melancholy eyes, sharp nose, thin lips and long fingers; she was casually dressed in a loose black shirt and faded blue jeans. She was holding a cigarette in one hand. "I have been sent here to study your set up," she said as she pulled a puff from the cigarette.

"And what have you studied here?" asked Sunita in a measured tone.

"What I have studied here has impressed me most," she replied, sounding sincere.

"Really?" asked a pleased Yogesh.

"It has impressed me so much that I have decided to quit Megatech and join Sonyog instead. I am sure you need an artist to design your campaigns?"

They were surprised to hear the unexpected offer. They looked at each other, not knowing how to react. Yes, they were in need of an artist and were planning to put an advertisement in the paper soon. That they would get a prized catch from Megatech without making any effort, was beyond their imagination. Could this be a clever move by the market leader to snuff their nascent company even before it was born?

"What made you take that decision, Natasha?" asked Sunita. "After all, we are novices in the field and you work for a company that can buy hundreds of Sonyogs out. Besides, we do not know you at all. How do we know whether or not you are our well wisher? How can we trust you?"

Natasha remained quiet for a while and then replied smilingly, "I am glad that you have been frank and blunt with me. I would have been disappointed if you had not been so. From the moment I saw you giving so much of respect to your mother, who is such a simple woman, I knew that you were both very genuine and very sincere. In today's world sincerity is one virtue that is extremely rare to find. One sees affectations everywhere. People say something, do something else and mean something else. I have changed jobs a number of times but haven't met any people who are absolutely sincere. I work for Megatech now and they pay me well but I am not satisfied with their work culture. I do not work for money. I work because it gives me a certain purpose in life, certain meaning. I am the only daughter of a well-to-do father who lives in Bombay. I am fairly well off without being paid. All that I am desperate to find is some decent people to work with. People, whom I can relate to. You know what I mean?"

They did not know what she really meant. But her words and the manner of her speech were oozing with sincerity. Instinctively they knew that they could trust her.

"But if you work for us, we really don't think we will be able to pay you anywhere near what Megatech might be paying," said Yogesh.

"Not to worry Yogesh," said Natasha. "I won't take from you a single penny till you are fully established. You two are making a new beginning in life and I want to share with you the thrill of it. My work will be my reward."

"But what about Megatech?" inquired Sunita.

"They will have to look for a new artist who can do the spy work for them. Natasha is not a spy. I did not come here to spy which they wanted me to do. I came out of curiosity and I am happy that I came."

Yogesh and Sunita again looked at each other. None of them said a word. But they both knew what to say.

"Natasha," it was Yogesh who decided to announce the decision. "Welcome to Sonyog."

Chapter 20

02 May

S. S. Dhillon, the new Director of the Special Protection Group (SPG), received the message when he was preparing to leave for work. He was wanted at the Prime Minister's Office (PMO) where he was required to meet Joseph, in connection with the security arrangements of the Prime Minister. Since SPG was responsible for the VVIP security in India, the security of the Prime Minister was directly under the control of the Director, SPG.

"Good morning Joseph!" said Dhillon as he entered his office.

"Good morning SS!" replied Joseph. This is how they had addressed each other when they had met for the first time and had continued to address each other the same way thereafter. "Let me congratulate you first on your well deserved promotion."

"Thank you Joseph. But with promotion come greater responsibilities. I need God's blessings and your best wishes to be able to discharge my duties well."

"My best wishes are always with you."

"Thanks again. So what is new?"

"Nothing new. I just wanted to give you some information about the PM's next tour outside the capital so that you could tie up the security at your end."

"When is the tour?"

"On the eleventh and twelfth of this month. Still more than a week to go."

"Good. It is always better to have advance information."

"Yeah, but---"

"What but, Joseph?"

"I know there is no need to say this but since you are new to the top job, the PM wanted me to stress upon you that certain parts of the information must be kept absolutely confidential."

"Of course! Of course! What parts?"

"See, the PM plans to visit Tehri Dam on the eleventh. He leaves Delhi early in the morning by aeroplane. Lands at Dehradun. From there he flies in a chopper to Tehri. He will inspect the Dam site and return to Dehradun by the evening. He will then go to Haridwar by road, address District Officers and spend the night there. So far, so good. This part of the programme will be public knowledge soon. But what needs to be kept confidential is the Prime Minister's night programme at Haridwar."

"Night programme at Haridwar? You must be joking."

"Not the one you understand. He is a deeply religious person, you know? He wants to say prayers at Har Ki Pauri on the river Ganges and take a holy dip there. He will be accompanied by his spiritual Guru, Swami Suryananda, when he visits Har Ki Pauri. The visit will take place in the wee hours of the morning, at 3 AM to be precise."

"Prayers at Har Ki Pauri - the Stairway to Heaven. But why so early?"

"He has his own reasons for that. But he desires that security at that time should be absolutely minimum. Not many people will be around at the river site that early in the morning. So heavy security is not required, in any case. He wants only that many security personnel as would not arouse the suspicion of the people around. In a way, he wants to go there unrecognised and return quietly after spending about twenty minutes or so at Har Ki Pauri."

"Well! I can understand his desire to keep the whole thing secret but we can't take chances with security. Times are bad, you know!"

"He is aware of that and he has promised to pass his instructions in writing. So no responsibility will devolve upon you. In fact, he has been holding such prayers at some other holy places earlier also and we had similar understanding with your predecessor as well."

"That is alright," said Dhillon after a pause. "But still I would insist that security of the Prime Minister should be left to us. There should not be any interference from anybody, not from the PMO and not even from the P.M.himself"

"I tried to reason it out with him myself," said Joseph. "But this is his wish."

"OK," said Dhillon as he prepared to leave. "His wish is our command."

"But remember the confidentiality," said Joseph as he got up to see him off.

"I know Joseph," said Dhillon reassuringly. "This information will be available to only those people who need to know it. I will take all precautions. You can trust me to handle it as competently as Mr. Lall did. But please send me the full details of his tour programme at the earliest."

"You will have it soon. Goodbye S.S."

"Goodbye Joseph!" Dhillon left his office already formulating the security plan that he would implement during his first assignment on the tour of the Prime Minister outside Delhi.

Natasha kept her word. The day after her meeting with Sunita and Yogesh she told the Megatech people that she had decided to quit. They were stunned to know her decision. Megatech had quite a reputation among the business circles. It was not often that people left Megatech just like that. What shocked them even more was the reason she gave for quitting. She had found the work culture at Megatech rather stifling and felt that she would be able to give free expression to her energetic spirit at the totally unknown Advertising Agency, Sonyog. Her leaving them and joining Sonyog was going to be a blow to their reputation. They pleaded, they cajoled and then they threatened her. But she refused to budge from her decision. She walked out on Megatech leaving them to lick their wounded pride.

"Hi Yogesh! Hi Sunita," she greeted her new employers as she entered the office of Sonyog.

"Have you bid goodbye to Megatech?" asked Sunita.

"Oh, yeah!"

"How did they react?"

"Mean. As expected."

"I hope they will give you all your dues?"

"I don't care," Natasha looked around at the newly furnished office. It was nicely done up. There were three cubicles divided by glass panel of the same height as the office table. Adjoining the third cubicle was a spacious room in which were kept the photocopier, a steel cabinet and a few steel racks. The first two cubicles had small but functional tables along with revolving office chairs. The third cubicle had a large table with a sloping surface. The last two rooms also had a PC each. A laptop adorned the table in the first room.

"That must be my slot," said Natasha pointing to the third cubicle.

"You are right," said Sunita. "The second room is mine and the first is for Yogesh."

"That is good," said Natasha as she walked into her cubicle. She looked around and saw an Apple Macintosh lying on the table. Apple had made inroads into Indian offices only in the last two years. "Lovely Mac! Has it got internet connection?"

"Yes it has. In fact all three of us have broadband internet connection."

"That is indeed very thoughtful of you," said Natasha. "Now where do we begin?" asked Natasha as she flung her cotton bag on to the table.

"We plan to design a few sample presentations for some well known companies and show these to their managements to get their response," replied Yogesh.

"Good idea," said Natasha. "I have worked with Megatech for more than two years and know some of their clients well. If you wish I can give you the names of some nice people who might be interested in what we do here."

"That sounds fine," said Yogesh. "I'll start visiting these guys as soon as we have our presentations ready."

Chapter 21

04 May

A beaming Yogesh parked the motorcycle in the parking lot of the World Trade Towers. He was very happy. It was only the fifth day since the inauguration of Sonyog. It was the first prospective client that he had visited with a sample presentation. This client was Sweet Drinks, the makers of Cool Kit, the new soft drink in the market. The Director, Marketing of the Sweet Drinks, was highly impressed with the Sonyog presentation. He had asked Yogesh to prepare a full-fledged presentation for his MD. He had, however, assured Yogesh that Sonyog could count on the Sweet Drinks as their first ever contract, as the approval of the MD was only a formality.

He kept his helmet on the motorcycle and took out a hair comb from his hip pocket. He hastily brushed his hair. He looked at the watch. It was already past 12 noon. He then opened the side box of the motorcycle and took out his laptop. Holding the laptop in one hand, he hurried to the main entrance of World Trade Towers. While on his way, he decided to give a small present to Sunita for his successful visit to their first prospective client. He decided to purchase a small gift for Sunita from one of the shops on the ground floor.

'What would be the appropriate gift for Sunita?' He wondered. 'Wasn't it a bit premature to present a gift?' His dilemma was resolved when his eyes fell on the flower shop. A large variety of fresh flower was displayed on the counter. The red roses in the middle indeed made an attractive sight. Red rose was Sunita's favourite, he remembered. 'It won't be expensive and would be appropriate for the occasion', he reasoned to himself.

"Please give me one nicely wrapped big beautiful red rose for presentation to someone." Yogesh ordered as he approached the flower shop. He knew that Sunita would be happy to hear the report of his meeting with the Director, Marketing of the Sweet Drinks. He had liked the concept and design of their sample advertisements. The idea was conceived by Yogesh but developed and refined by Sunita. The design was created by Natasha and brilliantly too!

"Beautiful!" commented Yogesh as he took the nicely wrapped red rose from the shop boy. "Please make one more, same type." How could he forget Natasha? She was an integral part of the team now. He took the second rose, paid twenty rupees and walked to the lift.

Little known to Yogesh, an ISI contact in New Delhi, who had come to deliver a message to his ISI handler, was observing him very closely.

The contact had arrived at the World Trade Towers ten minutes earlier along with his partner, a pretty young woman. He was in white kurta-pyjama made of khadi, the traditional dress of politicians in India, and was wearing dark glasses. She was wearing black top and dark brown corduroy trousers. They sat in the coffee shop whose side walls were made of glass. They carefully selected a table from where they could have a clear view of the hallway. They ordered coffee and lit a their cigarettes.

Ten minutes passed. The ISI contact and his lady partner finished their coffee. The woman excused herself to go to the loo. The man looked at his watch. He pulled another cigarette from the packet and lit it. Suddenly his eyes fell on a young man who entered the hallway and stopped. The young man looked around for a while. 'Could this be his man?' The contact fixed his eyes on him. He saw the young man purchase two red roses from the flower shop.

Just then the lady partner of the ISI contact returned to the table.

"Is he the one?" the man asked.

"Yes, he is the one" the woman confirmed.

"Good!" said the man. "You stay here. I'll be right back!"

The contact came out into the hallway. Many people were milling around. He followed the young man who was clearly heading towards the lift. The young man pressed the call button of the lift and the doors of one of the lifts opened instantly. He entered the lift. The contact followed him. One more person entered the lift just when its door was closing. The young man pressed the button for the seventh floor. The contact did nothing. The third man pressed the button for the third floor. All three of them were silent. The contact observed the young man. He was holding a laptop in his right hand and the two red roses in his left hand, both carefully wrapped in translucent sheet. After some time the young man placed his laptop on the floor, looked, first at the two roses, then at the two men and smiled.

The lift stopped at the third floor. The man, who had pressed the button for the third floor, got out. The doors of the lift closed.

"Lovely!" said the ISI contact.

"Pardon?" said Yogesh. He was too absorbed in the thoughts of Cool Kit, Sweet Drinks, Sunita and Natasha to hear what the man in khadi kurta-pyjama, wearing dark glasses, had to say.

"The roses are crimson red. Beautiful! Good choice!"

"Yeah!" said Yogesh. "But these are for someone else. My favourite is black. To me black is beautiful."

"Excuse me! What did you say?"

"I said that my favourite colour is black. To me, black rose is more beautiful than the rose of any other colour."

"That sounds too good to be true!" said the man as he pressed the button for the fifth floor. He pulled out a cover from his bag that hung from his shoulder.

The lift came to a stop on the fifth floor.

"Good luck! May Operation Red Rose succeed!" said the contact as he forced the cover into Yogesh's right hand. Having done that, he got out of the lift. Before Yogesh could realize what had happened, the doors of the lift closed and it began moving up again. A surprised Yogesh took his laptop as he got down on the seventh floor to go to his office. He walked down the corridor a short distance and then began to laugh. 'Who the hell was that fellow?' he wondered. He walked briskly to his office and pushed its door with some force.

"Congrats Natasha!" said Yogesh as he went to her first and gave her one of the roses.

"Thank you. But what for?" asked Natasha, sniffing the rose.

"Congrats Sony," said Yogesh, giving her the second rose.

"Red rose? Oh, so lovely! How thoughtful of you. But you didn't answer Natasha's query."

"My visit to the Sweet Drinks was a grand success!"

"Oh really!" exclaimed Natasha as she left her cabin and joined the two in the second cabin.

"How? What happened?" asked Sunita. 'Please tell all"

Yogesh told them all about his meeting with the Director, Marketing of the Sweet Drinks, and how much impressed he was with their work. Yogesh assured the two ladies of pocketing Sweet Drinks as their first contract. He told them as to how thrilled he was with the idea of giving a full fledged presentation to the Managing Director of the Sweet Drinks.

"Great! We will make it," shouted Sunita with delight.

"Well begun is half done," commented a happy Natasha. "Full fledged presentation means lot of work. Our presentation must be very very good. We must not lose Sweet Drinks at any cost." Yogesh and Sunita saw her going back to her work. She took a glass of water, opened the wrapper of the rose and carefully placed it in the glass. "It will remain fresh for at least three days," she said when she saw Sunita and Yogesh watching her.

"Beautiful," Sunita commented as she too sniffed the rose.

"And here is one more thing for you," said Yogesh, handing over to her the unopened cover that the man in the lift had given him.

"What is it?" she asked.

"I don't know," he replied.

"Then why are you giving it to me, without any rhyme or reason?"

"Because somebody gave it to me, without any rhyme or reason!" He then told Sunita how the man in the lift had given him the cover after exchanging some pleasantries.

"I hope it is not a love letter from one of your ex-girlfriends?" Sunita teased.

"I wish it is," Yogesh chuckled. "At least I would know that I have the personality to attract more than one girl!"

"You have the personality Yogesh. Don't you remember your girl friend Neena from the college days?"

"She was not my girl friend for God's sake!" Yogesh was amused. "She was not even a friend."

"You are lying!" Sunita chuckled. She opened the cover with the help of a cutter. She took out a paper and had a look at what was written. The paper contained only one paragraph which appeared to be some kind of coded message for somebody. But she could not make any head or tail of it. It read:

YCRWW2L HCR3RCH UPWWX MF4CR5 CRPJRCY
UPUWX CR882LY 2LPSDY 2L8YDW XHM3CR
5M8CRRC 9KCRBRCP XAM5Y 2LMUSM FCR82LX
UMPBCR 48MWCR UWXMW DJJCRRC 4WXMF
YUPUY DYF8M XCRJXU MPGU9K
9K3RCCRP WD8CR4 5M8AU YXU9K9K XACRPW
PUWAA UYM55 2LP4SL2 WAYU8 UWNMD
8YCRWW 2LHRCCRP 4W

"What language is this?" Sunita asked as she passed the paper to Yogesh. He took the paper and was as puzzled after looking at it, as she was.

"The script is Roman, alright," he said. "The numerals are the commonly used numbers but the words do not make any sense." Both continued to wonder for some time at the strange writing.

"Natasha, can you come here for a minute please?" asked Sunita.

"No, if that thing does not concern our work." She had obviously overheard their conversation. It was her way of advising them to concentrate on their work and not be distracted by other things.

"It is all rubbish," said Yogesh giving the paper back to Sunita. "May be some sort of joke. Throw it away."

She took the paper and got up to throw it in the dustbin. Suddenly she stopped, put the paper back in the cover and pushed it in her purse. 'Who knows it might be an important paper for somebody!' she thought.

The contact, to whom the paper was important, returned to the World Trade Towers in the evening. He had coffee in the same coffee shop where he had had it earlier in the day. After finishing his coffee, he left the coffee shop and took the lift to the seventh floor. On reaching there, he took position at the end of the corridor. He was certain that the people getting in or out of the lift would not be able to recognize him from that distance. He lit a cigarette and waited. He saw some persons closing their offices and catching the lift. None of them, however, was the man he was looking for. But he did not have to wait for long. Just when it was about 6.30 P.M, the contact spotted the young man closing his office. Two ladies accompanied him as he left the office.

Yogesh, Sunita and Natasha laughed and giggled as they approached the lift. They were not at all aware that they were being watched.

"Why don't you come to my place some time?" asked Natasha extending the invitation. "I live in Vasant Kunj, Number 1416, Sector K."

"Sure, we will come," replied Sunita. "You also come some time. We live in 177, Sector 3, R K Puram."

"Government quarters?"

"Yes, allotted to my ma you know?" replied Yogesh.

"It is not all that far from Vasant Kunj," said Natasha.

"Yeah, very close," said Sunita as they entered the lift.

The man in the corridor of the seventh floor of the World Trade Towers carefully noted down the number of the room in which Sonyog was located.

Chapter 22

05 May

As usual, Sunita and Yogesh reached their office at 10 A.M. When they opened it, they were shocked to see it in total mess. Most of the things were lying scattered on the floor. The drawers of the tables had been pulled out. The cabinet was also open. Its locks had been forced open by somebody. It was clear that the office had been ransacked at night.

"Who the hell has done it and why?" shouted Yogesh.

"We haven't done anybody any harm, then why should anybody do it to us?" asked Sunita. She was as bewildered as he was.

"I'll call the management. They are supposed to provide security at night!" Yogesh picked up the phone. It was working. He told the manager about the burglary. The manager turned up without wasting any time. He called the security personnel but none of them could provide any clue to the incident. They had not seen any intruders. Obviously, they had taken the security of the building for granted and spent most of their time sleeping while on night duty. The manager promised to take necessary action against the security personnel. He also decided to call the police to investigate the matter.

Natasha reached office before the police arrived on the scene. She was also upset to see the sight before her.

"Must be one of competitors," she spoke from her experience.

"Why should any competitor resort to this?" asked Sunita.

"You do not know how mean people in business can become," came Natasha's reply. "They would go to any length to finish their rivals off if the competition was cut-throat. Advertising is in the grip of cut-throat competition these days."

"I think Natasha is right," opined Yogesh. "Somebody must have come to know of our success with Sweet Drinks. Who handled their publicity campaign last year?"

"Megatech," replied Natasha.

Three of them looked at each other. They were sure that it was Megatech that did the dirty trick. They had every reason to feel hurt. First they lost out their senior artist to Sonyog. Then one of their important clients appeared to be slipping out of their hands.

"This is why people say you must have some hands on experience before getting into a new business," said Yogesh. "We are too inexperienced to understand these machinations. I often wondered how long our good times were going to last. Things had been going too well for us. Such a thing was bound to happen. In fact I wanted to purchase some nice gifts for the two of you after my meeting with the Marketing Manager of Sweet Drinks yesterday. But then I thought it might be premature. So I decided to present only those red roses instead."

The reference to the red roses made him sit up. He remembered Sunita had left her rose on the table when they left the previous evening. He also recalled that Natasha had left her rose in a glass. He looked for the two roses. They were missing.

"What are you looking for?" asked Sunita.

"Roses. They are missing."

"You are a strange person," said Sunita "You should check up if any item of the office equipment is missing instead of bothering about the stale roses."

"No, I mean, this whole thing could be linked to the red roses," said Yogesh. He then told Sunita and Natasha in detail about his conversation with the man in the lift before he forced a cover in his hand.

"Did you throw that cover away?" he asked Sunita.

"No I did not," replied Sunita. "For some strange reason I decided to keep it in my purse." She opened the purse and took out the cover.

Just then the manager returned with two police officers.

"I am Badri Prasad, DCP Central District, Delhi Police, and he is Inspector Rawat", the senior man introduced himself and his subordinate to Yogesh and did not bother to look at the two ladies. He moved his eyes all around the room.

"Anything stolen?" he asked.

Yogesh, Sunita and Natasha began to check up the various things that had been installed in the office. The office was new and the items were few. It did not take them long to do the check up. Surprisingly, none of the items was missing.

"Any damages?" asked the Deputy Commissioner of Police. The three of them carried out another check. Though most of the items lay scattered here and there, yet hardly any damage to any of the items could be seen.

"No theft, no damages. I think there is nothing for the police to do here," said the Inspector.

"But what about the fact that somebody broke into our office?" Yogesh pointed out.

"That can be investigated by the management of the World Trade Towers," replied the Inspector. "They have their own security arrangements. Besides, we in Delhi Police have far too heavy a workload. We are better off without these minor cases. So please cooperate with us."

The three of them felt stupid. They had called the police to seek its cooperation. But the police was counting on their cooperation.

"Hold on Rawat, let me deal with it," the DCP pulled up the inspector. Then he turned to Yogesh and asked, "Do you have any suspects? Or can you recall any incident that could somehow be related to this burglary?

"I can't think of any suspects," replied Yogesh. "But yes. There is one incident that might have something to do with this whole thing."

"What is it?"

Yogesh told the two officers all about the man who had handed over a cover to him that contained a paper on which was written something that appeared to be coded message for somebody. He told him that perhaps, the same man was behind the break in.

"Can I have that paper, if you still have it with you?" asked DCP Badri Prasad.

"Yes sir," Sunita intervened. "I had put it in my purse, thinking that it might be an important paper for someone." She took out the cover from her purse and handed it over to the DCP.

"Thank you!" said the DCP. He opened the cover, took out the paper and gave a casual glance to the writing on the paper before handing it over to the inspector who kept it in his diary.

"Now if you don't mind," said the DCP, "we will take leave of you. Let me see what we can make of this paper. Your break-in case however, will be treated as closed, if you permit, as nothing of value has been stolen." The DCP left the room without waiting for a reply. The inspector followed him.

"Delhi Police, friends of the people!" commented Natasha and then joined Yogesh and Sunita in setting the office right.

It took them less than half an hour to keep everything back in its place. They tried to get back to their work but were too shaken by the break-in to concentrate on anything. They decided to wind up for the day and get back to work only next day.

Chapter 23

06 May

Natasha was waiting for Sunita and Yogesh in the hallway of the World Trade Towers when they arrived to open their office. They greeted each other casually and walked silently to the lift.

"Let us hope that there are no more surprises for us in the office today," said Natasha when the lift started moving up.

"Yea," commented Sunita. "Let us hope so!"

Yogesh did not say anything. He was the first to get out of the lift when it stopped at the seventh floor. He hurried towards the Sonyog office. The two ladies followed him a little behind. On reaching the office, Yogesh took out the keys from his pocket and inserted the key into the door lock. He turned the key and pushed the door inside. The phone was ringing when the door opened. He looked at Sunita in surprise. She reached her cabin and picked up the phone.

"Hello!" she spoke.

"I want to speak to the young man," came a male voice from the other side.

"Which young man?"

There was no reply.

"Hello! Hello!" Sunita tried to elicit response but in vain. Yogesh observed the telephonic conversation. He took the receiver from Sunita.

"Hello! Who is there please?"

"Young man, listen to me carefully" came the voice. "Day before yesterday a cover was given to you by mistake. We want the cover back immediately. Otherwise you will be in trouble. What you saw yesterday morning was only a prelude to what we can do."

"Who are you and where are you speaking from?" asked a scared Yogesh. The use of word 'we' gave the impression that the man represented some dangerous gang.

"That is none of your business."

"But I don't have that cover with me anymore."

"Where is it then?"

"I gave it to the police yesterday when their officers came for investigating the break in."

"You fool! Why did you give it to them?"

"I could not, I mean, I didn't know!"

There was a pause on the other side.

"Hello! Hello!"

There was still pause.

"Hello!"

"Now listen you fool," the man finally responded. "The police officers must have come from the Connaught Place Police Station. If you want to save your life and the lives of the two ladies with you, then go to that Police Station immediately. Persuade the police to return that cover to you and come back to your office. I will call you up in an hour and give you further instructions on what to do only after you have retrieved that cover from the police. Remember, if you do not do what you have been told to do, you will be in big trouble." Then there was the sound of click. Yogesh slowly kept the receiver back.

"What happened Yogesh?" asked Sunita. "Who was he?"

"The same man who gave me the cover the day before yesterday. The voice was unmistakably his. He wants the cover back."

"What will you do?"

"I will have to get the cover back." Yogesh got up and reached the door. "Sunita, Natasha, don't be scared. Everything will be alright. I will be back soon. Take care."

There was lot of activity going on in the Police Station when Yogesh reached there. Men and women in uniform were moving in and out of the various rooms. Telephones were ringing all over the place. Police vans were coming in and going out. Some police officials were attending to the members of the public. Others were doing file work. Yogesh looked for Inspector Rawat and was relieved to find him in the main hall. The inspector was giving directions to some policemen. He faced Yogesh when he had finished giving his instructions to them.

"Is there some emergency?" asked Yogesh.

"No, why?"

"There appears to some commotion here."

"This is routine, Mister," said the inspector in reply. Yogesh could now understand why Inspector Rawat and his DCP were more than eager to close their complaint. If this was routine, what would the emergency be like? He sympathized with Delhi Police.

"What brings you here now?" asked the inspector.

"Sorry to trouble you like this but I thought I must tell you that we have found out the man who gave me that cover. He did so by mistake and wants it back."

"By all means," said Inspector Rawat. "But it is not with me. It is with DCP Sahib"

"Where is the DCP?" asked Yogesh.

"His office is on the first floor," replied the Inspector. "The ground floor is for the Police Station. You may take the stairs from that corner at the end of this corridor."

"Thanks!" said Yogesh as he rushed to the office of the DCP.

"Yes please!" queried a police constable who confronted Yogesh when he was looking for the chamber of the DCP.

"Hello! My name is Yogesh. I want to see Mr. Badri Narain, the DCP."

"You mean Mr. Badri Prasad?"

"Yes, Mr. Badri Prasad. I am sorry for the slip!"

"You have an appointment?"

"No, I don't. But I met him yesterday. He knows me."

"What is your name you said?"

"I am Yogesh. Yogesh Naqvi."

"Yogesh Naqvi?"

"Yes."

"Funny name. Are you a Hindu or a Muslim?"

"I am both." Yogesh was getting irritated.

"Interesting!" commented the constable. He looked curiously at Yogesh for some time. Yogesh managed to keep quiet. "You wait here. I will check up with sahib." The constable spared Yogesh any further questioning, much to his relief.

He saw the constable enter one of the rooms. He returned after a couple of minutes.

"You may go inside," the constable told Yogesh. "Sahib can see you now."

"Thanks!" said Yogesh as he walked into the chamber of the DCP.

"Hello Mr. Yogesh!" said the DCP from his chair. "Please sit down."

"Good morning sir," said Yogesh as he sat in a chair. "Thank you very much for sparing time for me. But I won't take more than two minutes."

"Take your time," said the DCP with a smile. "Tell me what can I do for you?"

"Sorry to trouble you like this sir but I thought I must tell you that we have been able to find the man who gave me that cover. He did so by mistake and wants it back. Can I take that cover back?"

The DCP thought for a while and then said, "Well normally anything we capture from the scene of the crime becomes property of the police. So we do not part with it. But in this case no police case has been registered. So technically it has not become police property. At least, not yet."

Yogesh felt highly relieved. "Can I get it back then?"

"I think you can," said the DCP as he opened the drawer of his table and took out the cover containing the coded message. "In any case, dealing with coded messages is not our job. It is the job of the intelligence people or the army. Our hands are full as it is." He handed over the cover to Yogesh.

"Thank you," said Yogesh.

"So we are over with it," said the DCP. "As of now, we have nothing to investigate."

"Yes," replied Yogesh.

"But I have a suggestion. You may hand over this message to the army. It might be of some use to them."

"Right sir!" said Yogesh as he got up to leave. "Let me see if I should do that. Thanks for your help. Bye"

"See you some other time," said the DCP as he bid goodbye to Yogesh. He then picked up the phone and dialed the number of a Cabinet Minister. He had to give him the completion report.

The telephone rang as soon as Yogesh entered his office. "I will take," he told Sunita and rushed to answer the phone.

"Hello!" called Yogesh.

"Could you get the cover back?"

"Yes. I have the cover with me right now."

"Just open the cover and see what is inside."

Yogesh did as told. He took out the paper with the coded message. "There is a paper having some kind of a coded message typed on it."

"Right. Now listen. Do not show this paper to any one, least of all to any governmental organization. Just tear it off and forget about all that has happened."

"I'll do as you have told. But I want no more trouble."

"You will have no more trouble from us if you do as you have been told. Goodbye!"

"Goodbye."

Yogesh told Sunita and Natasha all that transpired between him and the other man. Natasha advised the two of them to take the advice of that man seriously. "There is no use meddling in other people's affairs," she said. "It does more harm than good in the long run."

"But I think we must do something about it,' said Sunita. She recollected that she and Yogesh had taken a pledge after 26/11 Mumbai attacks to be vigilant citizens. "It is obvious that the paper that we have contains some very important information. May be highly sensitive! It might even relate to the security of the country."

"There are people who are being paid for ensuring the security of the country," said Natasha. "Each one of us must do our own job. Nothing more, nothing less."

Her argument did not satisfy Sunita. She felt bad at the way they were made to act. She was relieved that by retrieving the cover, Yogesh had managed to get some dangerous persons off their backs for the time being. But she could not reconciie to the fact that they had to bow to the threats of some bad people who might be planning something that could harm the interests of their motherland.

Sunita took the paper from Yogesh and made a photocopy of the same. She folded the photocopy and put it in her purse. She then handed back the original paper to Yogesh.

Yogesh, on his part, did not want to get any deeper into the episode. But deep down in his heart he knew that what Sunita said was right. He did not want his wife to think that he lacked guts.

"OK. Let me think about it" he said and put the paper back in the cover and kept it in the drawer of his table. "Now let us concentrate on our work. Remember, we have to prepare a nice presentation to the MD of Sweet Drinks!"

"Yes, back to work." said Natasha. "That should be our slogan now."

"We have duties as citizens of this country," Sunita tried to reason with Yogesh when they went to bed at night. "Country's security is not the responsibility of the Armed Forces alone."

"How do you know that the message concerned the security of the country?"

"It is just a feeling. Even if it did not concern the security of the country, whatever it did, must be having some serious angle to it. Otherwise why would people be so desperate to get the paper back from the police?"

"What you say appears to be right. But should we go deeper into it. Couldn't it land us in some trouble?"

"Yogesh, we are young. If the youth too fail to face up to the challenges, do we have any hope for this country? The message may or may not amount to much. But, I think, we must do our duty. Moreover, I think it is time to redeem our pledge that we had taken after 26/11."

"What do you suggest?" asked Yogesh earnestly, after being reminded of the pledge.

"I think we must hand over the paper to the concerned people in the government."

"I don't have much hope from the police. I could see today that they were terribly overburdened with routine work. I don't think they can do justice to this case."

"Then why not try the army?"

"That makes sense. Even the DCP Badri Prasad suggested that I should hand over this paper to the army."

"Then let us do that."

"OK! Tomorrow is Sunday. On Monday I will go to the Army Headquarters and see if there are any takers for this information, if it is indeed some information."

"I am so proud of you," said Sunita as she flung herself over Yogesh's chest.

"Proud of me for what?" asked Yogesh. "For what happened during the day or for what is going to happen now?"

He switched off the light and began to make love to her.

Chapter 24

08 May

Yogesh dropped Sunita at the entrance to the World Trade Towers and proceeded to Sena Bhavan. Sena Bhavan is located in the heart of New Delhi. It is a nine-storey building and houses the headquarters of the Indian Army. The building has a huge compound which is used as car parking by the officers working in the complex. It has many gates but most of them are now permanently closed, due to reasons of security. Only two gates are kept open during the office hours, manned by the security guards. The reception is located near gate number one.

Yogesh parked his motorcycle on one side of the main road, hung the helmet on its handle bar and walked into the main compound of Sena Bhavan.

"Excuse me!" called a security guard.

"Yes!" Yogesh responded.

"Can I see your pass please?"

"I don't have a pass."

"Then you go to the reception and get one made."

Yogesh looked in the direction pointed out by the security guard. He spotted a room marked as 'Reception'. Yogesh hurried into the Reception Room. He saw two officials in civilian clothes behind a public counter dealing with the visitors. His turn came.

"Yes please?" queried the receptionist.

"I want to meet someone in the army headquarters!"

"Whom?"

"Well! I don't know actually."

"Then come back when you know whom you want to meet," said the receptionist somewhat rudely.

"No, I mean, I know that I have to meet someone. But I do not know who the right person to meet is. I need your help to decide that."

"What help?"

Yogesh took out the coded message. "Someone handed over this coded message to me yesterday mistaking me for someone else. I have a feeling that this message contains some sensitive information. It might concern the security of the country. So I thought I might as well hand it over to the army, for whatever its worth."

"Hand it over to the police," advised the receptionist. "Next please."

"Wait a minute," Yogesh pleaded. "I tried with Delhi Police. But they do not appear to have any time for it."

"You think army officers are sitting idle? Don't waste my time. I have to dispose off other visitors too. Next."

Yogesh felt helpless. He left the room and began walking slowly back to the main gate.

"Excuse me," Yogesh heard someone call him. He turned and saw a smart looking young army officer walk up to him.

"Yes please," responded Yogesh.

"Hello, I am Major Raj Kumar." The young Major extended his hand.

"I am Yogesh," said Yogesh as he shook hands with the Major.

"I heard you say something about some sensitive information. What is it?" he asked.

Yogesh showed him the message and told him how he received it and why he suspected it to contain some classified information. The Major returned the paper to him, took his name and asked him to wait at the reception for some time.

Yogesh felt relieved.

After a short while the receptionist received telephonic instructions from inside the building and he issued a pass in the name of Yogesh Naqvi.

"Show the pass at the gate, leave your mobile phone with security guard, if you have one, take lift and go to room number 818 on the eighth floor," the receptionist gave directions to Yogesh.

Yogesh did as told.

"I am Colonel Bali," said a handsome looking officer when Yogesh entered room number 818.

"I am Yogesh Naqvi." The two men shook hands.

"Yogesh Naqvi? Are you a Hindu or a Muslim?"

"Well, actually my father was a Muslim and my mother is a Hindu."

"Was a Muslim? Is he not Muslim any more?"

"No. I mean he is no more. He died many years ago. In fact he too was in the army."

"Are you referring to Major Saif Naqvi of 13 Punjab who died fighting the ultras in the North-East?"

"You are right Colonel. Did you know him?"

"Of course, I knew him," said Colonel Bali as he gave a pat to Yogesh on his shoulder. "He was my course senior at the IMA." Colonel Bali was referring to the Indian Military Academy, Dehradun, where gentlemen cadets of the Indian Army get their pre-commission training.

"I am so happy to hear that," replied Yogesh.

"Sit down, Yogesh. Be comfortable."

"Thank you." Yogesh sat down in the chair.

"Yes. What can I do for you?"

"Nothing much Colonel. I just wanted to show you a piece of paper." Yogesh brought out the cover containing the message from his shirt pocket and gave it to the Colonel.

"A coded message," said Colonel Bali as he looked at the photocopy of that message. "Why do you want to give it to us?"

Yogesh told him the entire story, beginning with how the message came into his hands and ending with how his wife persuaded him to hand over the same to the army.

Colonel Bali had a friendly disposition. He offered Yogesh a cup of tea. Yogesh told him about his uncle Colonel Sanjay Sarang. Colonel Bali knew his uncle too and that piece of information further helped in removing the suspicion that two persons face when they meet for the first time.

"I am not sure if this message would be of any help to you," said Yogesh while leaving. "But we thought it was our duty to hand it over to you people. Who knows there might be some important information in it relating to the security of the country?"

"I appreciate your decision," said the Colonel. "In army we discount nothing. We will try to decipher it at the earliest and see what it contains."

"Decipher?" asked Yogesh, unable to comprehend the meaning.

"Yes," replied Colonel Bali. "The study of the coded messages is known as Cipher or Cryptography. Decoding the coded messages is called deciphering the code." Colonel Bali tried to help Yogesh understand the subject of Cipher.

"I see," said Yogesh. "Right Colonel Bali! I will take leave of you. Please inform me if something interesting comes out."

"Please give me your address and phone number," said the Colonel. "Some of our chaps might come to carry out a routine check with you. Ask them to show you their Identity Cards. The I - Cards will look like this." He showed him his own I - Card.

"Right!" said Yogesh.

"See you, Yogesh," said Colonel Bali.

"By the way," said Yogesh, while leaving, "That man also said something like 'May Operation Red Rose Succeed.' I do not know if this information is of any use to you. But I thought I might as well tell you about it."

"Operation Red Rose," repeated the colonel. "OK. Let me see if we can link it to something. Thanks again."

"Bye."

"Bye Yogesh."

Yogesh reached Sonyog after 11 A.M. Sunita looked at him inquisitively. He looked at Natasha who was busy with her work. He wished her good morning and she returned the wish with a smile continuing to do her work.

"Done," was all that Yogesh said in a low voice. He did not want Natasha to know that they had decided to pursue the matter against her advice. Sunita also got back to her work.

They continued to make preparations for their presentation to the M.D. of Sweet Drinks the following week.

It was 6 P. M. and it was time to close the office. Natasha had already left office and was gone. Sunita was not in a mood to go home yet.

"Yogesh, we have not been to Gurgaon for quite some time". Sunita told Yogesh about the most happening city in India which had come up as an up market suburban town just on the outskirts of South Delhi.

"You want to go there?"

"Yups!"

"Then let us leave the bike here and take the Metro".

"Good idea!"

They took the Metro that had only recently been extended up to Gurgaon.

"What happened at the Army Headquarters?" asked Sunita during the Metro journey. Yogesh told her about his meeting with Colonel Bali. He told her how the army chaps would try to decode the message with the help of cipher techniques.

They reached Gurgaon in less than half an hour. They got down at the MMCC Station. It came to be known as MMCC station because two of the most popular shopping malls of Gurgaon were located on the two sides of the station, right opposite each other. These were the Metropolitan Mall on the Western side and City Centre on the Eastern. Yogesh and Sunita chose the Metropolitan Mall for their outing. The fully air-conditioned building gave them ample respite from the sweltering heat outside. They walked around for a while and then settled down to have a cup coffee in Barista, the popular coffee joint on the ground floor.

"I wish I knew something about cipher," said Sunita when they were finishing their coffee.

"If you are that keen you can learn cipher now," said Yogesh.

"Don't be funny."

"I am not joking," said Yogesh, sounding serious. "If cipher is some kind of a study, there must be some book on it. We can go to some good shop and try to get a book on cipher."

"Good idea!" said Sunita.

"Let us go," said Yogesh when they had finished their coffee.

They went to the Om Book Depot located on the ground floor itself. They told the salesman their requirement and he produced half a dozen books on cipher within no time. They picked up one titled 'A Beginner's Guide to Cipher', paid and left for home.

Yogesh's mother had kept the dinner ready when they reached home. While Yogesh switched on the TV, Sunita went to their bedroom and began reading the book. She found the book quite interesting and informative.

Sunita learnt that the basic principle behind all cipher messages was the same. Each letter or number represented another letter or number. All that was needed to be done was to first, write down the message in original and then replace each letter by the chosen cipher letter or number. The coded message was ready. To decipher it, one needed to know the cipher codes. In deciphering, the process of replacing letters was reversed from the cipher code to the original. Having done that, the original message was ready once again.

Sunita found out that the use and effectiveness of a code lay in its ingenuity and novelty. No code could remain undeciphered for long. There were experts who could decipher a coded message within hours, without knowing the cipher code. This was done with the knowledge of grammar, syntax and structure of each language. All they had to do was to use this knowledge to tinker with the coded words and construct the cipher code. In fact it was because of this reason that all intelligence agencies frequently changed their cipher codes lest these became known to the enemy. Then there were customized softwares that the intelligence agencies used the world over to break the enemy codes. Such software applications were generally not available as off-the-shelf products as these have very few buyers.

One simple example of cipher that was given in the book was that it was an accepted fact that the most commonly used letter in English language was 'e'. One should try to find out the most commonly used letter, number or group of letters or numbers in the coded message and assume, with a fair degree of certainty, that the particular letter or number or group of letters or numbers stood for 'e'. Thereafter one should try to locate all such two letter words that have 'e' as their last letter. Such words could only be 'He, Me, We or Be'. Then one should experiment by replacing the concerned letter in other words by H, M, W or B. From there on, some two or three letter words would start making sense. With diligence and practice, one could go on identifying more and more letters and construct more and more words. This way the entire cipher code could be prepared and the entire message deciphered.

That night for the first time since their marriage, Sunita's mind was not in tune with what her body was doing when Yogesh made love to her. After the act, she switched on the reading lamp and returned to the book. Yogesh slept a blissful sleep.

Sunita finished the book before going to bed but could not resist the temptation of experimenting with the coded message with her new found knowledge of deciphering a code. She could not make much headway but had been hooked on to the challenge, nonetheless.

Chapter 25

09 May

The man who could make headway with the message was the Cipher Officer at Sena Bhavan. He had put the code on the computer and had run a special programme to detect and develop the code. The code turned out to be easy to break and it did not take the computer too long to decipher the complete message.

After deciphering the message, the Cipher Officer read it carefully. What he read sent a chill down his spine. He rechecked the code to ensure that the computer had not made any mistake.

It had not.

He looked at the calendar.

The date on the calendar was what it was.

He looked at his watch.

The time was ten minutes past ten in the forenoon. He could not afford to waste any time. He left his room hurriedly and went to room number 818.

"Yes officer!" said Colonel Bali. "Any luck with the message?"

The officer did not reply. He merely placed the paper containing the deciphered message on the table. Colonel Bali took the paper and began to read. His face turned blank, then stiff and finally pale as he finished reading the short message.

"Officer! Are you sure?" he asked.

"Positive," came the reply.

"Oh my God!" sighed Colonel Bali as he slumped into his chair. He looked at the ceiling and said, "What the hell are they up to?"

The Cipher Officer did not say anything. He had done his job and awaited further instructions.

Colonel Bali made up his mind. He got up from his seat. "You know the rules officer," he cautioned the Cipher Officer before leaving. "Not a word, I repeat, not a word is to be said to anybody. Understand?"

"I understand sir," assured the officer.

"Please get back to your job," directed Colonel Bali while marching out of his room. He did not take the lift as it might have made him wait. He did not want to wait. He rushed down the stairs to the sixth floor office of Lieutenant General P. N. Sehgal who was the Director General of Military Intelligence (DGMI). He had bypassed two levels of official channel. He knew that he was authorised to do so in the type of situation that he faced.

General Sehgal was having a meeting with two senior officers of the Indian Air Force. He was surprised to see Colonel Bali rushing in despite the red light outside.

"Top sec, Op I," said Colonel Bali.

The DGMI gave him a long and hard look. He knew that the information that Colonel Bali wanted to share with him was of the category of 'Top Secret and Operation Immediate.' As per the laid down rules, he was required to break all other engagements forthwith.

"Gentlemen, this is something most urgent," General Sehgal told the two Air Force officers. "Would you mind if we meet some other time?"

The Air Force officers too knew the rules and left without murmur.

"What is it Bali?" General Sehgal was eager to know the information that his officer had brought.

"Sir, yesterday I happened to come across a coded message. I gave it to our Cipher Section to decipher it. They have deciphered it today and the Cipher Officer gave it to me just minutes ago." He placed the message in front of the DGMI. The General Officer read the message but remained calm.

"Who gave you this message?" he asked.

Colonel Bali told his boss about Yogesh and how he had come to be in possession of the message and why he decided to hand it over to the army.

"Have you done a check up on this young man?" asked the General.

"Yes sir," replied the colonel. "His antecedents have been verified and he has come clean."

"Come with me," said General Sehgal as he left the room. Colonel Bali followed him as directed. Both went to General Surinder Pal, the Chief of Army Staff, whose office, along with that of the Defence Minister, had been shifted from the South Block to the Sena Bhavan only last year for reasons of security. It was considered to be too risky to have the Prime Minister and all the top Ministers of the Government of India in one building.

The chief was free and available. He looked at the two officers in shocking disbelief as he read the message.

"What is the background?" he asked

Colonel Bali told the chief all that he knew about the exchange of the message. He assured the chief that the medium could be relied upon. They would have to find the originator of the message.

General Surinder Pal took the two officers to see the Defence Minister. The minister had gone out to meet the Finance Minister to discuss some matters concerning the two ministries. The COAS spoke to his minister on his mobile phone and asked him if he could return to his office immediately. The minister assured the chief of the same and asked him and his officers to wait for him in his ministerial chamber.

They did not have to wait for long. The Defence Minister arrived in about twenty minutes. He was accompanied by Gyan Mehta, his Personal Secretary.

"What is the matter General?" asked Raman Kumar as soon as he saw the army chief and two of his officers.

"A matter of immense importance," replied the chief. He looked at Gyan Mehta who got the hint and left the room.

"What is it?" asked the minister as he took his chair.

"Sir, meet our DG Military Intelligence, General Sehgal and Colonel Bali, one of the officers working under him," said the chief, introducing the two officers to the Defence Minister. The minister shook hands with the two officers.

"Sir, yesterday," began the COAS, "a civilian young man gave a coded message to the Intelligence Branch of Army Headquarters which he, most certainly, had got hold of by accident. My officers have been able to decipher it after putting in some real hard work. You may kindly see it." The minister took the paper from the army chief and began to read it.

MESSAGE BEGINS (STOP) DEFENCE MINISTER RAMAN KUMAR MUST GO BEFORE ELEVENTH OF MAY IF OPERATION RED ROSE IS TO SUCCEED (STOP) MINIMUM PROTECTION WILL BE ENSURED FOR HIM TILL THEN (STOP) FINISH HIM OFF AND KASHMIR IS YOURS (STOP) MESSAGE ENDS.

Raman Kumar's face turned white as the full import of the murderous message dawned upon him. "General, what is this?" he asked.

"It is obvious from the reference to Kashmir," replied the chief, "that the message is for the Pakistanis who are plotting a major attack on India as a part of the Operation Red Rose and some bigwig in New Delhi is helping them in their plot. Being a capable and no-nonsense Defence Minister, you are a major stumbling block in their nefarious designs. That is why they want to assassinate you."

"So Swami Suryananda was right after all!" said Raman Kumar as he composed himself. "He had warned me of some threat of this nature to my life. But I am not worried about myself. I am worried about two things. Firstly, if the war breaks out with Pakistan, it might lead to nuclear conflagration which will have horrifying consequences for both countries. Secondly, this bigwig in our government that we are talking about might indeed succeed in handing over Kashmir to Pakistanis in return for some favours."

"I may also inform you sir," said General Surinder Pal, "that our Intelligence reports have confirmed that Pakistanis indeed are up to some mischief. They are working on plans for mobilisation of their forces near the border."

"But I am sure we can handle them. Isn't it?"

"About that there is no doubt. All we need is Presidential orders for mobilisation of our forces."

"Good. I will meet the Prime Minister and request him to convene meeting of the CCS today or tomorrow. Final decision on the mobilisation of our forces will be taken only after weighing all the pros and cons during the CCS meeting.

I will let you know of the government decision at the earliest."

"But what about your personal security?" asked the COAS. "Should I put some of my commandos on duty?"

"That will arouse suspicions," replied the Defence Minister. "Thanks for your offer. But I want to catch the traitor red handed. I will take precautions about my personal security but let things go on as usual. We must catch the traitors among us. I already have some suspects in my mind but I need to be absolutely sure before I reveal their identity to you or to any one else. For this purpose we must keep this information absolutely secret for the time being. Keep it fully confidential from everyone, including that brave young man of yours who gave this message. What is his name?"

"Yogesh Naqvi," Colonel Bali gave the name.

"I would like to meet this young man, Yogesh Naqvi. May be he can help us find out the man behind this so called Operation Red Rose."

"When would you like to meet him?" asked the army chief.

"Today itself." replied the Minister. "Let me see my engagements for the day." He opened his palmtop and checked the day's engagements. "I think I can meet him at 6 P.M. Please call him over around that time."

Yogesh looked at his watch. It was going to be 11.40 A.M. He was satisfied with the progress that they had made for the presentation to the M.D of Sweet Drinks. Despite the distractions, their work was going on at a good speed. Natasha had been very helpful in their preparations. Her experience at Megatech came quite handy. What they would have done if she had not joined Sonyog, Yogesh wondered. The telephone rang and Yogesh picked it up to answer.

"Yes please!"

"Can I speak to Mr. Yogesh Naqvi please?"

"Speaking!"

"Hello Yogesh! Good morning, Colonel Bali here."

"Hello Colonel! Good morning. I was thinking of giving you a ring myself. Was curious to know what happened to that piece of paper that I gave you!"

"There is some news for you. We are close to breaking the code. But we are sure already that the message you gave us contains some state secret. The matter has been brought to the notice of Defence Minister. He is deeply impressed by your sense of duty to the country."

"That makes me feel really good!" said a pleased Yogesh.

"You'll feel better when I tell you why I have called you."

"Is it so?"

"Yes. The Defence Minister wants to thank you in person. He desires that you meet him at 6 P.M. this evening. I hope it suits you?"

"It suits me fine," replied Yogesh. "I'll skip anything to meet Mr. Raman Kumar. But what about Sunita, my wife? Should I bring her along also? After all it was she who persuaded me to contact you!"

"Please bring her too with you," said Colonel Bali. "I am sure the minister will be only too happy to see both of you together. Now, do one thing. You leave your place by 5.30 PM or so and come straight to Sena Bhavan. I will arrange for you to be shown in at the gate."

"Right O," said Yogesh. "We will be at Sena Bhavan before 6 P.M."

"See you then."

"See you Colonel."

Sunita looked inquisitively at Yogesh.

"Mission Sena Bhavan successful," said a highly pleased Yogesh.

"Tell me in detail," asked Sunita.

"It was a call from Colonel Bali," replied Yogesh. "Colonel Bali is the officer to whom I have handed over that document. Nice fellow. He knew dad and he knows Sanjay uncle too."

"What did he say just now?"

"I am coming to that. It appears that the army fellows are close to breaking the code of the message. But they are sure already that the message contains some state secret. Colonel Bali has brought the matter to the notice of the Defence Minister."

"Defence Minister? Was the matter that important?"

"Must be so. Colonel Bali did not give me any details. But he said that the Defence Minister was highly impressed with our sense of duty to the country. He wants to meet and thank the two of us this evening at six."

"That is great!"

"What is so great?" asked Natasha from the hall where she was doing some work. Sunita didn't reply. She remembered that they had decided to approach the army headquarters against the advice given by Natasha. Yogesh got up from his chair and walked up to Natasha. Sunita followed him.

"Natasha," Yogesh called her.

"Yes," she continued to do her work.

"I hope you didn't mind."

"Mind what?"

"We decided to pursue the matter against your advice."

Natasha left her work and stood up. She put her hands on her waist and looked affectionately at Sunita and Yogesh. "When I advised you against getting any further into the matter, I did my duty," she said. "When you decided to go ahead with it, you did your duty. So the question of anybody's minding or not minding is irrelevant."

"We discussed the matter among ourselves," said Sunita. "We weighed the pros and cons of pursuing the matter or dropping it and we felt that we couldn't live with the guilt of suppressing what could be a classified information of great importance for the country."

"My dear Sunita," said Natasha, "When I advised you against that line of action, I knew you wouldn't follow my advice. You are too young to bother about the consequences. In fact I would have been disappointed if you hadn't done what you did. But remember, I am older than either of you and have seen more of this world. I wish you the very best in life but my experience tells me that there might be some trouble ahead. If there is one, be prepared to face it."

"I think there is nothing to worry now," said Yogesh. "The army chaps have found the information so valuable that they thought it wise to bring to the notice of the Defence Minister. The minister has invited us to thank us in person. We have to leave at 5.30 P.M."

"What a great moment it would be," said Sunita, when getting ready to leave office in the evening. "Meeting Mr. Raman Kumar in person. I heard him once when I was in college. He had come to address the students to win their support for the reforms in our education system. He spoke so well! Imagine, we'll be able to know him personally now!"

"I am happy for you," said Natasha. "It is going to be 5.30 P.M already. You better be going."

"What about you?" asked Yogesh. "I think we can close the office early today!"

"That sounds fine," said Natasha. "I have got some shopping to do. Groceries and stuff like that. I think I'll also call it a day."

The three of them left the office together. Sunita and Yogesh bade goodbye to Natasha in the parking lot and left on their motorcycle. Natasha followed a short distance behind in her car. They were excited at the prospect of meeting one of the most popular politicians in the country.

They had hardly covered about two hundred meters when Yogesh sensed something wrong. He had casually looked into the rear view mirror of his bike and had a feeling that a speeding white Scorpio, that was about twenty meters behind, was rushing towards them. Instinctively, he swerved the motorcycle to the extreme left of the road. But despite his effort, he could not avoid the accident. The Scorpio hit the motorcycle from behind and sped away. Yogesh's maneuver, however, helped in minimizing the force of the impact and saved them from being run over. He pressed the brake pedal with his right foot and put the left foot on the ground trying to bring the motorcycle to a halt. The rear of the motorcycle turned a full circle due to the sudden application of the brakes.

"You bastard!" Yogesh shouted at the Scorpio but it soon sped out of sight. Yogesh couldn't see the license number of the vehicle. He had, however, a vague impression of the sticker that he saw on the rear glass-screen of the vehicle. It was the picture of a white stallion in running stance with some caption below. He couldn't read the caption.

"Are you alright?" Sunita asked in a trembling voice.

"I am OK," replied a shaken Yogesh, trying to control himself. His eyes were still fixed in the direction in which the Scorpio had disappeared.

"My leg Yogesh!" said Sunita. "It is badly injured."

Yogesh looked at her right leg. It was bleeding.

"Oh no!" he said. He tried to get down from the motorcycle but could not swing his leg over the pillion as Sunita was still sitting there.

"Can you get down?" he asked Sunita. She tried to lift her right leg but her body was still shaking with fear. She couldn't stand. As Yogesh tried to recoil his right leg to jump free off the motorcycle, some passers by rushed to help them.

"Sunita! Yogesh! Are you alright?" asked Natasha as she came running out of her car.

"I am alright," said Yogesh. "But she is badly injured. Help her get down please!"

Natasha and a couple of other persons helped Sunita get down and stand on her feet. Blood had soaked her right shoe.

"Police. Call the police," shouted someone in the swelling crowd.

"Call the ambulance first," shouted someone else.

"Help me in taking her to the car," said Natasha. Yogesh had already pulled his motorcycle on its stand. He took Sunita's right hand in his hands and put it around his shoulders. Natasha did likewise with the other hand from the other side. They made her lie on the rear seat of the car. Natasha took the wheel and Yogesh sat in the passenger seat in the front. He looked around and saw one of the security guards of the World Trade Towers coming towards them. He gave him the keys of his motorcycle and said, "We had an accident and madam is injured. We are going to take her to the hospital. You please take care of the motorcycle and tell the police, if they come, that we are in the hospital."

"Which hospital sir?" asked the security guard.

Yogesh looked at Natasha. They had not decided which hospital they would take her to. Yogesh gave a quick thought and decided to take her to a private nursing home.

"Niramay Nursing Home in Jor Bagh" said Yogesh. Natasha started the engine and they were on their way to the hospital. None of them spoke a word for sometime. They were still trying to recover from the shock of the accident. Yogesh tried to recall the sequence of events that led to the accident. They had just left the World Trade Towers and turned to the right to join the traffic on the left hand side of the road. The turning was alright. The traffic was not too heavy. He recalled that when he looked into the rear view mirror the first time, he saw Natasha taking the turn and following them. When he looked there the second time, Natasha's car was not visible but a white Scorpio was speeding towards them. He recollected that there were two persons in that vehicle but things happened so quickly that he could not get any clear view of either of the two. The Scorpio hit the motorbike at the rear just when he had very nearly pulled it to the extreme left of the road. If he had not done so, the accident could have proved fatal. Was it just an accident or was an attempt to knock them off?

Yogesh began to worry.

"Yogesh," it was Sunita who broke the silence. "I think Natasha can take me to the nursing home? You go and see the Defence Minister."

"To hell with him," said Yogesh. He felt sorry immediately thereafter for having used that phrase for Raman Kumar. "I mean, I can't leave you in this condition. We must find out how serious the injury is. We can always meet the Defence Minister some other time. I am sure he will understand. Unfortunately, I don't have Colonel Bali's number. Otherwise I would have called and informed him."

"I hope the accident was not related to your new adventure?" asked Natasha.

"Can't say," said Yogesh after a long pause. He was beginning to doubt the wisdom of ignoring Natasha's advice. He came out of his thoughts when Natasha brought the car to a halt outside the main door of Niramay Nursing Home.

The nursing home was located in a four-storey building in the posh Jor Bagh Colony. It was an exclusive set up that provided excellent treatment, though at a price. Only the well-to-do could afford it.

The helpers came running to the car with a stretcher. Sunita was taken to the emergency room where a male doctor and a lady doctor gave her immediate attention. They removed her shoes and folded her trousers upwards. The wound was on the lower part of the right leg, just above the ankle. It was a deep cut but there was no apparent sign of any bone fracture. The doctor on duty hurriedly took an X-ray of the leg and it confirmed that there was no bone fracture.

The bleeding from the wound had not yet stopped. It required six stitches before it did. But the doctors did not allow her to be taken home. "She would have to be under observation for at least two days as there is every chance of the wound getting infected," they ruled. Despite Sunita's protests, Yogesh told her firmly that she would have to stay at the nursing home as advised by the doctors.

The police arrived at the nursing home shortly afterwards. They recorded the statements of Yogesh and Sunita and assured of all help before leaving.

"What happened Colonel?" asked the Defence Minister when he saw Colonel Bali enter his chamber at about 6.45 P.M.

"I don't know, sir," replied Colonel Bali. "Yogesh promised that they would be here before 6 P.M. I waited at the reception till 6.30 P.M. I gave a ring to his office but there was no reply. I checked up at his residence. There was no response from there either. I can't understand why they haven't come. At least they could have given us a ring. Or may be he doesn't have my number!"

"I hope everything is alright with them," sighed the Defence Minister.

"I hope so sir," commented the Colonel.

"Don't you have his cell number?"

"No sir."

"Then why don't you check up with the police?"

"Police? Why?"

"Just to find out that no untoward incident has taken place."

"I'll just check up, sir!" the colonel turned to leave.

"Check up from here only," said the minister as he pushed one of the phones lying on his table towards Colonel Bali. The colonel dialled 100.

"Police Control Room," came a male voice from the other side.

"Hello I am Colonel Bali, speaking from Sena Bhavan. We were expecting a young couple here to call on the Defence Minister. They were to reach here by 6 P.M. It is already approaching 7 P.M. but the couple still haven't turned up. They haven't reached home either. I wonder if you have any information about them!"

"What are their particulars?"

"A young man named Yogesh Naqvi and his wife. They were to come from World Trade Towers to Sena Bhavan. I think they were to come on a motorcycle."

"Wait a minute please."

Colonel Bali held the receiver in his hand. He heard the clatter of typewriters and printers in the background. The Defence Minister sat quietly, watching him.

"Mr. Yogesh Naqvi and Mrs. Sunita Naqvi. Is that right sir?" queried the Police Control Room.

"Yes," replied Colonel Bali. His heart skipped a beat as he heard the Control Room give full name of Mrs. Naqvi.

"Sir, this couple has met with an accident. They have been admitted to Niramay Nursing Home in Jor Bagh."

"I hope they are alright?" asked Colonel Bali with more a wish than a question.

"Details not known sir."

Colonel Bali told the Defence Minister about the reason why Yogesh and Sunita could not keep their appointment.

"Are they alright?" asked the minister.

"Sir the Police Control Room does not have any more details. Should I check up from the Nursing Home?"

"Please do."

Colonel Bali enquired the number of Niramay Nursing Home from the directory enquiry and dialled it. He was greatly relieved when the nursing home informed him that Yogesh was not hurt at all and his wife was injured but was out of danger.

"Thank God," the Defence Minister sighed. "Well Colonel, I am beginning to suspect something. It was not an accident. It can't be an accident. Somebody has tried to kill that young man."

"You really think so?" asked a bewildered Colonel Bali.

"Yes," said the minister emphatically. "And since this so called accident has taken place after my meeting with the Home Minister and the Prime Minister, I think I also know who is behind this plot."

"Who is he, sir?" asked Colonel Bali in astonishment.

"That I will let you know after my meeting with Yogesh Naqvi. I am so relieved to know that he is safe. You must bring him to see me tomorrow. For the time being we must ensure adequate security for him and his wife at the nursing home."

Raman Kumar picked up the phone and personally spoke to M.S. Bedi, the Commissioner of Police in Delhi, to provide security cover to Yogesh and Sunita. He then turned back to Colonel Bali and said, "Colonel, can I bank upon you to do one thing?"

"Please sir!"

"Have one bouquet of flowers and a get-well card delivered to Mrs. Naqvi on my behalf. Tell the young couple not to get scared. Their safety is our responsibility from now on. I wish I could visit the nursing home personally but you know the security regulations. Moreover, we still haven't found out the source of that message of the planned attack on me."

"I think, sir, Yogesh might be of some help," said Colonel Bali. "After all, he is the only person who saw the man with the message."

"That is precisely why I wanted to meet him," said the minister. "But now we have this accident. Do one thing Colonel, please try to get this young man to meet me tomorrow some time. Let us see if he can really throw more light on the whole subject. I am becoming more and more certain that some dangerous game is being played right in front of our eyes and we must expose it. But to do that we need Yogesh Naqvi to identify some people."

Yogesh's mother and Sunita's parents and brother rushed to the nursing home as soon as they received the news of the accident. Sunita, Yogesh and Natasha decided not to tell anything to anybody about their adventure with the coded message. They feared that their people would get scared and link the accident to their action. They told their folks that it was an accident caused by the heavy rush. They, in turn, cursed the Delhi Traffic for the mishap. 'People do not observe the rules of the road'. 'DTC buses are the worst offenders.' 'Young children of the rich are too incorrigible; they drive like mad', so on and so forth.

Colonel Bali also came to see Yogesh and Sunita at the nursing home. Yogesh saw Colonel Bali asking the receptionist about the room where Sunita was staying. He hurried to meet him half way in the corridor. "Please do not mention anything about our meeting with the Defence Minister," Yogesh requested the Colonel. "Our folks are standing outside my wife's room and they do not know anything about it. We do not want them to know, yet."

"I understand Yogesh," said Colonel Bali. Yogesh took the Colonel towards Sunita's room. "Papa, meet Colonel Bali. He is a friend," said Yogesh, introducing the Colonel to his father-in-law. Colonel Bali shook hands with Sunita's father and bowed to the ladies.

"Please come this way," Yogesh escorted him to Sunita's room.

"Must be Colonel Bali," said Sunita as soon as she saw Yogesh enter the room with an army officer in uniform. She was feeling better now.

"Yes Mrs. Naqvi. I am Colonel Bali."

"Sorry we could not come," said Sunita with a smile. "I hope the Defence Minister is not cross with us. We wanted to meet him so badly."

"He understands perfectly well," said Colonel Bali. "You can meet him when you are alright. I hope the injury is not too serious?"

"It is nothing really," said Yogesh, "It could have been worse. It was not an accident. It was an attempt to kill us."

"Must be the man who gave you that cover by mistake," said Colonel Bali. "He must have got a wind of the developments. But it won't be long before we are able to get him. The Defence Minister is taking personal interest in the matter. He has also spoken to the Police Commissioner to ensure your safety. So do not get scared of any one or anything."

"Has the message been fully deciphered?" asked Sunita. "I am curious to know what exactly it contained."

"Not yet," Colonel Bali lied. "But we will be able to break the code soon. I think in about two days time, we will be able to know the full details."

"Please let us know the details as soon as you have them," said Sunita.

"Sure," replied Colonel Bali. "By the way Yogesh, will it be possible for you to spare some time tomorrow? The Defence Minister wants to have a chat with you on the whole affair."

"Tomorrow I think, would not be a problem," said Yogesh.

"You must go Yogesh," said Sunita.

"Yes I will go," Yogesh confirmed to Sunita. Then he turned to Colonel Bali and asked, "What time?"

"Come some time in the forenoon," said Colonel Bali. "Or rather, to be on the safe side, I will arrange for you to be picked up. Can I contact you on your mobile tomorrow?"

"Sure! Take my number. I will be with Sunita the whole day," replied Yogesh.

"Fine," said the Colonel as he noted down the mobile number. "I will inform you about the exact time of appointment on phone tomorrow. An army vehicle will come to pick you up. So be ready."

"My privilege," said Yogesh as he bade goodbye to Colonel Bali.

"Yogesh, can I ask you for a favour?" asked Sunita.

"You don't have to ask for a favour," replied Yogesh. "Just tell me what you want!"

"I think the nursing home will allow only one person to stay with me."

"Yes. I will stay here for the night."

"Then you kindly take everybody home. They are just wasting time here. Have your dinner and come back soon. Sumit can stay here till you come back."

"No. I will stay here till Yogesh returns," said Natasha as she entered the room.

"But you are getting late?" Yogesh pointed out.

"Never mind," replied Natasha. "There are certain advantages of being single."

"OK. If you so desire!" said Yogesh.

"Please bring that cipher book and the message," said Sunita. "The message is lying in the book. The book is in the cabinet in our room. Also bring a pen and some papers."

"Relax Sunita," said Yogesh. "These things can wait!"

"Please Yogesh, I am quite OK! That message will keep me busy. Otherwise what will I do here over the next two days?"

"Alright," said Yogesh. "If you want it that badly!"

Yogesh left with his family members and returned after about one and a half hour. He brought home made food for both Sunita and Natasha. They were famished by then and relished their dinner. Natasha left for her home soon afterwards. Sunita continued to fiddle with the code till late at night but could not make any progress.

Yogesh dosed off in the adjoining bed that had been kept for the attendant.

Chapter 26

10 May

When Yogesh got up in the morning he saw a posse of policemen on duty in the premises of the nursing home.

"Good morning, Yogesh ji," said a police inspector when he saw Yogesh coming out of the room. "I am Inspector Vasudev. We are on duty here to ensure your safety. We came here at night. I did not meet you as it was late. I did not want to disturb you."

"That is nice of you," said Yogesh. He felt grateful to the caring Defence Minister. He had been worried about their safety after the accident. The enemy would not dare strike in the nursing home now, he thought. The thought made him feel safe.

Sunita's parents came to see their daughter early in the morning. Natasha also came to see her. She left soon thereafter for Sonyog. 'The show must go on,' was her advice.

The call from Colonel Bali came early in the forenoon. The appointment of Yogesh with the Defence Minister was fixed at 2 P.M. An army Gypsy came to pick him up, as promised by Colonel Bali.

Yogesh was received by Colonel Bali at the reception. He took him to the chamber of the Defence Minister.

"Sir, meet Mr. Yogesh Naqvi," Colonel Bali said by way of introduction.

"Good afternoon sir," said Yogesh, quite excited to see the popular minister.

"Good afternoon Yogesh!" the minister returned the greeting. "I am so glad to see you!"

"My privilege sir."

"Please sit down," Raman Kumar offered seat to Yogesh. He then turned to Colonel Bali and said, "You mind getting General Surinder Pal and General Sehgal here, Colonel?"

"Not at all sir," replied Colonel Bali while leaving. "I will be right back."

"I must congratulate you on taking a very wise decision on handing over that paper to us," the minister assured Yogesh as the two took their seats. "Well done! How is your wife?"

"She is fine sir," replied Yogesh. "She is likely to be discharged from the nursing home tomorrow. She is sorry; we could not make it here last evening."

"That was not your fault. I wish I could find out the man who tried to run you over!"

"He could have tried again but won't succeed now. I am extremely grateful to you for providing adequate police security at Niramay Nursing Home."

"That was my duty. I will provide you all the necessary help."

"Sir!" Yogesh decided to ask the question uppermost in his mind. "Has the message been fully deciphered?"

"Not fully," replied the minister. "You know these codes are not easy to break. They require time and patience. But we are sure by now that the message relates to the security of our country."

"I see," said Yogesh.

"Well Yogesh," spoke the minister as he got up from his chair. "Tell me, will you be able to recognize from the photograph, the person who gave you the cover?"

"I think so," replied Yogesh. "I had a clear and close view of his face."

Raman Kumar opened a cabinet. He brought out a photo album and placed it on the table in front of Yogesh. "It is possible," he said, "that the man who gave you that cover, works in our government. We have received some intelligence reports earlier also that there is someone in our government who is a spy of some enemy country. But we have not been able to establish his identity so far. It is extremely important that the traitor is recognized and punished before he can cause any major damage to the security and interests of our country. Here are photographs of some government functions that I have attended in the past. It is quite possible that the man, who gave you the cover, is present in some photograph. Go through the album carefully and see if the traitor is present in any one of these photographs."

Yogesh did as told. He started examining each photograph carefully. He had hardly flipped through half a dozen sheets when he looked with amazement at the photo of the man in white kurta and pyjama wearing dark glasses. The photograph showed Raman Kumar and Sukhraj Malik sharing a joke and two other persons looking at them with smiles on their faces. The man wearing dark glasses stood a little behind but he was the man Yogesh was looking for. No question about that!

"Sir, this is the man," Yogesh shouted in excitement as he showed the photograph to the Defence Minister.

"Let me see," said Raman Kumar. He took the album and looked at the man on whose photo Yogesh has placed his finger. "Balwant? Is he that man?"

"You know him, sir?" asked Yogesh.

"Of course I know him," replied Raman Kumar. "This innocent looking man is the son-in-law of our Home Minister!"

Yogesh was stunned to hear the identity of the man. He could not believe that the son-in-law of one of the most powerful men in the country could be engaged in some dirty work against the interests of the nation.

"Are you sure he is the man?" asked the Defence Minister.

"I am hundred percent sure," replied Yogesh. Suddenly the hazy picture of one of the men in the white Scorpio that had hit the motorcycle also began to become clear to him. "I can also see now that he was the man who was sitting with the driver in the Scorpio that tried to kill us."

"Oh my God!" sighed Raman Kumar. "I suspected as much."

Both remained silent for some time. The silence was disturbed when the army chief, the DGMI and Colonel Bali walked in.

Raman Kumar introduced Yogesh to the army chief and the DG MI. "This young man has done a most commendable job for us," he said. "He deserves to be awarded Ashok Chakra."

"Yes sir," said General Surinder Pal. "That message might contain some state secret."

"More than the message General, he has been able to identify the traitor," said the minister. The statement startled the three officers. They looked at the minister inquisitively. "He was able to pick up the man from the photographs of various government functions that I have attended from time to time," told the minister.

"Who is that man, sir?" asked the army chief.

"He is the son-in-law of our honourable Home Minister," said Raman Kumar with a sigh.

"What?" asked the three men, almost in one voice.

"Here is that S.O.B," said the Defence Minister, pointing at the photograph and pushing the album towards the three officers.

"Unbelievable!" the COAS lamented.

"Too shocking," General Sehgal despaired.

Silence fell in the room. They were all trying to comprehend the consequences that will follow when this devastating information became public.

"OK Yogesh," said Raman Kumar, finally. "I can't tell you how grateful we are to you for your invaluable assistance. I think when the history of the present government is written, your name will find a prominent place in it for lending your hand in helping the nation to nip the evil in the bud and busting a dangerous spy ring. I will see to it that your efforts are suitably rewarded. Please contact me anytime you need my help on any matter. But don't tell anybody anything about Balwant or the message. We will see how to go about it. It is a sensitive matter and has to be dealt with delicately. Give my best wishes to your wife. Bye!"

"Bye sir!"

A happy and satisfied Yogesh took leave of the Defence Minister leaving him to chalk out further strategies with his senior officers.

"Let us get back to business," said the minister. "We are faced with a grim situation. We will have to handle the affair very carefully. Balwant is the son-in-law of the man who could have become the prime minister of the country.

He lost only by very few votes."

"I wonder if the Home Minister is aware of the activities of his son-in-law!" queried General Sehgal.

"That is indeed a moot question," said General Surinder Pal.

"Though I pray it is not true," said the minister, "yet I have a feeling that the plot of my assassination could not have been hatched without the blessings of the Home Minister. Probably his ambition has overtaken his judgement. It is obvious that he wants to assassinate me, dislodge the Prime Minister, invite Pakistani army into Kashmir and hand over Kashmir to them. He is doing all this to ensure that he becomes the Prime Minister of India, even if it means choosing a bloody path to realize his ambition. And General, my suspicions are not unfounded. Yesterday when Colonel Bali told me that Yogesh Naqvi had met with an accident, I knew that it could not be a coincidence that the accident took place barely half an hour after I had told the Prime Minister and Sukhraj Malik about the coded message given to us by Yogesh Naqvi. I suspected that someone close to either of the two could be the man behind the message. That is why I called Yogesh here and got this man picked up from the various photographs. My observation was also based on an earlier report submitted to us by the RAW. They had warned us of the existence of a CIA mole in our government. This Balwant is the CIA mole."

The three officers looked with disdain at the photograph of Balwant.

"Sir, you must persuade the Prime Minister to cancel his Tehri - Dehradun trip," said General Surinder Pal. "The ISI may launch their so-called Operation Red Rose any time. We need the Prime Minister in New Delhi at the time of this emergency. And we do not know what this father-in-law and son-in-law duo is up to."

"I spoke to him this morning about it," replied Raman Kumar. "But he insists that he must go. It appears that he wants to offer prayers at Haridwar on the no moon night. But more importantly, he is of the view that by letting things go as per the schedule is the best way to capture the man who would try to kill me. I also tend to agree with him that we must capture the would-be assassin and extract from him the truth behind the 'Operation Red Rose'. Yogesh's statement alone will not suffice to lay our hands on Malik and Balwant. I have a feeling that Malik and Balwant might still go ahead with their assassination plot against me. History shows that such maniacs find it extremely difficult to withdraw when fighting against odds. They find their salvation only in pushing ahead with their ghastly deeds with renewed determination. When I met Sukhraj Malik yesterday he told me that he would ensure adequate SPG cover to me at all times. I would take the risk and go along with what he has told me. But should something happen to me, you must not be found lacking in your duty to the motherland. What I want you to do is to put the army on full alert because should the Pakistanis go ahead with its plans to invade Kashmir, war with Pakistan will be inevitable."

"You will not find us wanting in any way sir," the army chief assured his minister. "But please look after yourself. We need you to lead us."

"Thank you General for your kind words," said Raman Kumar. "God is on our side and I am sure, we'll win."

"Ma, if you don't mind," said Yogesh as soon as he entered the hospital room where Sunita was recuperating, "I want to talk to Sunita in private for a moment." Yogesh's mother had come to see her daughter-in-law, straight from her school. She was surprised at Yogesh's request. Her face, however, remained expressionless. Years of a lonely, disciplined life had taught her the difficult art of holding her emotions in control. She left the room without saying a word.

"Why did you do this to Ma?" asked Sunita as she kept aside the cipher book, the pen and the papers she was writing on.

"The news is such," replied Yogesh. "I wanted to tell you in strict privacy."

"What is it?"

"I have been able to identify the man with the message, the man who tried to run us over."

"Really? Who is he?"

"Hold your breath and listen." Yogesh looked at the door. There was no one else in the room. "His name is Balwant. He is the son-in-law of Sukhraj Malik, the Home Minister!"

"Son-in-law of the Home Minister?" asked Sunita in disbelief. "Isn't he the person who assists him in his political work?"

"You are right. He is the husband of Sarla, Malik's only daughter."

"What is there in the message and for whom it was meant? Why did he want to kill us?"

"They have not been able to decipher the whole message yet. But the Defence Minister told me that whatever it was, it indeed concerned the security of the country."

"But why kill us?"

"Obviously because we handed over the message to the army despite his threats on the phone asking us not to do so," said Yogesh.

"How crooked and cruel people can be!" Sunita sighed.

"The Defence Minister really appreciates our decision to approach army headquarters. He said that we might even be suitably rewarded."

"If they can put that traitor in jail, that would be our greatest reward."

"It is only a matter of time. Balwant, probably, along with his father-in-law, will be behind bars soon. I am sure of that."

"But I am still surprised, why doesn't anybody give us some details of the message?"

"Any luck with your efforts?"

"Not much really," replied Sunita. "I have tried various permutations and combinations. But things haven't come right yet."

"I knew it wasn't going to be that easy," said Yogesh. "It has taken three days for the professionals in the army but they have not been able to fully decipher the message yet. However, there is no harm in continuing to try. Who knows with persistence and bit of luck you might succeed!"

Just then Natasha entered the room, holding a bouquet of roses for Sunita. "Good evening and get well soon," she said as she handed over the bouquet to Sunita. "How is your leg?"

"It is fine," replied Sunita. "It is much better. The pain has mostly disappeared. The only problem is the stay in the nursing home. They look after me well but I want to get back home."

"That is unfair," Yogesh teased. "You have complete rest here and friends come and present you flowers. I have to do all the running around but not one rose for me."

"I'll give you one," Sunita chuckled.

"In fact I thought of bringing some roses for you also," said Natasha, knowing fully well that Yogesh was just pulling her leg. "But your favourite colour was not available."

"You know my favourite colour?" asked Yogesh.

"Black," replied Natasha.

"How do you know?"

Natasha just smiled back.

Sudhir Nanda decided that he had had enough. He confronted Sanjana, his wife for ten years. "Enough Sanjana, enough!" asserted Sudhir with conviction. "Ten years I have tolerated you. For ten years I have been trying to make you understand that you will have to learn to live within my salary. I have never compromised on my integrity and I never will. I don't care what other officers do. But I am not going to take any favours or any bribe from anyone. Rather than being proud of me for what I am, you tease me and taunt me on my lack of guts. You know what? One does not require guts to take bribe. One requires guts to refuse bribe when it is readily available and every other person is taking it. But Sudhir Nanda has never been for sale and never will be. And as for my guts, I'll show you my guts tonight. I am going to throw you out of my house, and my life. I don't give a damn what happens to my carefully cultivated reputation tomorrow. Get out, you bitch!"

It did not bother Muniappa's conscience any more. He knew that he was cheating his wife who had been a fine companion. She was a homely, God fearing and simple woman. Muniappa loved her deeply. But he found her too cold in the bed. Muniappa tried to make her more adventurous in the bed by showing her blue movies and giving her erotic books and magazines to read. But to no avail.

One day an exporter offered Muniappa the services of a call girl in return for his help in getting a file cleared from his minister. Muniappa's boss had already cleared the file and it was lying on Muniappa's table. He found no harm in claiming credit for getting a favourable decision for the exporter from his boss. It enabled him to spend an evening with a pretty girl and live out his fantasies.

Muniappa had made his choice. He was going to enjoy a happy family life in his marriage and seek sexual satisfaction outside marriage.

Anand Mishra was neither shocked, nor dismayed when he returned home from office and found his sister Kumkum hanging from the ceiling fan. He had seen her getting into deep depression and had refused to be treated. He too had gone into depression many times but managed to pull himself out by immersing himself in his work. Kumkum had no such diversion.

Kumkum had been staying with her brother ever since he was posted in Delhi two years ago. She had moved to Delhi from Varanasi after a quarrel with her parents. They wanted her to marry a particular boy whom she did not like. She refused to do their bidding. Since she was quite close to Anand, she moved to Delhi to live with him. Anand Mishra had not yet married and lived single in a two bed room government flat on the Minto Road.

One night Anand Mishra went to Kumkum's room to inquire something and found her naked in her bed, playing with a dildo. He did not know what came over him. Like a man possessed, he undressed himself and hopped into the bed with Kumkum. She too could not control her urge. They made wild, passionate love and soon lay exhausted. None spoke a word. But they were no more brother and sister. The trust had been broken. From that night onwards they were hardly on speaking terms with each other. But before going to bed every night, they would find themselves indulge in sex, without sharing a word of communication.

Both felt terribly guilty. Both felt highly miserable. But both felt helpless.

Anand Mishra was relieved to find that Kumkum had finally decided to put an end to their misery. Had she not done so, he himself would have committed suicide one day. For him, the burden of the guilt of the incest was too heavy to carry.

Sarla and Balwant were happy that they had made their decision and had already started implementing it. They had made friends with Mini and Mayank Oberoi about a year ago. Mini and Mayank Oberoi were an upwardly mobile couple. Mini was a ramp model, smart and very pretty. Mayank was a fashion designer, very handsome and very rich. Mini and Mayank had a farm house in Chhatarpur, on the outskirts of South Delhi. When they invited Sarla and Balwant first time to their farm house, they offered them to join in group sex with them. Balwant was not very keen but Sarla persuaded him to try it out, just for the heck of it. Initially, it was only two couples, Mini and Mayank, Sarla and Balwant. But slowly the Oberois began to enlarge their group from two to four and four to ten. Now there were a dozen couples having wild parties in their farm house at least once a fortnight. It was a free-for-all sex. Anyone with anyone. All couples came from the upper class families but none from as powerful a family as Sarla and Balwant. The risk of exposure had begun to scare them. They began to rue the day they fell for the bait of the Oberois.

Finally, they decided to end their sexual adventures. They were not going to take chances with the political fortunes of Sukhraj Malik. They had refused invitation from Mini and Mayank for tonight's party and were going to stay that way in future as well. They had taken the call and were sure of that.

Chapter 27

11 May

05.00 A.M.

Sunita looked at the adjoining bed. Yogesh was still sleeping. She decided to let him sleep. She took the cipher book, the coded message, a blank sheet of paper and a pen and began to tinker with the code again. Once again it appeared to be a vain attempt.

Many times during the last two days, Sunita had felt that she had come close to breaking the code but something would go wrong somewhere and she had to start all over again. She had begun to wonder if the exercise was worth all the effort that she was putting into it. But despite the setbacks, she could not get herself to throw away the message. Every time she wanted to do so, the message would appear to stare at her in the face, daring her to unravel the secret.

06.00 A.M.

Yogesh got up from the bed and was surprised to see his wife's doggedness and relentless pursuit of the code. "At this rate you might succeed in fully decoding the message even before they do it in Sena Bhavan," he said with a smile.

"Who knows?" said Sunita, keeping aside her papers.

"Have you had your morning tea?"

"Not yet. I was waiting for you to get up."

Yogesh pressed the call bell and one attendant arrived with tea within five minutes. Sumit arrived shortly afterwards.

"Hi didi ! Hi jijaji !" said he, extending his wishes. "Mom and Papa will come at eight. I'll be here till then," he said matter-of-factly.

"That is so nice of you Sumit," said Yogesh, finishing his tea. "So I can go home and change and also bring some breakfast for Sunita."

"Ask ma to make 'Aloo-ka-Pratha' for me," said Sunita. "I want to have some spicy stuff for my breakfast."

"By all means my dear!" said Yogesh and left for his home.

09.00 A.M.

Yogesh returned to the nursing home and found Sunita in the company of her mother who was busy reading some film gossip in Stardust. Sunita was still engrossed in the coded message.

"Leave that damn thing aside, I say," Yogesh told Sunita. "Let us have breakfast first."

"What is that you are so busy with since yesterday?" asked Sunita's mother.

"It is nothing much mom," replied Sunita. "It is a book relating to cipher. We plan to use it in our work."

"Thinking up some new idea on ads?"

"Yes, mom."

Yogesh gave a knowing look to Sunita. She merely smiled back at him.

"Mom, please come. Join us for breakfast." said Yogesh.

"Thanks Yogesh. I am on fast today. I had brought some sandwiches for you two but she wants to have only Aloo-ka-Pratha made by your Ma!"

"And that is what she is going to have," said Yogesh with a smile.

Sunita's mother got back to her article. Yogesh joined Sunita to have breakfast. The prathas were really good but he could make out that her mind was not on the prathas, despite her avowed desire, to have the same. He knew that she was still thinking about the code. He decided to let her continue with her preoccupation with the code.

"It could be two letters or two numbers standing for one letter," Sunita blurted out, in the middle of her breakfast.

"I beg your pardon!" said Yogesh in surprise. He could not make anything of what she said.

"No, I mean, I think my whole approach has been wrong," said Sunita, leaving her half finished prathas in the plate. "Please remove these plates and let me see if I can succeed with my new approach."

"Come on Sony, finish your breakfast first," Yogesh said, still puzzled.

"No Yogesh, I am over with it. Thanks for the prathas. These were great!"

Yogesh knew that she did not mean what she said. But he decided not to disturb her chain of thoughts. He quickly finished his breakfast and removed the empty plates from the bed.

"What is going on Sunita?" asked her mother. She was even more surprised than Yogesh to see the sudden change in her daughter's behaviour.

"Nothing mom," assured Sunita. "Mom, may I request you for one thing?"

"What?"

"You please go home now,"

"Why so early?"

"Please mom! I want to devote undivided attention for some time to my work. As it is, I am quite alright and will be discharged from here in the evening."

"But Sunita -------------?"

"Please mom! My good mom! You please go home now."

Her mother looked at Yogesh. He merely shrugged and said nothing.

"Ok Sunita," said her mother finally. "I will go if you insist. But you come to us when you are discharged from here and stay with me till your wound gets completely healed. Since Yogesh's mother has to go to school every day, there won't be anybody to look after you there."

"That makes sense," it was Yogesh who spoke. "Sony, you better stay with mom and papa for a few days so that I can attend office. At least one of us must be at Sonyog now."

"It suits me fine," said Sunita. "But let me be alone for some time now. And mom, please don't take it otherwise. It is something that I must attend to."

"Never mind Sunita," said her mother with a smile while leaving. "I know you are just like your father when it comes to reading a book and solving a problem. You won't give up till you finish it. Wish you the best of luck. But before I leave, tell me what would you like to have for lunch?"

"Anything mom, anything," said Sunita, rather impatiently.

"Alright," said her mother and left.

"I'll drop mom home and return soon," Yogesh told Sunita. "Take care."

"I will," said Sunita and eagerly got back to the code. She tried various combinations of letters with letters, numbers with numbers, letters with numbers and numbers with letters. As if through some inspiration, she began to see a pattern in the linkages of the various letters and numbers with each other.

1.30 P.M.

Yogesh returned to the hospital with the lunch box. Sunita was still busy with the code. She felt that she had the full text of the message before her. But she could not grasp it as the decoded letters were written here and there due to too much of overwriting and too many corrections.

"That is too much Sony," said Yogesh. "Your obsession with this coded thing is beginning to irritate me."

"Please Yogesh" Sunita pleaded. "It should not take very long now."

"I know how much is your 'not very long'," said Yogesh. "It is two hours at least and I can't wait for two hours to have my lunch." Yogesh snatched the papers from Sunita's hands and placed them on the side table. "Now be a good girl and let us enjoy our meal."

"OK baba!" said Sunita. Yogesh laid the home made food. Sunita tried to forget all about the coded message when the aroma of the home made curry filled her nostrils.

"Smells great!" she said.

They ate their lunch and had some casual conversation.

02.15 P.M.

"Yogesh, you should leave now," said Sunita. "Ma will be waiting for you. But give me my papers before you leave."

"Come on Sony," said Yogesh a bit indignantly. "You are supposed to be taking rest. But here you are getting more and more into this coded message."

"Yogesh, I think I am almost there. I just have to put in all the letters in the proper place and I think I'll be able to get the message right."

"You are not going to do anything now. You will just take rest. You appear to be too exhausted."

"Yogesh please!"

"No Sony, no. You must take rest. Last night also you did not sleep well, courtesy that coded message."

"In that case, why don't you take those papers home Yogesh?" asked Sunita. "Who knows you might succeed in putting the final message in place. I think I have already been able to finalize the code key. Just start from where I left. Each letter, number or a combination of them stands for another letter or number. Just substitute them in the code and you might get some meaningful message."

"I am going to do just that. But I do not want you to waste any more energy on this code any more." He collected the papers and the lunch box and walked out of the room.

03.00 P.M.

Yogesh was impressed with the work that Sunita had put in. Once he started working on the message himself, he too was hooked to it. After about half an hour of tinkering with the various letters deciphered by Sunita, he had some kind of a message before him.

MESSA GEEBEG INSST OPDEF ENCEM INIST ERRAM ANKUM ARMUS TGOBE FOREE LEVEN THOFM AYIFO PERAT IONRE DROSE ISTOS UCCEE DSTOP MINIM UMPRO TECTI ONWIL LBEEN SURED FORHI MTILL THENS TOPFI NISHH IMOFF ANDKA SHMIR ISYOU RSSTO PMESS AGEEN DS

Yogesh knew that all the groups of five letters each did not make independent words. He would have to put extra effort in linking and delinking the various letters to form proper words. It did not take long. After about fifteen minutes of effort, he had a message that sent a chill down his spine when he read it.

MESSAGE BEGINS STOP DEFENCE MINISTER RAMAN KUMAR MUST GO BEFORE ELEVENTH OF MAY IF OPERATION RED ROSE IS TO SUCCEED STOP MINIMUM PROTECTION WILL BE ENSURED FOR HIM TILL THEN STOP FINISH HIM OFF AND KASHMIR IS YOURS STOP MESSAGE ENDS

Yogesh's heart began to pound hard against his chest. He understood why Balwant was so desperate to get the message back that he had, obviously, given to him by mistake. He was plotting the assassination of the Defence Minister Raman Kumar, with or without the knowledge of his father-in-law. No wonder, he wanted to kill Sunita and him as they had gone to the army with the message. He was glad that Sunita had persuaded him to go to the army. It might help in unearthing the murderous plot and saving the life of the Defence Minister. It was sure to help save the country from plunging into turmoil. But what if the army authorities were not able to fully decipher the message and Balwant succeed in his bloody game? It was already the eleventh of May. Should he not rush to the Sena Bhavan?

He made his decision. The magnitude of the seriousness of the information made it mandatory for him, not to take any chances. There was no time to inform Sunita about the message yet. He must hand over the message to Colonel Bali without wasting any more time.

03.45 P.M.

"I need a pass," said Yogesh as he approached the reception counter at Sena Bhavan. "I want to meet Colonel Bali in room number 818."

"What for?" asked the receptionist in an indifferent tone.

"I have to discuss something with him."

"You have an appointment?"

"No, but what I have to discuss with him is very urgent," replied Yogesh, trying to control his irritation.

"I need his instructions to make pass for you," said the receptionist as he pushed the telephone towards Yogesh. He went through the list of telephone numbers in Sena Bhavan and said, "His number is 52163."

Yogesh dialled number 52163. There was no reply. He waited for some time and dialled again. Once again there was no reply.

"I think he is not in his seat," said Yogesh.

"You will have to wait here," said the receptionist as he took the phone from Yogesh.

"I would prefer to wait in Colonel Bali's room," pleaded Yogesh. "You see, I met him on a number of occasions in the last few days."

"Sorry," was all that the receptionist said.

Yogesh felt helpless. He had a devastating piece of information with him but he could not bypass the receptionist to hand over the information to the people who needed it. He thought of showing the message to the receptionist. But then he remembered the advice of the Defence Minister to keep everything confidential. He thought of speaking to General Sehgal or General Surinder Pal. Why not? After all, the two generals knew all about the exchange of the message.

"Excuse me,"said Yogesh as he approached the receptionist again.

"I have already told you that you will have to wait till Colonel Bali answers the phone," said the receptionist in a stern voice.

"I don't want to see Colonel Bali. I want to see the Defence Minister. Give me the phone." Yogesh surprised even himself at his demand to see the minister. Yes, why not? The minister had categorically told him that he could contact him anytime for anything. The seriousness of the message demanded that it should be brought to his notice without wasting any time. The receptionist gave a long, hostile look to Yogesh. Reluctantly, he again pushed the phone towards Yogesh.

"What is the number of the PS to the minister? "Yogesh asked.

"52100" replied the receptionist, without looking at the phone list.

Yogesh dialled the given number.

"Yes please!" came a female voice over the phone.

"Can I speak to the PS to the Defence Minister please?" Yogesh asked.

"May I know who is calling?"

"My name is Yogesh Naqvi. I had met the Honourable Defence Minister yesterday. I have to see him again. For that I wish to speak to his PS."

"Hold on for a second please!"

Pause.

"Hello! This is Gyan Mehta, PS to the Raksha Mantri!"

"Good afternoon Mr. Mehta! My name is Yogesh Naqvi."

"Yes Mr. Naqvi," said Mehta. "I know about you. You wish to see the RM?"

"Yes Mr. Mehta! It is something very urgent."

"The minister is not here at the moment. But he is likely to arrive soon. You may come over here, if you wish."

"Yes, I would like to come there and wait for the minister," said Yogesh. "Will you please speak to the reception?" Yogesh handed over the receiver to the receptionist with a feeling of victory of sorts over him.

"Reception?" called Gyan Mehta.

"Yes sir."

"Mehta, PS to the RM here."

"Yes sir."

"Please issue one pass to Mr. Yogesh Naqvi. He is a guest of the RM."

"Right sir," the receptionist looked at Yogesh in awe as he made a pass and gave it meekly to Yogesh.

"Thank you," said Yogesh. "And here is my mobile which I am going to deposit with the security guard. I will collect it on my way back. Security regulations!" Yogesh winked at the receptionist and rushed into the building.

The receptionist merely smirked back.

04.00 P.M.

Mehta received Yogesh warmly and said, "I have heard about you from the Raksha Mantri. I am sure he will be happy to see you."

"When is he likely to come to the office?" asked Yogesh.

"He is expected anytime," replied Mehta. "You may sit here or you may wait for him in the ante room of his chamber, if you like."

"I think I'll sit inside," said Yogesh. "Please give me something to read, some book or some journal."

Mehta gave him some old issues of 'India Today' and 'Outlook'. Yogesh made himself comfortable in the ante room adjoining the chamber of the Defence Minister. He flipped through the pages of the two journals. But he could not concentrate on reading. His mind was preoccupied with the contents of the message. He took out the deciphered message from the cipher book and read it again. 'How could the Home Minister and his son-in-law ever hatch such a bloody conspiracy? God forbid, what would happen if they actually succeeded in carrying out the assassination of the Defence Minister and really hand over Kashmir to Pakistan or to whosever the message was meant? Yogesh feared an unprecedented national crisis if the traitors were not exposed.

04.30 P.M.

Yogesh got up from his seat and began to pace up and down the ante room. He casually looked outside from one of the side windows. He could have a clear view of the portico where the official cars were allowed to pick up or drop the VVIPs. He was about to move when he saw an Ambassador car drive into the portico with the Indian tricolour waiving on its bonnet. 'Must be the Defence Minister,' he thought. The right hand side rear door of the car opened first and a man in white khadi kurta-pyjama, stepped out. He turned back and walked by the rear of the car towards the left side of the car, carrying a brown brief case in his left hand and a cotton bag slung on his right shoulder. The man was wearing dark glasses. Yogesh had a clear view of the man from the window. The recognition was instantaneous. The man was unmistakably Balwant.

Balwant opened the rear left door of the car. Yogesh saw the Defence Minister get out of the car from the rear left door. He said something to Balwant and both started laughing. Then they walked towards the main entrance to the Sena Bhavan, still engaged in a warm, friendly chat.

The sight of Raman Kumar having a warm, friendly talk with the country's number one traitor shocked Yogesh. He could not reconcile to the totally unexpected and unlikely happening. He felt uneasy and failed to make out why Raman Kumar had become so friendly towards Balwant. Yogesh wanted to know the truth behind his strange behaviour. He made his decision quickly. He looked around the room. In one corner of the room was the attached toilet. Yogesh picked up the journals and hid them behind the sofa. He picked up the cipher book and rushed to the toilet. He closed the door and positioned himself behind it from where he could easily overhear the conversation in the room

Raman Kumar entered the room first, followed by Balwant. He hurried to his chair and picked up the phone. He pressed the buzzer and said, "Mehta, I want the red light on and make sure that I am not disturbed by anybody till I give a green signal."

Mehta was not surprised to get such instructions. He knew that when Yogesh was around, the minister did not want to be disturbed. Unknown to him or his minister or Balwant, Yogesh heard the conversation from behind the door of the toilet.

"Sit down," said Raman Kumar. Balwant took the chair lying on the other side of the table.

"Well Nikhilesh," said Raman Kumar, "You are not only my nephew; you are also my Political Advisor and my accomplice in the conspiracy. It is time that you know everything about me and Operation Red Rose."

The statement stunned Yogesh. What he heard was too shocking to believe. The man who handed over the murderous message to him, the man who tried to run over him and Sunita, the man whom he had identified as Balwant from the photograph and the man who was sitting with the Defence Minister whom he was planning to assassinate, was not Balwant. He was Nikhilesh, the nephew of Raman Kumar, the Political Advisor to the Defence Minister and his co-conspirator in an operation called Red Rose. But why was he planning the assassination of his own uncle? Yogesh was desperate to know the truth.

"You often ask me," began Raman Kumar, "Why I have chosen this dangerous path. I will tell you now why I did it because today, on the 11th day of the fifth month of this year, you and I are standing on the biggest turning point in the history of free India. Today we will give a new direction to the course of events that are about to unfold from midnight tonight. Dear Nikhilesh, the day has finally come when, with the help from our Chinese comrades and their friends in the ISI, your uncle will indeed become the Prime Minister of India in the next twentyfour hours or so."

"But how can the comrades and the ISI help you become the Prime Minister of India?" asked Nikhilesh in an excited voice.

"Well!" Raman Kumar drew a deep breath. "They will help me by launching Operation Red Rose tonight."

"What exactly is Operation Red Rose?" asked Nikhilesh.

"Operation Red Rose has been planned by the ISI in collaboration with the Chinese. It has its origins in a proposal mooted by the Americans. They have taken the concurrence of all five permanent members of the UN Security Council to pass a resolution urging India to hand over Kashmir Valley to Pakistan and then put pressure on us to accept the UN resolution. But our comrades are more practical than the Americans. They know that unless they have a friendly government in New Delhi, this pressure simply will not work. They want a Chinese type government in place here under my leadership. After all it is for nothing that they have invested their time, effort and money in me. To enable me to do this they have conceived Operation Red Rose. They have put the ISI of Pakistan in touch with me. This is what the ISI is planning to do in the Operation Red Rose. You may read it here," said Raman Kumar as he opened his brief case and brought out a yellow coloured file. He pushed the file towards Nikhilesh. "Read the paper on the left side which the ISI has sent me last week."

Nikhilesh opened the file and casually glanced through the other papers in the file and asked, "What about the other papers?"

"They are other messages and the key to the code," replied Raman Kumar. "You read only the decoded message that I have pointed out to you."

Nikhilesh took about five minutes to read the message. "Fantastic!" he exclaimed, sounding quite impressed with what he had read.

Yogesh cursed Nikhilesh for not reading out the message aloud. He prayed to God to let him know the truth behind Operation Red Rose.

"So, in nutshell, this is Operation Red Rose for you," Raman Kumar began to speak as he took the file back and put it in his brief case. God seemed to have answered Yogesh's prayer. "It promises me the prime ministership of India if I assist the ISI in their plot to assassinate Prabhat Rai. It promises ISI the merger of Kashmir with Pakistan, it promises the comrades a friendly government in New Delhi and rights over river waters in Tibet and, I believe, the Americans will get Al Qaeda in the bargain. It is a dangerous operation for us but I have decided to go ahead with it. So far things have gone as per plan. In fact it all appears to have gone too smoothly for those brilliant men in the ISI. They must be patting each other on their backs for getting a man like me from the Chinese to do their bidding. But they are sadly mistaken. They think that I am so ambitious that I won't mind handing over Kashmir to them in return for the prime ministership of India. They hope to attack Kashmir and reach Srinagar virtually unopposed with help from me and then use international pressure to formally merge Kashmir with Pakistan. You think, I will allow them to get away with their game plan? Forget it."

"So what is your game plan now?" Nikhilesh was curious to know the details.

"Presently my game plan is that the events will be allowed to take their destined course as of now," Raman Kumar continued. "Prabhat Rai will go to offer prayers and take a holy dip at Har Ki Pauri at about 0300 hours tonight. The ISI has already put one sniper on the job. He will take a snipe shot at Prabhat Rai and that would be the end of him and his prime ministership. The entire blame for taking Prabhat Rai to Har Ki Pauri without adequate security will be put on Swami Suryananda, Joseph and Dhillon. As for Balwant and Sukhraj Malik, well, they are condemned men already. We have enough witnesses in the army who will swear that Balwant and Malik were guilty of plotting mine and Prabhat Rai's assassination. People will believe easily as they would think that Malik could not tolerate his narrow defeat at the hands of Prabhat Rai three years earlier for the leadership of the party."

"Uncle, how did you manage to get the details of Prabhat Rai's yagna at Haridwar?" asked Nikhilesh.

"Nikhilesh!" Raman Kumar smiled. "On the second or so of the last month I went to see Prabhat Rai to invite him to be the chief guest at the test-fire of Rudra. The test was slated for the eleventh of May by the army. Prabhat Rai expressed his inability to accept my request as he had other commitment on the same day. Swami Suryananda was also with Rai when I went to see him. I always believed the Swami to be a charlatan. But he amazed me by predicting some kind of role for me in shaping Prabhat Rai's destiny. But what he failed to foresee was his own role in shaping my destiny. He told me in confidence that Prabhat Rai was committed to performing the last of a series of eleven yagnas at Haridwar on the no-moon night, that fell on the eleventh of this month, that is tonight. Prabhat Rai has gone to Tehri and Haridwar for the twin purposes of pleasing the environmentalists and performing his yagna. When I received this message from the ISI, I knew that this was the opportunity when I could put the ISI on the trail of Prabhat Rai and get the deed accomplished. I prepared a message and gave it to you for delivering it to their man in the lobby of the World Trade Towers."

"That I had delivered as directed by you," interjected Nikhilesh. "But why did you ask me to hand over the second message to some patriotic looking young man?"

"That was a ploy to implicate Balwant Naik and Sukhraj Malik. The idea came to me after that conversation I had with the Swami at Prabhat Rai's residence. The ploy worked. I made that message showing a plan to assassinate me, instead of the Prime Minister. This message that I wrote was deliberately put by me in a simple code which even an amateur could have deciphered. I wanted the message to reach army headquarters in a manner that won't arouse suspicions. I wanted the army chaps to decipher the message quickly so that I could use the army top brass in my game plan against Sukhraj Malik. You spotted the right man to hand over the cover."

"Uncle, I did that with the help of my girlfriend. But I was quite amazed to find that by a sheer coincidence, this young man even exchanged the same password with me as the ISI man had done earlier. When I told him that the two red roses that he was holding were beautiful, he replied that to him black was more beautiful or some words to that effect."

Yogesh heard Nikhilesh in total disbelief. Everything became clear to him. He had come into the possession of the message just by chance. 'Perhaps it was God's will, to create a way to save the life of the Prime Minister and catch the culprits before they succeed in their nefarious designs', he thought.

"Providence my son, providence!" said Raman Kumar. "Luck is on our side. But to make sure that the young man indeed delivered the message to the army, I used our friend Badri Prasad of Delhi Police. Badri Prasad too has been on the payroll of the comrades since the time he was on deputation to the Intelligence Bureau from Delhi Police.

"How did you handle the situation thereafter?" asked Nikhilesh.

"Easy! Army chaps soon deciphered the message as expected. I asked you to knock off Yogesh in a hit and run manner as I did not need him any more. You did hit him but could only injure his wife and the bugger survived. I, however, did not let your effort go in vain. I decided to use the accident to our advantage. When the news of the accident reached us in army headquarters, I arranged police security for Yogesh and his wife in the nursing home on the one hand and led the army fellows to believe that the accident was an attempt on Yogesh's life by the man behind the message. Yogesh Naqvi finally came to see me here yesterday. This is where I played a masterstroke. I gave him an album of photographs and asked him to identify the man who gave him the message. He quickly spotted you, as expected. This was a photo that had both you and Balwant in the picture. I identified you as Balwant, the son-in-law of Sukhraj Malik. I shared the news with the two Generals and that Colonel and led them to believe that Yogesh had pointed out at Balwant and not you. Courtesy Yogesh Naqvi, we have enough witnesses in the army against Balwant now."

"Yogesh Naqvi, some patriot!" Nikhilesh chuckled. "But what do you plan to do with him now?"

"Poor man!" commented Raman Kumar. "Yogesh is the only person who knows the truth behind your identification as Balwant. He is a real threat now. So he must go. This deed will be performed by our accomplice Badri Prasad. He will ensure that Yogesh goes to his grave before midnight tonight. Tomorrow I'll see to it that the blame of his death is laid at the door of Balwant for the obvious reasons. The events, no doubt, will move at a very fast pace tomorrow. The Prime Minister would be dead. The Home Minister would be discredited. Pakistan will invade Kashmir and there will be chaos all around. The whole country will look up to some powerful person to hold the reigns of the government. Who else will be more powerful than the Defence Minister of the country? In any case the five major world powers will also use their clout in projecting me as the right candidate for the top job in India. This will be ensured by the comrades in Beijing."

Yogesh was stunned to hear the ploy created by Raman Kumar to implicate Balwant by using him as a tool. He could make out that while General Surinder Pal and his colleagues were correctly shown Balwant's photo, he was made to look at Nikhilesh as Balwant by Raman Kumar.

"So there you are!" said Raman Kumar with an air of finality. "Tomorrow I will become the most powerful man in the country. But I will not accept merely the prime ministership of India. I will persuade the President, the Cabinet and the three service chiefs to declare martial law and make me the Chief Martial Law Administrator. The three service chiefs already hold me in awe and in a moment of national crisis, they are bound to rally behind me. The Pakistanis will help me in making my task easier through their misadventure in Kashmir. From their point of view that is what Operation Red Rose is all about. But they are in for a rude shock. I am going to ditch them. They are not going to find Raman Kumar waiting for them with open arms. They will be repulsed by our armed forces with a resolve never seen before. In a way, Pakistanis will actually help me in strengthening my position as the undisputed dictator of this country. No doubt, the ISI will try to expose me as being their man but who is going to believe them? We will also use the political turmoil and the martial law to physically eliminate Sukhraj Malik, Balwant, the Swami and whosoever dares to oppose me. As for our comrades in Beijing, I think I can handle them by offering them what they want in Tibet. In any case if they can tame Brahmaputra, it might eliminate the scourge of recurrent floods in Assam once and for all. I am sure that I can convince them to ditch Pakistan and work with India to raise a formidable joint front as a counter to the Americans in the world affairs."

Yogesh could not stand it any more. His head began to whir with the mind-blowing information with which it had been bombarded. He squatted on the floor in the toilet. He closed his eyes and held his head in his hands. His senses had become numb and he felt as if his thinking faculty had deserted him.

Yogesh did not know much about Raman Kumar's past. In his college days, Raman Kumar used to be a committed Maoist. He had been a great admirer of the Chinese brand of communism. It was not a surprise when the Chinese Agency for Overseas Intelligence (CAOI), the agency whose name starts with a capital C, recognised the Maoist in him and put him on their payroll. CAOI began to support Raman Kumar both financially and politically. He managed to visit China under a cultural exchange programme when he was in college. It was during that visit that he was able to develop a deep bond of friendship with his benefactors. It was at their advice that he joined the ruling party, rather than one of the communist parties. They convinced him that it was only by siding with a mainline bourgeois party that he could succeed in capturing power and put a Chinese type system of government in place in India.

For over fifteen years Raman Kumar had been working relentlessly to achieve that end. So much so that he did not even marry. He, however, befriended some women who were drawn to him for his intellect. He joined the ruling party and also started the literacy movement in India in a big way. With his hard work in the field of adult literacy, which was to be his road to success, and some assistance from the leftist but influential journalists, he was able to influence Prabhat Rai hard enough to be inducted into the Union Cabinet as Minister in charge of the HRD.

His induction into the ministry, however, created a problem. All of a sudden he was a VIP, a very important man in the Indian government. The problem did not relate to his official work. It related to his maintaining contact with the CAOI and to get him women for the physical gratification. He did not want any scandals. So he decided to terminate all his affairs and took recourse to paid sex. He needed someone whom he could trust to help him hire women and maintain contact with the Chinese. Nikhilesh was the only one who he fitted the bill. Raman Kumar made him the offer to join him as his Political Advisor. He was happy that his nephew accepted his offer.

Raman Kumar was a role model for Nikhilesh. Like him, Nikhilesh never married and like him, he had his share of girlfriends. His latest girlfriend was Neena whom he also used occasionally as a courier to exchange messages and documents with the CAOI and the ISI. Neena loved to live her life in the fast lane. She did not bother to find out what information she was passing from Nikhilesh to the foreign agents. She liked Nikhilesh and he looked after her well. When Nikhilesh told Neena about locating a patriotic looking young man, she suggested the name of Yogesh. She had a score to settle with him.

Neena and Yogesh had been classmates in Kirori Mal College. Neena was known to be a man-eater. At one time she got enamoured of Yogesh but he spurned her advances. Neena never forgave him for that. When Nikhilesh told her his requirement, Neena immediately decided to take her revenge upon Yogesh. She was certain that being the son of an army officer who died in harness, Yogesh could easily be lured into handing over the coded message to the army headquarters.

"My only reservation is that this may be the end of democracy in India," commented Nikhilesh, trying to strike an intelligent conversation with his uncle.

"You think this country deserves democracy?" chided Raman Kumar. "Democracy is a luxury that only the rich can afford. In India our corrupt politicians use democracy only to perpetuate their hegemony over the political system of the country. Democracy has no meaning for the hungry millions. To them, a loaf of bread holds more value than the right to vote. Democracy has, in fact, slowed down the progress of our country and this trend must be reversed. Once I become the ruler of this country, I will make people realise that they have been fooled all along by the petty politicians. I will make India a superpower, just like China, within ten years."

"Alright uncle," said Nikhilesh after a long silence. "I will sink or swim with you. Tell me my instructions now."

"Just be with me for now," replied Raman Kumar. "In the evening we will try to steal some rest. We got a long night ahead."

Nikhilesh nodded in agreement and then spoke, "Uncle, can I have a cup of tea?"

"Why not?" said Raman Kumar as he pressed the buzzer of his phone.

"Yes sir!" came Mehta's voice.

"Mehta, please arrange to send two cups of tea for us," said Raman Kumar.

"Two or three?" asked Mehta.

"Why three?" queried Raman Kumar. "We are only two of us here, Nikhilesh and me."

"Sir, what about your guest, Mr. Yogesh Naqvi?"

"He is not here. Why? Did he come to see me?"

"Yes sir, he came barely ten minutes before you came. I asked him to wait for you in your chamber. It is surprising that he is not there."

"It is alright," said Raman Kumar, trying hard to control his anxiety. "Please send the tea."

Nikhilesh looked at the changed expression on the face of his uncle. "Anything wrong?' he asked.

Just then Mehta entered the room from the side door. He went to the ante room, looked around and said, "It is indeed strange, sir! He entered the ante room and, to the best of my knowledge, he didn't leave till the time you came. Or may be he left from the other door without informing me. But why should he go like that, without meeting you?"

"Never mind," said Raman Kumar. "He will come again if he is interested in seeing me."

Mehta looked around once again and went back to his cabin, still surprised at the strange behaviour of Yogesh Naqvi. Nikhilesh could not make out anything from the conversation.

"Who came here and when?" he asked.

Raman Kumar gave some quick thinking to the unexpected crisis and said, "Yogesh Naqvi came to see me about ten minutes before we came. That fool Mehta asked him to wait in this chamber. I did not expect that boy here today at all. I don't know why he came. He might have left the room before we entered it. But it is equally likely that he is still here, hiding somewhere and may have overheard our conversation. If that be the case, we are in big trouble."

Nikhilesh looked at his uncle in horror. "Then what should we do?"

"You have your revolver with you?"

"Yes, it is in my bag," he replied.

"Take it out and be ready to shoot," said Raman Kumar coolly. "Now listen to me carefully. If Yogesh is still in this room, he came to my chamber to ...... to kill me. Since he is a Muslim, we'll brand him a terrorist, in fact a jihadi who used the coded message to come near me and kill me. But before he could shoot, with that revolver, you grappled with him and managed to snatch it from his hand. Then .... then you shot him dead in self defence. Now get up and see if that blighter is hiding somewhere behind the sofa or in the toilet. Remember, no mistakes. Don't hesitate to shoot me in my arm or shoulder, if the need arises. This might be the only way to silence Yogesh Naqvi, by making him a terrorist, a spy or a criminal. He shot at me and was in turn shot by you."

Just when Raman Kumar was trying to tackle the unexpected jolt to 'Operation Red Rose,' Lt Gen Raheel Ginai was preparing his team for the big day which was only hours away.

"Friends," began the ISI chief, "though we must not forget to be grateful to the Americans for swinging the world opinion on Kashmir in our favour, yet, we must remember that as always, it is our trusted friends in China who have given us the real hope that Kashmir will be a part of Pakistan now. UN Security Council resolution, fully backed by all its members, and the international pressure, might not have succeeded in forcing the Indians to accept the final resolution to the Kashmir problem but with a pro-China government in place in New Delhi tomorrow, we have every reason to believe that they will accept the same. In fact it was only when Mr. Li Yongding, our trusted friend from the CAOI, called on me some time ago and offered the services of Raman Kumar, their mole in the Indian government, that I became certain of our success. I must also compliment you for coming with a brilliant plan to make Operation Red Rose our road to success. Though I feel sorry for Prabhat Rai for the fate that awaits him, yet, I have no remorse because all means are justified so long as we achieve our ends."

"When will the invasion into Kashmir take place?' asked S-5.

"I have already taken the COAS into confidence. Our forces are ready to launch an all out offensive at six hours notice," replied the chief. "It all depends on how things go in Haridwar. If our man succeeds in his mission, which I am sure he will, we will force the President to give orders to the army to invade Kashmir tomorrow itself. In fact it is our invasion which will pave the way for Raman Kumar to seize power there."

"I cannot wait to see their democracy destroyed forever," interjected S-2. "For far too long the Indians have been berating us for the absence of democracy in Pakistan. Tomorrow they will be in much deeper political mess than what we have ever been in Pakistan."

"Is there any chance that some of their states might also break away?" asked S-1.

"That will be our next move," assured the chief. "But let us not get too greedy at this juncture. Let us first get Kashmir from them. We will concentrate on the break up of the Big Brother later."

In Beijing, Li Yongding, the Director of the Chinese Agency for Overseas Intelligence, the agency whose name starts with a capital C, was chairing a meeting of his top functionaries. He reminded them of the philosophy of the CAOI which was contained in the ancient Chinese treatise on the art of war, Sun Wu. It read:

Skilful military leaders conquer the enemy without fighting any battle. They capture cities without attacking them. They overcome nations without protracted warfare. They strive for supremacy without stationing their troops abroad, yet, they win complete victory over their enemies.

"Gentlemen," Li Yongding was giving final instructions to his officers, "we are all set to move a step closer to our objective of making China number one superpower of the world. With India as a vassal state of China, we will easily control half the population of the world with all the attendant benefits. But caution has been the hallmark of all our operations the world over so far and the same it will be even now. Whatever be the situation in New Delhi tomorrow we must keep a low profile for some time. We will take command of the situation when the time is right. At this moment we should hope for the best but be prepared for the worst. As you know, we had managed to send the CCS papers to the RAW via our man in Washington. People in New Delhi have been made to believe that they have a CIA mole in their government. Nobody knows that Raman Kumar is our man. Should Operation Red Rose fail, CIA will get all the blame. But if it succeeds, we will move in for the kill."

05.05 P.M.

Yogesh knew that he would literally have to run for his life. He heard Nikhilesh's footsteps approaching the toilet. As soon as Nikhilesh turned the door knob, Yogesh pulled the door inside and hit his hand that held the revolver with the cipher book. The sudden blow unsettled Nikhilesh. Yogesh pulled him inside the toilet and pushed him hard into a corner. Nikhilesh fell on the floor. That gave Yogesh the crucial few seconds in which he could make his bid to escape. He jumped out of the toilet and ran to the main door of the room without looking back. He pulled the door and rushed out of the room, barely escaping the shot of Nikhilesh that hit the door.

A nervous Yogesh ran towards the lift. While running, he heard two more shots being fired inside the Defence Minister's room. When he reached the lift, the door of the lift had started to close and he just managed to squeeze in.

But he had enough time to get a glimpse of Nikhilesh rushing out of the room with revolver in his hand and shouting, "Catch him. He is a terrorist." Yogesh looked at the other men in the lift. Besides the operator, there were only two other officers there. They were engaged in some deep conversation. To his relief, neither they nor the lift operator heard Nikhilesh. The lift began to move. Yogesh looked at the floor indicator in horror as he found the lift moving up, rather than down.

"Where will you go sir!" asked the lift operator.

Yogesh was about to say 'ground floor' but it struck him that he might have to face Nikhilesh holding a loaded revolver in his hand there. He was bound to shoot him dead to silence him forever.

"Eighth floor," said Yogesh, hoping that Colonel Bali might have returned to his room by then. He knew that he must save his life first before he stood any chance of exposing Raman Kumar and Operation Red Rose.

The lift came to a stop on the eighth floor. Yogesh got out and ran to room number 818. He pushed the door open. There was no one inside. He took a chair and sat. He looked around and his eyes fell on the telephone. He grabbed the phone and dialled his father-in-law's number. But he could not get the call through. He soon realized that this was an Army telephone that did not have direct connection with civil telephones. He gave up and decided to wait for Colonel Bali. He thought of Sunita, of Sonyog and of Natasha. He cursed himself for not following the advice of Natasha. He and Sunita should not have gone to the extent of handing over the message to Colonel Bali, he thought. Their enthusiasm had landed him in deep trouble where his own life was in danger. He was not sure how he would be able to leave Sena Bhavan with his life and limb intact.

Yogesh knew that Colonel Bali was his last and only hope. If he could meet him early and tell him of the plot to assassinate the Prime Minister of India, he would certainly help him. The thought of the assassination plot filled his mind with revulsion. He felt a sense of outrage at the way Raman Kumar had hatched the plot. Yogesh felt horrified at the planning that had gone into the plotting of Operation Red Rose. It was obvious that if the ISI succeeded in assassinating Prime Minister Prabhat Rai at Haridwar, the blame will fall on Balwant. Home Minister Sukhraj Malik will be forced to resign and Raman Kumar would have excellent chance of becoming the Prime Minister of India. A chill went down his spine at the very thought of seeing a Chinese spy, an ISI collaborator and a traitor to the nation at the helm of her affairs. He shuddered at the prospect of seeing the country in a deep political turmoil and in war with Pakistan. He knew that he was the only person at the moment who could bring back the country from the edge of the precipice where it stood. The thought made him feel less scared. His life had a purpose. He must live up to it. He must not allow Raman Kumar, Nikhilesh and their masters in China and the ISI to succeed in their murderous designs.

He got up from his chair and looked through the window. Soon the sound of the police sirens started coming from all directions. Just then the door opened behind him and Yogesh saw Colonel Bali enter the room.

"Yogesh!" asked a surprised Colonel Bali. "When did you come?"

"Ages ago," replied Yogesh as he hurried towards the Colonel.

"Colonel, I am in deep trouble and I need your help. In fact the country needs your help."

"What are you talking Yogesh?" asked Colonel Bali.

The conversation was interrupted by an announcement over the Public Address System for which the speakers had been permanently installed in the corridors at each floor, mainly to warn people of some emergency like fire.

"Your attention please! Here is an important announcement. It is brought to the notice of everybody present in the Sena

Bhavan that there has been an attempt on the life of the Honourable Defence Minister. A young man in civilian clothes came to meet the Honourable Minister. He fired two shots at him and injured him seriously. After shooting the Honourable Minister, he ran towards the upper floors of the Sena Bhavan. All are requested to help the police in capturing the man either dead or alive. His name is Yogesh Naqvi and he is having a gate pass with him issued in his own name. Please hear the announcement again."

The man over the P.A. system began to repeat the announcement. Colonel Bali looked at Yogesh with shocking disbelief. "What is this Yogesh?" asked Colonel Bali.

"Colonel, please listen to me carefully," pleaded Yogesh. "I did not shoot Raman Kumar. He has been shot by his nephew Nikhilesh with his consent. This is a trap to kill me as I have just found out the details of Operation Red Rose and also the fact that it is Raman Kumar and Nikhilesh and not Sukhraj Malik and Balwant who have planned Operation Red Rose which involves the plot to assassinate the Prime Minister Prabhat Rai."

"I can't believe it!" said a bewildered Colonel Bali.

"Colonel," said Yogesh, "You please try to understand. This man Raman Kumar and his nephew Nikhilesh have hatched the assassination plot against the Prime Minister. If we do not act fast, they will first kill me as I know the truth and then kill the Prime Minister early tomorrow morning at Haridwar. If you don't believe me I would request you to kindly go to the room of the Defence Minister. There is a yellow coloured file that contains the details of the plot and irrefutable evidence against him. The file can be found in the brown briefcase of the Defence Minister. It might still be lying on his table. I will give you the rest of the details later. You please believe me and bring that file. It will not only save me, it will also help save the life of the Prime Minister."

Colonel Bali gave a long, probing look to Yogesh and then got up saying, "Okay Yogesh. Let me see if I can get the file. Meanwhile, please stay here only. I am going to bolt the door from outside."

Raman Kumar lay in his room, bleeding profusely. He was shot in the right shoulder and the right arm. Mehta and other staff of his office had already removed his shirt and were trying to control the bleeding by placing cotton on the wound.

The ambulance did not take long to arrive. Two attendants ran to the chamber of the Defence Minister with a stretcher. They put the minister on the stretcher and ran back to the ambulance carrying the injured minister with them.

"Nikhilesh," shouted Raman Kumar as he was being taken inside the ambulance. "Please call my nephew. Don't move. I must talk to Nikhilesh before we move."

Nikhilesh was busy coordinating the police cordon around the Sena Bhavan. Police personnel had already been posted at the stairs, the two main gates and near the lifts on the ground floor.

Nikhilesh ran to his uncle as soon as he got the message that his uncle wanted to see him.

"Yes uncle? Are you alright?"

"I am going to be alright," Raman Kumar replied though his shoulder had started giving him lot of pain. I have some confidential papers in my briefcase that is lying on my office table. Please get hold of those papers. Those papers are very important."

Nikhilesh looked into the eyes of Raman Kumar and said, "Don't worry uncle. I know their importance. I will collect them right away."

"Also, get in touch with Badri Prasad. You will need his assistance."

"Right uncle! I'll do that. Please take care of yourself."

The ambulance sped to the Ram Manohar Lohia Hospital.

Nikhilesh rushed back inside. He took lift to the first floor and ran to the chamber of the Defence Minister. He pushed the door with force and barged in. He got a shock when he saw an army colonel reading from the file.

"Who are you?" shouted Nikhilesh.

Colonel Bali looked at Nikhilesh and said with a straight face, "I am Colonel Bali from the Army Intelligence."

"What are you doing with RM's papers?" asked Nikhilesh as he grabbed the file from Colonel Bali but not before the colonel had read what he had come to read.

"I gave him an important document which contained a coded message. I was looking for it," replied Colonel Bali.

"Could you find it?"

"No. I don't know where he has kept it. Perhaps the man who shot the minister came for that document. I thought we might as well keep it safely with us in our branch."

Nikhilesh looked at Colonel Bali with suspicion. But the colonel kept his nerve. He did not allow any expression on his face.

"Don't worry Colonel," said Nikhilesh. "All your documents are safe with the minister. Please do not waste your time and energy here. Go and get that terrorist now."

Nikhilesh left the room with the file and the briefcase.

Colonel Bali went straight to the room of his boss Lieutenant General Sehgal. He told him the truth behind the alleged attempt on the life of the Defence Minister and the plot to assassinate Prime Minister Prabhat Rai.

The General shrugged his shoulders. "Listen Bali," he said with firmness. "I don't want to get into all this and if you take my advice, nor should you. We are not supposed to know of any plot to assassinate the Prime Minister because from what you say it is clear that one of them is a liar. It is either the minister or that young man of yours. By training and by judgement, I would rather go along with what the minister says than believing what an outsider has to say."

"But what happens if the Defence Minister turns out to be the liar?" asked Colonel Bali.

"That will not affect you and me," replied the General. "But if that young man is indeed a terrorist, then nobody will spare us. So better go along with what the minister says and save your skin rather than run the risk of having a noose around your neck by siding with that young man. As for the Prime Minister, you and I do not know anything. That is the truth and nothing but the truth. But I hope you are not hiding Yogesh Naqvi anywhere?"

"No sir," Colonel Bali lied. "I told him to be on his own and not count on my help."

"Well done!" said the General. "Now please go and stay in your room."

Colonel Bali left, feeling depressed. Despite knowing the truth from the file of the Defence Minister, he could not convince his own boss. He knew that General Sehgal was certain that Yogesh was hiding in his room but as far as he was concerned, he had washed his hands off him. Yogesh was Colonel Bali's responsibility and if something went wrong, no one would come forward to help him.

PA System was blaring another announcement when Colonel Bali walked down the corridor to his room on the eighth floor.

"Your attention please! All civilians, officers, JCOs and Other Ranks, who are present in Sena Bhavan at the moment, are directed to go to their respective seats. No unauthorized official should be seen moving around in the corridors till further announcement is made. The terrorist who tried to kill the Honourable Defence Minister is still holed inside the building. Your cooperation is solicited for the capture of the terrorist."

Colonel Bali entered his room and bolted it from inside. "Yogesh?" he called.

"Yes Colonel?" answered Yogesh as he turned away from the window. "Could you get that file?"

"Sorry buddy. I could not bring the file. I was able to get it and glance through it too. It confirmed what you stated. But before I could do away with it, Nikhilesh charged in, looking for the file. He snatched the file from my hand. I could not fight him, partly, because I was too shocked to think clearly and partly, because I knew that he would be armed."

"With that goes, perhaps, our only hope of convincing the people that Raman Kumar is a mad man, a traitor and a murderer," said Yogesh.

"You are right," said Colonel Bali. "No one is going to believe you and me without incontrovertible evidence against him. After all, he is the Defence Minister of the country. I went to see the DGMI before coming here. He refused to believe what I told him. If my own boss is not convinced with what I told him, it is naive to believe that others would believe us. But tell me all that you know about Operation Red Rose and what exactly happened in the minister's room?"

Yogesh told Colonel Bali all that he knew. He also told him that actually he came to see him to show the text of the message that his wife had been able to decipher. Yogesh proceeded to tell Colonel Bali that he had to go to see the minister because he was not in his seat. He told him all about his hiding in the toilet and overhearing the detailed conversation in which Raman Kumar and Nikhilesh had been engaged. He informed him of their plans for the future. He showed him the cipher book as well as the decoded message.

"The deciphering is absolutely correct," said Colonel Bali. "It is amazing how an amateur is able to break the code so easily."

"Not so easy Colonel. My wife spent three days on it and I too gave it about thirty minutes. I know that our enthusiasm has landed me in deep trouble but there is no going back now. I implore you to help me in exposing Raman Kumar, not for my sake but for the sake of this country."

Colonel Bali was aghast at the prospect of seeing the country in a bloody mess and losing Kashmir to Pakistan. Thousands of lives laid down in the cause of the unity and integrity of the country would go in vain.

"The life of Prime Minister must be saved at all costs," said Colonel Bali finally. "But before we can do that, we will have to save your life first. The odds are heavily staked against us. But my friend, I will do all that I can, to see you safely out of Sena Bhavan."

"So what do we do?" asked Yogesh. "I don't think I can escape being detected by hiding in this room for too long."

Just then another announcement came over the P.A.system.

"Colonel S.K. Bali and Mr. Gyan Mehta are requested to come to the reception on the ground floor immediately." The announcement was repeated twice.

"Good luck Colonel," said Yogesh. "It might enable you to find a way to get me out of this place."

"That is possible," said Colonel Bali. "I don't know why they have called me. But you stay here till I come back. I will lock the door from outside so that no one else can open it."

"Right Colonel," Yogesh sighed. "I hope and pray that you will succeed in finding a way out for me."

"I hope so too," said Colonel Bali, handing him a jug of water. "Take this. It might take some time before I return. You might need it. I am sorry I am not able to look after you better than this."

"Never mind," said Yogesh with a smirk on his face.

Colonel Bali walked out, leaving his friend to spend his time all by himself. Yogesh walked up and down the room for a while and then slumped in the chair.

Colonel Bali went to the ground floor where General Surinder Pal, the army chief, and M.S. Bedi, the Police Commissioner of Delhi, were conducting the proceedings.

"Yes sir," Colonel Bali addressed the COAS when he approached him. "What are my instructions?"

"Bali, since you recognize Yogesh Naqvi well, you have to stand at one of the two gates of Sena Bhavan and let people move out of the building after checking their I-cards," said the General. "Mr. Gyan Mehta will stand at the other gate. Please make sure that we don't lose him at any cost."

"Why two gates?" queried Nikhilesh. "Why not let people march out of only one gate?" He did not want the job of identification of Yogesh to be entrusted to Colonel Bali.

"Nikhileshji, we have got more than five hundred persons inside the building," replied the army chief. "If we use only one gate we will be stuck here for more than two hours."

General Sehgal, who was standing close by, came forward with a suggestion. "Nikhileshji, we'll do one thing. Since both Mr. Mehta and I recognise Yogesh Naqvi, let Mr. Mehta stand at one of the two gates and I will stand at the other. You may keep watch on the two gates as second line of monitoring. I am sure between the three of us we will definitely be able to capture the rascal."

"That sounds fine," said a relieved Nikhilesh. "Let Mehta be at gate number one and you be at gate number two. I will monitor from behind."

"Fine," said General Surinder Pal. "Let us get on with it now. Please make an announcement on the PA System that people can leave the building, one by one, after showing their I cards at the gate."

Nikhilesh and Mehta proceeded to occupy position at gate number one and General Sehgal began walking towards gate number two.

"Bali, I am positioned at gate number two," General Sehgal told his officer with a wink.

Colonel Bali could not immediately grasp the meaning behind the wink. He went back to his room, trying to draw a plan to get Yogesh out of the building. He knew that if Yogesh had to spend the night inside the Sena Bhavan, he would never come out of it alive. Raman Kumar would become the Prime Minister of India the next day and the truth behind Operation Red Rose would never be known.

Colonel Bali could think of only one way in which Yogesh could be smuggled out. The wink in the eye of his boss gave him an idea.

Yogesh looked pale and weary when Colonel Bali returned to the room. He had very nearly given up all hope of ever getting out of the Sena Bhavan alive. He felt sorry for Sunita and his mother whom he loved so much but reconciled to what he thought was going to be the most likely way in which his life would end.

Colonel Bali, however, had something else on his mind. He decided to put into action a plan that had a fair chance of succeeding.

"Yogesh, a thorough check is being made at the two main gates of the building of each person leaving Sena Bhavan. The only way to escape and that too, before Raman Kumar and Nikhilesh are able to seize power, is to simply walk through the tight security."

"But how is that possible? That rascal Nikhilesh will cut the life out of me even before I take a step out of the gate."

"That is a chance we have to take. There simply is no other option. Take off your clothes!"

"Take off my clothes?" asked Yogesh. He saw Colonel Bali remove his belt and start unbuttoning his shirt.

"Yes," replied the colonel. "We are going to exchange our clothes."

Yogesh saw the point. He too started taking off his clothes.

Within five minutes Yogesh was wearing Colonel Bali's uniform and Colonel Bali was wearing Yogesh's civilian clothes. There was not much difference in their height. But Colonel Bali was slightly heavier of the two. As such, his uniform came a bit loose on Yogesh. He managed to keep it tight with the help of the belt.

"You think I can make it?" asked Yogesh, seeking assurance to quell his anxiety.

"If I know my boss well, yes," replied Colonel Bali.

"But what about the Identity Card? I don't have any with me."

"Don't worry about that. Just hang your driving licence around your neck. Take this chain." Colonel Bali removed the chain from his Identity Card and gave it to Yogesh. "I will keep my card in my pocket."

Yogesh took out his driving license from his purse and put the chain through its eyelet. He then hung it around his neck as advised by Colonel Bali.

"That looks fine," assured Colonel Bali. "You will pull it off. I am sure of that."

"Thanks for the encouragement." Yogesh did not sound too sure of himself. "But what about you? When will you come out?"

"Only after Nikhilesh has left the scene," replied the colonel. "I will tell the security personnel that I was on leave and had come to the office to attend to some urgent work. But you don't worry about me. I can take care of myself. I will get in touch with you as soon as I am able to leave Sena Bhavan. But you better go now. If they find you here, you are a dead man. And if they find out that you are with me, I am a dead man too! Once you are free, you can approach the Home Minister, the President or whomsoever you like, to thwart all their bloody plans. But remember, you must leave the building through gate number two only."

At gate number two, General Sehgal personally examined the identity card of each person coming out of the building. Nikhilesh did likewise at gate number one. People were impatient to leave the building and get back home. They marched through either of the two gates in single file and left as soon as they were permitted to leave by the inspecting teams at the two gates. Most of the people marched silently. They were sure of establishing their bona fides and leaving the building without any hitch.

The only person who was nervous was Yogesh in the army uniform. He had pulled the cap closer to his eyes and wore Colonel Bali's glasses. He reached gate number two and felt as if he would collapse on the floor before showing his driving license to General Sehgal. He recalled the assurance given by Colonel Bali that there was every chance of General Sehgal coming to his rescue at the crucial moment.

Yogesh took a deep breath and steadied himself. His turn came and he showed the driving license to General Sehgal.

"Move on Colonel," said General Sehgal. "Next please!"

Yogesh put his head down and marched out of the gate. He looked around for Nikhilesh and saw him standing some distance away. Nikhilesh did not even give a second look to the 'Colonel' coming out of gate number two. Yogesh heaved a sigh of relief and briskly walked to the road. Once on the road, he hailed a taxi and jumped into it. He thanked his stars for having made it with help from two well meaning soldiers.

"Where will you go, sir?" asked the driver.

"Go straight first," replied Yogesh. "I'll tell you later where to go."

The taxi driver gave him an indifferent look but did as told. However, he kept looking at the army Colonel through the rear view mirror every now and then.

"Take me to Ashoka Road via India Gate," Yogesh instructed the driver after deliberating on the various options available to him. His father-in-law lived in one of the bungalows on the Ashoka Road. The driver took turn towards Raj Path and raced towards India Gate at a steady speed. From India Gate, he took left turn and entered Ashoka Road.

When the taxi approached the bungalow of Yogesh's father-in-law, he could see a posse of policemen posted outside the house. Yogesh let the taxi continue its drive towards Patel Chowk.

He looked at his watch. It was 6.25 P.M. He knew that Sunita might have been discharged from the hospital by then and there was little possibility of her being in the hospital. He decided to go home to RK Puram. He directed the driver to take him to Africa Avenue in South Delhi.

The driver did as told.

Yogesh noticed a few barricades being put up by the Delhi Police on the road. But seeing an army officer in the taxi, the police waived it to move on without checking.

While driving down the Africa Avenue, Yogesh could have a clear view of his house in Sector III of R.K.Puram. He saw a group of policemen waiting for him at his mother's house as well. He, then, decided to go to Natasha's house in Vasant Kunj, hoping and praying that the police might not have suspected him to be there. "Please proceed to Vasant Kunj," he told the taxi driver.

"Where exactly you want to go sir?" asked the driver, unable to control his growing irritation.

"Why are you bothered?" asked Yogesh in reply. "You will get your fare as per the meter." The driver did not comment. He put his car on the way to Vasant Kunj.

06.40 P.M.

Virtually everybody had left the Sena Bhavan. Nikhilesh was feeling desperate at not having been able to corner the man who knew too much. He began to feel certain that Yogesh had somehow managed to give him slip with the help of Colonel Bali.

"Mehta!" called Nikhilesh. "You know which is that Colonel's room? Colonel Bali, I think is his name."

"Yes I know," said Mehta.

"Take me to his room. I want to satisfy myself before we give up."

They reached room number 818 in a matter of minutes. Nikhilesh turned the knob on the door. He found the knob loose, indicating that the room was unlocked. He took out his revolver and pushed the door open. To his shock, he found Colonel Bali sitting in his chair, wearing civilian clothes. It didn't take Nikhilesh long to realize that the clothes belonged to Yogesh. Colonel Bali stood up and confronted Nikhilesh bravely. The look of defiance in his eyes confirmed to Nikhilesh how Yogesh was able to escape from the Sena Bhavan.

"Here is Yogesh," shouted Nikhilesh and pumped three bullets into a helpless Colonel Bali. The colonel slumped in the chair and was dead within no time.

"Why did you shoot him?" asked Mehta.

"In self-defence," replied Nikhilesh. "He is armed you know!"

Mehta moved forward and recognized Colonel Bali. "He is not Yogesh," he said. "This man is Colonel Bali."

"Don't tell me. I recognize Yogesh from his clothes."

"Clothes may be of Yogesh, but he sure is Colonel Bali. I know him well."

"If what you say is right then how did he come to be in Yogesh's clothes?"

"That I don't know. But I think you have killed the wrong man."

"Even if he is Colonel Bali, I have killed the right man."

"How can you say that?"

"Mehta, try to understand. This colonel collaborated with that terrorist and helped him escape wearing his own uniform. It is just as well that he is dead. If you have any loyalty towards the Defence Minister, then keep mum on it." He moved forward and took out the room key from the pocket of Colonel Bali's trousers. "We will handle this case tomorrow," said Nikhilesh. He and Mehta left the room after locking it.

"Your arrangements Commissioner, are deplorable and the army fellows are no better," Nikhilesh shouted as soon as he reached the ground floor. "I am sure that the terrorist has simply walked through one of the gates. Commissioner, please get his photo flashed on the TV and get the announcement made for a suitable reward for his capture. We must have that man within the next hour!"

"We have already collected his photograph and are going to reveal his identity to the press shortly."

"Not shortly. Please do it now!"

The Police Commissioner did not like taking instructions from Nikhilesh. But keeping in view the crisis at hand, he thought it wise to keep silent. He called one of his officers and directed him to arrange an impromptu press conference near the main gate of the Sena Bhavan.

07.00 P.M.

Sunita was at her wit's end. She had come to her father's house from the nursing home with her parents after her discharge. She and her parents had received the news of involvement of Yogesh in the shootout at Sena Bhavan from Badri Prasad, DCP Central District, Delhi Police, who had arrived at their house with a police party. They were aghast on hearing from Badri Prasad that Yogesh was the prime suspect in the shootout in the Sena Bhavan. Sunita was unable to comprehend what Yogesh was doing in Sena Bhavan in the first place. Was he able to put the deciphered message in place? Did the message contain some highly dangerous information? She had no answers to these queries.

"Madam," the DCP addressed Sunita, "you and your family must cooperate with us fully. You must not leave your house under any circumstances. Very soon Yogesh Naqvi's identity will be disclosed to the press. You can well imagine how people will react once they know the man who shot at the popular Defence Minister. If they find out that you are his family, you might have to face the fury of the mobs, which are gathering at various places in the city. So be here as it is only in your interest. You are safe under police protection."

07.15 P.M.

"Stop here!" Yogesh told the taxi driver when they reached the block in Sector K of Vasant Kunj where Natasha's flat was located. "What is the fare?" Yogesh asked, his right hand reaching out to his hip pocket to take out the purse.

"Rupees one hundred and ninety two." The driver read out the meter reading.

"Oh shit!" blurted Yogesh.

"What happened sir?" asked the driver.

"I left my purse in the office." Yogesh recalled that he had put his purse on the side rack in Colonel Bali's room after taking out his driving license. Being in a state of nervousness and anxiety, he forgot to pick it up before leaving Colonel Bali's office.

"So what do we do now?" asked the driver. "You want me to take you back to Sena Bhavan?"

"No," replied Yogesh. "You please wait here. I'll be back in a minute."

Yogesh left the taxi and took stairs to reach Natasha's flat on the second floor. He pressed the door bell.

Natasha opened the door. She took some time before she could recognize Yogesh standing at her door, in army uniform. "Yogesh, what is this?" She asked. "You in army uniform?"

"I will explain it in a minute," said Yogesh. But first give me two hundred rupees. I have to pay the taxi fare."

"Alright!" said Natasha as she walked back to her drawing room, picked her hand bag and took out two hundred rupee notes. She gave the money to Yogesh who ran downstairs and returned soon, after disposing off the taxi driver.

"Tell me now," said Natasha. "What is this all about? Is this some kind of a joke?"

"No joke Natasha," said Yogesh as he followed her in to her apartment. "I need your help."

"What help?" asked Natasha, "You have been missing from the nursing home since lunch. Sunita was worried, you know?"

"Did you see her today?" asked Yogesh.

"Of course I did," said Natasha while offering him a seat.

"I went to the nursing home from office. They had discharged her at 4 P.M. but she insisted that she would leave the hospital only after you arrive there. By the way, have you heard of the shootout in the Sena Bhavan in which the Defence Minister has been injured? I hope it has nothing to do with your adventure?"

"You mean Sunita is still at the nursing home?" Yogesh asked, ignoring her question.

"Oh no," replied Natasha. "We finally managed to persuade her to leave the nursing home. She is now at her father's place and feeling much better. I am coming from there only. I was there till about 6 P.M."

Yogesh looked at the ceiling and drew a deep breath. He stretched his legs and closed his eyes. "Oh God!" he sighed.

"Yogesh, is anything wrong?" asked Natasha.

"When did you hear the news of the shootout in Sena Bhavan?" asked Yogesh, again ignoring her query.

"I heard it from a policeman when I was coming home after leaving Sunita. The police had put up a roadblock on the way and when I asked reason for the same, I was told that somebody had shot the Defence Minister and the police was carrying out the search for the shooter and his possible accomplices."

"Could you please switch on the TV? Put on some news channel."

Natasha did as requested. She began to worry about Yogesh but dared not ask him anything again. She decided to wait till he was ready to share his anxiety with her.

All news channels were running the story of the attempt on the life of Raman Kumar by a terrorist in Sena Bhavan. Natasha settled for CNN IBN news.

"Ladies and gentleman," Rajdeep Sardesai came on the air. "Here is an important announcement. The young man who tried to kill the Honourable Defence Minister has been identified. His name is Yogesh Naqvi. It is suspected that he has managed to give slip to the police cordon outside Sena Bhavan. If you see him anywhere, please give a ring to the police control room at the number one zero zero. Anybody who gives clue that could lead to his arrest will get a reward of fifty thousand rupees. We have managed to get the photograph of Yogesh Naqvi which you are seeing now."

Natasha was dumbfounded. She looked at Yogesh with horror. "Yogesh I can't believe it is you who did it?"

"I did not shoot him Natasha," said Yogesh with anguish in his voice. "This man Raman Kumar is a megalomaniac. He is going to kill me because I have found out that he is plotting to assassinate Prime Minister Prabhat Rai at Haridwar tonight!"

"What are you saying Yogesh?" Natasha asked in utter disbelief.

Yogesh told her in brief about the dangerous web in which he was caught and the harrowing time that he had to undergo in Sena Bhavan.

"The thing that hurts me most is that not many people are going to listen to me, what to talk of believing me." The feeling of anguish and helplessness was written all over the face of Yogesh.

"What do you want me to do Yogesh?" Natasha asked in a calm voice.

"Please tell me Natasha, how far you are willing to go to help me?"

"How far, you think, I should go to help you?"

"I want you to accompany me all the way to Haridwar in your car. I must first get out of Delhi to save my life. Then I must reach Haridwar before 3 A.M. tonight. If I can save the life of the Prime Minister, there is no way that Raman Kumar can realise his dream of becoming the Chief Martial Law Administrator. After that it is only a matter of time before he gets exposed and punished for his heinous crimes. But God forbid, if he succeeds in assassinating the Prime Minister tonight, he will become the undisputed dictator of this country tomorrow and use his powers to suppress the truth forever. It is imperative, therefore, that I leave Delhi immediately. It will be a big help if you take me to Haridwar in your car."

Natasha thought fast and said, "Well Yogesh, you went ahead with your adventure against my advice. Somehow I had suspected some trouble in it from the beginning. But to hell with it! I have accepted you as a friend and I will do all that is expected of a friend. I am with you and together we will attempt to make it to Haridwar in time. But we can't leave with you in this uniform. The police will find you out at the first checkpoint. In fact, they might already be on your trail. Who knows the taxi driver might have watched the announcement on the TV by now!"

"You are right," said Yogesh as he jumped out of his chair. "We must leave immediately. But I don't have any other clothes!"

"My jeans and shirt won't fit you. So what do we do?"

"Wait a minute! You have some ladies suit, I mean salwar kameez?"

"Just one or two. I usually wear only jeans."

"One is enough, if it is not too tight."

"You must be joking. You in a salwar kameez?"

"Natasha that is the only way to avoid being detected by the police."

"I see," said Natasha. She went to her bedroom and brought out a set of salwar kameez and a headscarf. "Try this," she said. "I'll see how much money I have got at home."

Yogesh went to the bathroom and came out five minutes later. He looked funny in the salwar-kameez but Natasha could not bring herself to laugh. "I've got only eight hundred rupees in my purse," she said "Would that be enough for the petrol?"

"Not enough," said Yogesh. "Unfortunately, I don't have any money with me right now. I left my purse in Colonel Bali's office. So what do we do?"

"Not to worry Yogesh," assured Natasha. "I have my ATM cards with me. We will draw some cash on the way."

"That sounds good," said Yogesh.

"Then let us hurry up," said Natasha.

"Give me a minute. Let me speak to Sunita first. She will be highly worried." Yogesh dialled his father-in-law's number. It was engaged. He tried Sunita's cell phone. It was busy too. 'Must have been trying to make enquiries about me!' Yogesh said to himself.

"Hurry up Yogesh."

"Let me try ma!" Yogesh pleaded.

"Come on Yogesh, leave the phone," implored Natasha. "It is too risky to stay here any longer."

"You have a cellphone?" Yogesh asked Natasha.

"No. I stopped using one long time ago. Too much of a nuisance. You speak to Sunita and your mother from some pay phone in Connaught Place."

"OK. Let us go."

They left the apartment in Natasha's car. They had hardly gone about one kilometre when they saw about half a dozen police jeeps racing towards the block where Natasha's house was located.

"That was a close shave," said Yogesh as he adjusted the headscarf.

"I told you, fifty thousand bucks is a lot of money for a taxi driver," said Natasha.

"I hope the police won't break into your house."

"I hope not. But you better be careful. We are approaching the first police check point."

Yogesh opened the dashboard of the car as soon as they reached the police check post. He saw one police officer coming towards their car. Yogesh started fiddling with the CDs and finally selected one for the playback. He inserted the CD into the car CD player and began to adjust its volume, tone and bass. The police officer peeped inside and found nothing suspicious. He waived to the two ladies to move on. The police check was carried out at two more places before they reached Connaught Place. Each time they approached a police check point, Yogesh repeated his exercise with the car stereo and the CDs.

"I think it is too risky to travel by my car all the way to Haridwar," said Natasha.

"Why?" asked Yogesh.

"Soon they will find out that you entered my apartment in that block. It won't take them much longer to find out that together we left in my car."

"You are right. Let us do one thing. Let us leave your car in some parking lot here and hire a taxi."

"Done," said Natasha. "We'll go to the underground parking. You can speak to Sunita also from one of the pay-phones there. And you better change to some male dress. Two ladies travelling in a taxi from Delhi to Haridwar at night is a sure recipe for arousing suspicions. Besides, your short hair is a dead give away."

Natasha selected a parking lot near the place where a couple of public call booths had been installed. She gave Yogesh some coins from her purse. "Take these and remain inside the booth till I return with some male dress and disguise material for you. I'll also draw some cash from the ATM." She was gone within seconds.

Yogesh slowly walked into one of the call booths and closed the door from inside. He dialled Sunita's cell number. It was still engaged. He tried her father's number. He was relieved to hear the ring on the other side. He inserted the coin when he heard his father-in-law's voice.

"Papa, Yogesh here. What is wrong with all the phones? I have been trying for the last half an hour. Can I speak to Sunita urgently?"

"Yogesh, are you alright son?" asked his worried father-in-law. He could not bring himself to tell Yogesh that the phones were busy because too many people were calling to know about him.

"Yes papa. But let me talk to Sunita please!" Yogesh pleaded.

"Hello,"it was Sunita's voice.

"Sunita, are you alright?"

"Yogesh you tell me. Are you alright? We are so worried on seeing this announcement on the TV."

"Listen Sunita. I am OK but I'll be able to meet you only tomorrow. Trust me. I did not shoot the Defence Minister. I have been trapped."

"OK Yogesh, I trust you completely. But, you save yourself first. They have tapped our phone and will reach from wherever you are speaking within minutes. So please get out of there as quickly as you can and...." Yogesh heard the sound of click. Clearly, somebody had snatched the phone and stopped her from speaking any further.

Yogesh hung the phone and burst out of the underground parking. He could no longer afford to wait for Natasha to return. He halted a passing auto rickshaw. "Daryaganj please," he said.

The auto rickshaw driver stared at the clumsy looking lady speaking in a male voice. Yogesh realized his mistake. "Eunuch, you know!" he said with a forced smile on his face. "We have a big family living there in Daryaganj."

"I see," said the driver with a mischievous smile and started the auto rickshaw. They had barely left the outer circle of the Connaught Place when a number of police jeeps converged on to the area where underground parking was located.

In Islamabad, the seven wise men of the ISI were glued to the TV in the Operations Room of the agency. They were surfing the various Indian news channels, all of which were running the shooting of Raman Kumar as their main story. They were trying to make out what exactly had happened in New Delhi and why. They had no idea as to who Yogesh Naqvi was and why he had shot Raman Kumar. The chief had contacted Li Yongding also over phone but the Chinese were as clueless about the developments in New Delhi as the ISI was.

08.00 P.M.

Yogesh got down in front of a four-storey building. Shafi, his friend from the school days, lived in a second floor one room flat in it. Yogesh asked the auto rickshaw driver to wait and ran up the stairs. On reaching Shafi's flat, he pressed the door bell.

"Coming!" It was Shafi's voice from inside. Yogesh heaved a sigh of relief that Shafi was at home. Shafi opened the door of his flat but could not recognize Yogesh.

"Let me in Shafi, I am Yogesh," he said as he walked into the flat. Shafi closed the door behind him. "Before you ask any questions, please go downstairs and pay thirty rupees to the auto rickshaw driver. I hope you have some money with you?"

"Of course I have," replied Shafi. "I'll be back."

Shafi left his room to make payment to the auto rickshaw driver. He returned within five minutes.

"Yogesh, my friend!" Shafi confronted his friend. "You in this condition? Salwar kameez, shootout. What is all this?"

"Shafi, while I answer your questions, you have to do three things for me," said Yogesh. "Firstly, you have to lend me whatever money you have with you. Secondly, I'll write a letter that you will have to deliver safely to Sunita as early as possible. Thirdly, you have to display all your theatrical skills to help me get into some disguise so that I can travel incognito to Haridwar tonight."

08.15 P.M.

The assassin had arrived in Haridwar earlier in the day. He moved around on the banks of the river like any other pilgrim. He slung a bag on his shoulder, which contained the three parts of a rifle that would become the deadly AK-74 when assembled. He also carried a silencer that he proposed to attach to the barrel of the gun. He had about fifty rounds of ammunition with him, though, he was certain that he would not need more than one. The assassin reached Har ki Pauri

Har ki Pauri or Staircase of God, if translated literaly into English, consists of about a dozen stairs of concrete that lead from the southern bank of the river Ganges to a forty metre wide river channel of the river Ganges. It is in this channel of the holy river that pilgrims take bath to wash away their sins. There are three small temples about thirty feet downstream on the eastern side, most famous of these temples being the Temple of Laxmi Narain. Across the river channel is a fifty feet wide and about two hundred feet long platform where the pilgrims gather in the morning and in the evening to sing devotional songs and chant hymns. A two- storeyed clock tower stands right in the middle of the platform. The main channel of the river Ganges lies across the platform. An overbridge joins the southern bank with the platform.

The assassin looked at his watch. Enough time, he thought. He recalled his instructions. He was to enter the clock tower at around midnight. He knew that though the clock tower would have been sanitised and closed by the police earlier in the day, yet, the lure of one hundred dollars had made an unsuspecting caretaker allow a 'documentary film maker' to enter the clock tower and take a few shots of the early moning Aarti from a vantage point. The assassin was to occupy a vantage point behind the parapet of the balcony on the first floor of the clock tower. He was to lie down there and wait for Prabhat Rai to arrive. He was to shoot him either in the car parking on the southern bank when he would get down from his car or when he came to have bath in the holy water at Har Ki Pauri. "Mr. Rai, you better say your prayers now," said the assassin, speaking to himself. "Tomorrow you may not get any time for that."

08.30 P.M.

Defence Minister Raman Kumar returned to his bungalow from the hospital. His right shoulder and arm had to be bandaged as one of the bullets had hit him on his right shoulder and the other had grazed past his right upper arm, causing a minor bruise there. The pain in the shoulder had subsided a great deal as a result of the administering of the painkillers. The doctors, however, wanted to keep the minister under close observation for at least another twenty-four hours. Little did they know that these were the twenty-four hours for which Raman Kumar had staked his reputation, his position and his life. There was no way they could keep him in the hospital tonight. He insisted and got himself discharged from the hospital about ten minutes earlier.

Raman Kumar had not been able to keep track of the day's events due to his confinement to the hospital. He called for his nephew Nikhilesh as soon as he left the hospital. There were a number of ministers, MPs and other dignitaries who had visited him in the hospital. There were many more who were present at his residence when he reached there. But he didn't have time for anyone of them.

Nikhilesh arrived soon. He requested everybody with folded hands to leave his uncle alone so that he could take complete rest as advised by the doctors.

"Yes Nikhilesh?" said Raman Kumar as soon as the last of the visitor left his room and Nikhilesh bolted the door from inside. "What is the latest? I hope things are going as per plan. Has that boy been silenced?" He had too many questions to ask.

"Uncle," replied Nikhilesh. "Things have not gone exactly as per our plan but they have not gone out of hand either. It was stupid of me to have accompanied you to the Sena Bhavan. Yogesh saw me and decided to overhear our conversation. As ill luck would have it, we chose that very time to discuss everything in detail."

"I had to tell you all my plans," said Raman Kumar. "I had to take you into confidence before the Operation Red Rose unfolded itself. Unfortunately, we didn't carry out a thorough check of the room. But tell me what happened after I was taken to the hospital?"

"After the shootout in the room, Yogesh managed to enter the lift that was going up," replied Nikhilesh. "I decided to wait for him at the ground floor, thinking, that I would get him when he would try to make an escape. But he didn't come out of the building. When you were being taken to the hospital, you told me to get hold of your briefcase and the secret papers."

"Could you get them?"

"Yes, I could. But when I entered your room I saw one army colonel going through the yellow file!"

"Bloody hell. Who was he?"

"He introduced himself as Colonel Bali from Intelligence Branch," Nikhilesh continued. "I suspected that he had read the papers but he behaved as if he had not. He said that he had come to make sure that the deciphered message was not misplaced. I was not fully convinced with his explanation but I had to accept his statement on its face value. The police arrived on the scene and Sena Bhavan was completely sealed. It was then decided that people should be allowed to leave the building, one by one after showing their I-cards at the two gates. General Surinder Pal wanted Colonel Bali to man one of the gates but I intervened. Accordingly, one gate was manned by a senior General and the other by Mehta. But when the last of the officials was reported to have left and Yogesh didn't turn up I became suspicious of Colonel Bali's involvement in the whole affair. I went to his room with Mehta and that bloody Colonel was there wearing Yogesh's clothes. Obviously, Yogesh left Sena Bhavan in his uniform and with his I-Card. When you see hundreds of I-Cards, one is bound to make mistakes. So Yogesh made good his escape. But I didn't spare your Colonel. I shot him dead there and then and I have cautioned Mehta to keep mum."

"I see,' said Raman Kumar. "So this Colonel also knew the truth. It was good thinking on your part to finish him off. At least half the threat has been eliminated. But what about that boy Yogesh? Did you get any lead on him?"

"We did," replied Nikhilesh. "His photograph and his particulars have been flashed on all TV channels. A reward of fifty thousand rupees has also been announced to anyone who helps the police in arresting him. In fact at this moment, virtually everybody in this country believes that Yogesh is a terrorist who tried to assassinate the Defence Minister of India. People are after his blood."

"Good going!" said Raman Kumar. "But you haven't told me about the lead on Yogesh."

"About Yogesh, we got our first lead that came from a taxi driver," replied Nikhilesh. "This man told the police that he had dropped a man of this description wearing army uniform at Vasant Kunj. The police reached there but a bit too late. The bastard had already left Vasant Kunj with a lady friend of his. Her name is Natasha and she works for Sonyog, the Ad Agency of Yogesh and his wife Sunita. His wife is the daughter of the Chief Postmaster General of Delhi and she is presently staying with him at his Ashoka Road residence. We have tapped their phones, expecting that he would give a ring there some time soon. We have also deployed police in sufficient numbers at their house. I have already spoken to DCP Badri Prasad about this development and he is taking care of Yogesh's family."

"Did Yogesh give a ring?" asked Raman Kumar, showing his impatience.

"Yes uncle," replied Nikhilesh. "He gave a ring about an hour ago. The call was traced to a public call booth in the underground car parking at Connaught Place. But that girl Sunita proved to be a clever person. She warned her husband to save his life as she suspected the phone to be tapped. The police reached the underground parking within minutes. That was not good enough. The bastard once again gave a slip to the police."

"If the chase continues till about 3 A.M," said Raman Kumar, "we need not fear anything. So tell Badri Prasad to keep the police on its toes. Keep the heat on. Meanwhile ask the army chief to meet me immediately. We will need him the most tomorrow morning. And keep me informed of the developments. There is no going back now."

"Right uncle!" said Nikhilesh. "So I'll take leave of you now."

"Before you leave, please switch on the computer. I must send a report to the ISI on the net. They might be highly worried. I have to reassure them so that they do not call off Operation Red Rose."

09.00 P.M.

Natasha had been wandering aimlessly in Connaught Place for more than an hour. She recalled that she had left Yogesh in the public call booth and had come out of the underground parking to draw cash and do the required shopping for him. She had drawn ten thousand rupees from an ATM but before she could enter any shop, she saw a number of police jeeps speeding towards the car parking. It was clear that the police had somehow managed to find that Yogesh and she were in the parking area and were preparing to arrest them. She felt extremely scared. She did not know whether or not the police were able to capture Yogesh. 'What would they do to him if they capture him?' She was highly worried. She began to feel less scared when she saw the police jeeps leaving the area, one by one after about half an hour of wait. The manner of their dispersal showed that, in all probability, they had not been able to lay their hands on Yogesh. But she still could not prepare herself to go to the car parking. She continued to be part of the evening crowd in Connaught Place, hoping and praying that she would not be recognised by anybody. As the time passed, she regained control of herself. She went to a shop and using their phone, she dialled Sunita's number.

"Hello!" she said.

"Yes," came a male voice, sounding rude. Must be a policeman!

"May I know who is speaking please?"

"May I know who you are?"

"I am a friend of Sunita."

"Sunita is not in a position to talk," came the curt reply and the phone on the other side went dead. Natasha left the shop and decided to while away some more time before taking out her car from the parking. She decided to leave Yogesh to take his own care wherever he was.

Yogesh was still with his friend Shafi. He had discarded the female dress and put on a white Dhoti Kurta, the traditional dress of the elderly gentlemen in India. Shafi was busy giving him the make up of an old man. Being a man from the theatre, he had the required material as well as the necessary skills. He applied the oil and the white paint on his hair, eyebrows and eye lashes. He was busy creating false wrinkles on his face so that he could easily pass off as an old man going for an early morning bath in the holy Ganges at Haridwar on the no-moon night.

"Shafi," called Yogesh. "The letter that I have given you contains very important information. Make sure you deliver it safely to Sunita and that too as soon as you can. Remember, no one else should get to know of this letter otherwise they will find out that I am on my way to Haridwar. At the same time, any delay or failure on your part to deliver it to her might cost me my life and the country too might have to pay a heavy price in such an eventuality."

"Don't worry Yogesh," said Shafi. "This letter will be in Sunita's hands as soon as you are on your way to Haridwar. I am sorry I have not been able to help you much financially. Perpetual broke, you know! You will have to travel by bus."

"Never mind Shafi," said Yogesh. "So long as I can reach there before 3 A.M, my purpose will be served. The mode of conveyance doesn't matter. Five hundred rupees that you have given me is more than what I need."

"Any other message for Sunita?"

"Just tell her, if you can, not to worry about me. She should try her best to do her part of job as suggested by me in the letter. I only hope she is not troubled by the police for her efforts."

Sunita and her father were mad at the police officers on duty. The police believed that Yogesh was indeed a terrorist who tried to kill the Defence Minister of India. The worst part was that Sunita and her parents were not even aware of what actually happened at Sena Bhavan. Sunita had a chance to know the truth but to her the life of her husband was dearer than anything else. The brief telephonic conversation had made her feel better and she was able to take control of herself. She knew that Yogesh could not kill anybody. So she decided to warn him to save his life first. She was certain that the truth would emerge in the end and

Yogesh would be exonerated of the false charges. The police, however, did not take kindly to her action. They wanted her to continue the conversation on the phone so that they could trace the call and nab him in the call booth itself. They felt let down when she cautioned Yogesh against the plan of the police. They had been behaving badly with her and her parents since then. They decided to answer all the calls themselves thereafter. A lady police officer was posted in Sunita's room so that her conversation with other persons could be monitored to get some clue to her husband's likely movements.

Sunita's mother-in-law had also come there on hearing the news of her son's involvement in the shootout. She had gone into deep meditation, obviously, praying for her son's safety. To her, the behaviour of the police did not bother much. But Sunita's parents, especially her father, felt highly enraged. He had known the Police Commissioner Bedi well. He lived in a nearby bungalow. Moreover both were from the same batch of the Civil Services of India. But he could not contact the Police Commissioner as he was busy in the Control Room with the Home Minister. None of the other officers proved to be of any help. Little did he know that the police officers on duty at his residence were simply complying with the instructions given by DCP Badri Prasad.

09.30 P.M

Yogesh indeed looked like an old man in his seventies as he walked into the Inter State Bus Terminal at Kashmere Gate. He had bent his back slightly forward as he walked. He had put his right hand over the shoulder of Shafi. On the way from Daryaganj, the police had stopped their auto rickshaw many times and peeped inside. None of the policeman could suspect the old man to be Yogesh. He had passed the test and he was sure of travelling undetected right up to Haridwar. He prayed to God to help him reach Haridwar before 3 A.M.

Yogesh and Shafi left the auto rickshaw at the gate of the bus stand. Yogesh looked at his watch. He calculated that if he could get a bus in the next ten or fifteen minutes, he was sure to reach Haridwar in about four hours, thanks mainly to the newly opened National Highway on which the buses easily did more than ninety kilometres per hour. But when they reached the bus counter, they were in for a rude shock. The last bus to Haridwar was ready to leave but it was already fully booked. There were many people like Prabhat Rai who wished to have a holy dip in the river Ganges on the no-moon night.

"My grandfather must go to Haridwar tonight," Shafi pleaded with the booking clerk at the ticket window.

"You should have come earlier," the counter clerk replied.

"We tried our best," Shafi decided not to give up. "But our auto rickshaw broke down on the way. We have come walking the last one kilometre. No auto rickshaw or taxi would carry a short distance passenger."

"Not my fault," replied the counter clerk. "I can't help you as not a single seat is available. You can see for yourself."

"I don't mind going standing if I have to," said Yogesh, trying to make his voice sound like that of an old man.

"For that you have to talk to the conductor," said the counter clerk.

Shafi ran towards the bus and began to plead the case of his grandfather before the conductor. "You see he has taken a vow to take a holy dip in the Ganges on sixteen consecutive no moon nights. Tonight it is his fifteenth. He will have to do the sixteen all over again if he could not go tonight."

"But there is no seat and I can't take an old man standing in the bus all the way to Haridwar," said the conductor. "It is two hundred kilometres, you know, and it won't take less than four hours for us to reach there."

"I'll manage son," said Yogesh. "But please don't leave me behind." He was beginning to feel helpless.

Just then a young man got down from the bus. He had seen Shafi and Yogesh pleading with the bus conductor.

"Grandpa!" the youngman addressed Yogesh respectfully. "If you are in such an urgent need, then, I can spare my seat for you."

"God bless you my son," said Yogesh with tremendous relief. "I will pray to mother Ganges for your well being and long life."

"There is no need for that," said the young man. "But you will have to do something else for me in return for my seat."

"What is it son?"

"I was going to Haridwar with my grandfather. He is a real old man you know! He needs assistance for doing his routines. You appear to be in much better health than him. If you promise to take care of him, you can occupy seat number 23. He is in 24. Here is the ticket."

"Don't worry my son," said Yogesh. "Don't worry at all. Your grandfather is my responsibility." He paid him one hundred and eight rupees, the amount of the fare, and the young man disappeared. Shafi also bade goodbye to Yogesh and left the bus stand to try his talent to find a way to meet Sunita. Yogesh entered the bus and went to occupy his seat next to a man who looked to be in his eighties.

"Nikku?" called the old man.

"I am not Nikku," replied Yogesh. "I am Yogi, your friend. Nikku has gone home."

"Yogi, my friend," said the old man. "I am so happy to see you. Nikku gone home? Good riddance. None of them ever wants to come with me, you know!"

Yogesh let out a sigh. So it was not a case of a kind hearted young man doing favour to an old man. It was a case of finding a means to escape. Strange are the ways of the world, he thought!

The driver entered his cabin and took the wheel. Just when he started the engine, the old man sitting next to Yogesh began to shout, "Hold on! Hold on! I must go to the loo."

"Hurry up, grandpa," said the driver. Yogesh gave a helping hand to his fellow old man and slowly they got down from the bus and made it to the urinal. Seeing the old man, Yogesh also could not control the urge to ease himself.

"Still going strong?" asked the old man without looking up.

"What?" asked Yogesh, unable to comprehend his question.

"I asked, how strong are you there?" asked the old man pointing towards Yogesh's loins and then looking at him with a smile. "Still going strong or is it as flaccid as mine?"

"Carry on grandpa," said Yogesh trying hard to suppress his laughter. "Finish your job. The bus is waiting for us."

"I am not your grandpa," replied the old man, sounding offended.

"I mean, Nikku's grandpa," said Yogesh, realizing his mistake.

The two old men slowly walked back to the bus and took their seats. The bus was on its way to Haridwar.

10.00 P.M.

Natasha finished her food and left the restaurant. She looked for the police near the underground parking. There was not a single police jeep there. She slowly walked towards the parking. She was careful not to arouse any suspicions. Not many people were left in the Connaught Place at that hour. All shops except the bars and the restaurants were closed. The shooting of the Defence Minister by a young man named Yogesh Naqvi was a common topic of conversation among people. Natasha recalled a group of young men in the restaurant who were pulling a colleague's leg, asking him to let them hand him over to the police as Yogesh Naqvi and claim fifty thousand rupees as reward. 'How ignorant people can be?' she thought. 'They do not know that the very man whom they suspect of having shot the Defence Minister was risking his own life to save the nation from plunging into a bloody and uncertain future. Only if they knew the truth!'

She entered the parking and casually walked towards her car. She looked around. There were just two persons who had come to take their vehicles. She made sure that no one was watching her. She sat in her car and started it. Slowly she reached the exit gate and handed over the parking card and a fifty rupee note to the man at the counter. No sooner had she done so, a group of policemen piled on to her car from all directions.

"Please come out!" said a police inspector.

"Why? What have I done?" asked a scared Natasha. She had faced police for the first time in her life.

"Please step out!" said the police inspector with authority.

Natasha knew that she had been cornered. She opened the door and got down from her car.

"Follow me," said the police inspector. "Varun, you follow us in Madam's car," said the inspector, addressing a colleague. Natasha followed the inspector meekly. He took her to a police van that had just pulled to the left of the road. The rear door of the van opened and about half a dozen lady police officials came out of it.

"Inspector Rachita," the inspector accompanying Natasha called his lady colleague. "Please take madam to the police station. We'll follow you."

Inspector Rachita escorted Natasha to the police van and asked her to get inside. The sight of women police officials made Natasha feel less scared. She got into the van along with them. The van took her to the police station in a matter of minutes.

"What is your name?" asked Inspector Rachita as soon as Natasha took a chair in the police station.

"Natasha!"

"Natasha what?"

"Only Natasha."

"Where do you live?"

"At 1416, Sector 'K', Vasant Kunj."

"Where do you work?"

"At Sonyog. It is an advertising agency."

"Owned by whom?"

"Mr. Yogesh Naqvi and his wife."

"He is the man who shot the Defence Minister and tried to kill him today?"

"No. Yogesh didn't shoot him," Natasha spoke in a loud voice. "He is innocent!"

"You think he is innocent and that is why you helped him escape from the police?"

Natasha remained silent.

"Where is he now?"

"I don't know."

"He was with you when you left Vasant Kunj and now you don't know where he is?"

"I swear I don't know."

"You are telling a lie,"

"I have never told a lie in my life," said Natasha and began to cry.

"If you don't know where he is right now, then could you please tell us where have you been after leaving your car in the underground parking?"

Natasha wiped her tears with her handkerchief and took control of herself. She told the police about her remaining in Connaught Place all through the evening, as she was too scared to face the police.

"You have no reason to fear the police if you are innocent," said Inspector Rachita. "But you have been conniving with a terrorist. So you will have to face the consequences."

"He is not a terrorist!" protested Natasha. "He told me it was not he who shot the Defence Minister."

"Then who shot him?"

"He said it was Nikhilesh, the minister's nephew."

Nikhilesh heard the statement as he entered the room. "That innocent looking man is a master criminal. He said that I shot my own uncle and you believed him? It is gullible people like you who unwittingly become the tools in the propagation of terrorism."

Natasha found herself at her wit's end when she heard the voice of the man she feared and hated. She wanted to protest but could not utter a word out of fear. She had never seen violence even in her dreams. To be in the presence of an arch villain was too unnerving for her.

"Your life can still be spared if you tell us where he has gone?" shouted Nikhilesh.

"I don't know," said Natasha, the words coming out of her lips with great difficulty.

"Did he tell you where he wanted to go?" asked Nikhilesh.

"Haridwar." The information came involuntarily. She looked up at Nikhilesh, realizing that this was one occasion on which she should have told a lie. "No, I mean, he wanted to leave Delhi. I am not sure whether he wanted to go to Haridwar, Ambala, Agra or some other place." Natasha tried in vain to retrieve the situation.

Nikhilesh became red in his face. He kept silent for a while, trying hard to control his mental turmoil. He knew that Yogesh was on his way to Haridwar to save the life of Prabhat Rai. "You keep this lady in custody," he told the police, "and I will see as to what is to be done to apprehend that terrorist before he leaves Delhi."

He rushed out of the police station.

10.45 P.M.

Raman Kumar was taking rest in his room when General Surinder Pal arrived to see him. "Welcome General!" he said as he came to a sitting position in his bed.

"Thank you, sir and good evening!" said the army chief. "How is the wound, sir? I hope it is not hurting too much?"

"Not much," replied Raman Kumar with a smile. "But it is a fresh wound and will take time to heal."

"We couldn't believe that the innocent looking young man could be so dangerous!"

"Appearances are deceptive General. I also believed him completely till he pulled out a revolver from nowhere, took aim and started taunting me. He said that he had given me adequate warning about the plot to assassinate me. He laughed that he had even told me clearly as to who was the person who had hatched the plot of my assassination. He said that he could not be blamed if we fell into his trap. Having said so, he fired at me. I ducked for cover. Fortunately the bullet hit me only on my shoulder. I am grateful to Nikhilesh that he did not panic. He grappled with him and snatched his revolver. Had he not done so, Yogesh would have killed both of us."

"Thank God your life has been saved. We, in Sena Bhavan would have never forgiven ourselves if something had happened to our honourable minister. Not that we are going to forgive anybody now. I have already ordered enquiry as to how he was able to walk into your room with a loaded revolver."

"That is very nice of you. But right now we should focus our attention on the events that are likely to happen rather than on the ones that have already taken place. My injury and your enquiry should in no way deviate us from our main objective of thwarting the conspiracy of Sukhraj Malik and his son-in-law for whatever they are planning in that operation called Operation Red Rose."

"I hardly know Sukhraj Malik but sir, you know him well. Are you sure that Malik too is involved in planning this operation?"

"There is not an iota of any doubt in my mind about it," replied the Minister. "Without Sukhraj Malik there is nothing that Balwant can gain by plotting anything. I am sure that Operation Red Rose involves something really dangerous. The bid on my life is only a tip of the iceberg."

General Surinder Pal was a simple soul, a soldier to the core. He did not know much about politics or political conspiracies. He listened attentively to his minister whom he admired. He believed every word of what he said. "This man Sukhraj Malik must be stopped in his tracks. We can't allow free hand to the traitors and conspirators against our motherland! Should I speak to the Police Commissioner about taking him into custody?"

"Easy, General," said Raman Kumar, highly satisfied with his own performance. "It is too early yet. We have no solid evidence against him. But God forbid, if something goes wrong then together we will see to it that Malik and Balwant are exposed and punished for their ghastly crimes."

"Right sir," said the General as he got up to take leave. "As Chief of the Army Staff and as Chairman of the Joint Chiefs of Staff, I assure you that the three services are fully behind our beloved Defence Minister in this hour of crisis. Just pass me your orders for whatever you want me to do."

Raman Kumar had already started dreaming of becoming the Prime Minister of the country when the morning came the next day.

11.00 P.M.

Shafi got down from the auto rickshaw in front of Mathur's house on Ashoka Road wearing a white overcoat of a doctor. He had decided on his plan to reach Sunita when Yogesh told him about their accident and the resultant injury to her. Shafi had obtained the necessary details about Niramay

Nursing Home and Sunita's treatment from Yogesh. Slowly he approached the gate of the bungalow.

"Is this the house where the Chief Postmaster General lives?" Shafi asked the police personnel on duty.

"Yes," replied a head constable. "What do you want?"

"Officer, I am Dr. Shafi from Niramay Nursing Home. Mrs. Sunita Naqvi, who is the daughter of the Chief Postmaster General, was discharged from our nursing home this evening. She forgot to collect a very important medicine. Her wound might get infected if this medicine is not administered to her immediately."

"What medicine?" asked the head constable.

"Histrionicin," said Shafi. He was thinking of his histrionic abilities when the policeman asked him the unexpected question. The policemen were as ignorant about the medicines as Shafi was. They looked at each other but did not offer any comments.

"Where is the medicine?" asked the head constable.

"It is here," said Shafi as he pulled out a small bottle containing a colourless liquid from his coat pocket. The head constable took the bottle from his hand, opened its lid and smelled it. It gave slightly pungent smell.

"Where is the label of the bottle?" he asked.

"I have poured Histrionicin into this bottle from a jar," replied Shafi. "Histrionicin comes in jars, you know! It has to be imported from Germany. Very expensive!"

"Okay," said the head constable. "We will deliver it to the lady. You may go."

"I can't go like that," said Shafi. "I have to give the first dose to her under my observation. There might be some adverse reaction. Some people are allergic to it."

The head constable stared at him for a while and then said, "Hold on." He took the walkie-talkie from one of his colleagues, pulled its antenna and spoke, "Hello! Inspector Khan sir? Over"

"Yes. Inspector Khan here. Over," came a voice on the walkie-talkie that was audible to everybody around.

"Sir, Havildar Hari Ram here. Sir, there is a doctor at the gate. He insists that he must give some medicine personally to the Chief PMG's daughter. Over."

"What is his name? Over"

"What name did you say?" Havildar Hari Ram asked Shafi.

"Dr Shafi. Tell that I have been sent by Dr S.S. Sharma from Niramay Nursing Home."

"Sir, he is Dr Shafi. He has been sent by Dr Sharma from Niramay Nursing Home. Over."

There was a brief pause. Then the voice of the inspector came again.

"Send him in. Over and out."

A policeman carried out a cursory body search of Shafi and then asked him to move on. Shafi heaved a sigh of relief. He walked briskly into the house. He saw Sunita's parents sitting in the drawing room. Also sitting there were two police officers. Shafi walked up to Sunita's father and said, "Good evening sir. You remember me? I am Shafi, Doctor Shafi. Where is Sunitaji?"

"She is inside," replied Sunita's father. He knew that he had seen the doctor somewhere but could not recollect where and when.

Shafi went hurriedly into the bedroom. Sunita was lying in her bed. A lady police officer sat in a nearby chair. She gave him a hostile look.

"Hello Sunitaji," said Shafi. "I am Doctor Shafi Yogi. You remember me? I have brought something very urgent for you which you need very badly. If you don't take it now, the situation will go out of control and tomorrow may be too late. That is why I came personally. How is the wound otherwise?"

"It is paining," said Sunita as she recognized Shafi and began to grasp the meaning behind what he said. She could make out that Yogesh had met Shafi and he was carrying some message from him for her.

"I have to give you this dose of antibiotics," said Shafi, taking out the bottle from his coat pocket. "It is Histrionicin, you know! Imported from Germany! You forgot to bring it from the nursing home. Can I have a glass?"

Sunita saw him picking up a glass from the side table. The lady police officer kept watching them but did not say anything. Shafi examined the glass and said, "I must wash it absolutely clean." He entered the adjoining bathroom and cleaned the glass. He came out after a couple of minutes. "Now it is clean," he said. He opened the bottle and poured the liquid into the glass. He, then, kept the glass on the side table and said, "But you must clear your bladder completely before you take this medicine. Please get up."

Shafi gave a helping hand to Sunita as she got up from the bed. She entered bathroom and closed the door from inside, unable to make out anything from his strange behaviour. Her dilemma was resolved when she saw a cover prominently displayed on the flush tank of the commode. It was a cover from Yogesh to her. She opened the cover and tears came to her eyes the moment she saw a letter in Yogesh's handwriting. She read the letter from top to bottom. All her questions were answered. Yogesh had written everything in detail about what happened at Sena Bhavan and how he managed to escape with the help of Colonel Bali and General Sehgal. He had written why he chose to go to Natasha's flat and how he got separated from her. Then he told her of his plans to reach Haridwar before 3 A.M. so that he could try to save the life of the Prime Minister. In the end he had suggested to her to somehow contact the Home Minister in person and inform him of the details of

'Operation Red Rose'.

"What are you still doing inside?" came the lady police officer's voice from outside the bathroom.

"Coming," said Sunita, as she cleaned her face and pulled the flush. She put the letter under her bra and came out of the bathroom.

"I am ready," she spoke to Shafi with a look of gratefulness. "You may give me the medicine and go, I will take care of myself as advised by you."

Shafi let out a smile and gave Sunita the glass containing the medicine. Sunita took a sip. She was grateful to him for offering her a drink of 7'UP. She was badly in need of a cold drink.

Sunita finished the drink and called, "Papa! Can you come in for a minute please?"

11.15 P.M.

"Nikhilesh, we'll have to do something about it," said Raman Kumar as he heard from him that Yogesh was, most probably, on his way to Haridwar. "We have gone so far into it that we just can't afford to withdraw at this stage."

"Then, what should we do?" asked Nikhilesh.

"I will speak to Sukhraj Malik and ask him to order a thorough checking of all vehicles leaving Delhi tonight," said Raman Kumar. "He will be made to understand that Yogesh is attempting to leave Delhi to save his life. But we just can't take any chances now. You will have to do one thing. Take some of your trusted men with you and be on your way to Haridwar. Ask Badri Prasad to help you get the right men. If you can get hold of the bastard, finish him. Otherwise, if need be, go after Prabhat Rai. He must go now. If the ISI man can get him, fine. Otherwise you shoot him. Take enough arms and ammunition with you. We will see what should be done to cover the tracks later. Take your official I-card with you so that no search is made of your vehicle on the way."

"Right uncle. I will be on my way soon."

"Please remember," said Raman Kumar. "You must give me a ring between four and five in the morning from Haridwar. Simply say 'Hello' three times. I'll get the message that the mission has been accomplished. Leave the rest to me. God willing, we will be the masters of the nation by tomorrow morning. Good luck!"

11.30 P.M.

"Please stop the bus. I have to go to the loo," shouted the old man.

The bus to Haridwar had covered about seventy kilometres since it left Delhi and had just crossed Meerut. It was the third time since Delhi that the old man had got the bus stopped. To Yogesh, the frustration of the delay bothered more than the irritation of giving a helping hand to the old man every time he had to ease himself. But he kept his cool.

"Blood sugar, my friend," said the old man as they got down from the bus. "I envy you. Very good health you have kept."

Yogesh didn't respond. The ritual over, they returned to their seats and the bus started again.

"How many children you have?" asked the old man.

Yogesh was lost in his thoughts when the question came."Children? None! I was married only last month."

"No children? Married only last month?"

Yogesh bit his lips. He had slipped again. "Yes, my friend he decided to continue the game. "I remained a bachelor till last month."

"Why?"

"You see, I loved a girl when I was in college."

"You went to college?"

"Yes. I fell in love with her. Her name was Sunita. She also loved me deeply. But we were both innocent, you know! A bit stupid, you may say. We were in love but we could never express our true feelings to each other. We lost contact after our college. She left with her parents to live in some other town. I remained in Delhi with my mother. I was sure that she would have married someone else. But I did not marry. I couldn't even dream of any other girl. I loved her so much. I decided to remain a bachelor forever."

"Very interesting," said the old man. "But then, why did you marry now?"

"Last month I happened to meet Sunita in some social gathering. We had met after fifty years. But I recognized her instantly. She had the same glow on her face, same spark in her eyes, and same magic in her gait. I asked her about her husband and her family. She told me she had remained unmarried like me."

"Oh! How very romantic!" gushed the old man.

"Well, my friend," Yogesh continued. "We knew that we could not afford to waste any more time. So we got married the same day."

"Tell me something about your wedding night," pleaded the old man lustily.

"Wedding night!" asked Yogesh. "It was a memorable night. We celebrated our wedding night in a beautifully decorated room in Hotel Hyatt Regency. She was great. She was gorgeous. She was absolutely breathtaking."

"How many times did you do it?" asked the old man, breathing hard.

"My friend, we continued our good morning till morning."

Yogesh suddenly recalled the joke of a caring father who had three grown up daughters. The father was very rich and wanted to find the most deserving bridegrooms for his daughters. He found three smart, strong and virile bridegrooms for his three daughters and had them married on the same day. To find out how manly his sons-in-law were, he directed each of his daughters to wish her morning greetings to him as many times as her husband made love to her on the wedding night.

The eldest daughter was the first to meet her eager father the next morning. 'Good morning dad! Good morning!' she said. 'Twice was not bad', thought the father.

Then came the second daughter who said, 'Good morning dad, good morning and really very good morning!' 'Three times was indeed very good,' the father concluded.

Then came the youngest daughter who looked tired and sleepy. 'Good morning till morning dad!' said the daughter while yawning.

Yogesh had begun to enjoy the conversation, despite the circumstances in which he was caught.

"Why didn't you bring your wife to Haridwar?" asked the old man.

"She met with an accident," replied Yogesh. The mention of the accident brought an abrupt end to his chain of thoughts.

"Accident?" asked the old man.

"Yes," Yogesh replied indifferently. "I am going to Haridwar to pray for her early recovery." He got up from his seat and walked to the driver's cabin. He did not want to answer any more of the queries of the old man. He knocked at the door. It was the conductor who opened the door.

"Excuse me," said Yogesh a he entered the cabin. "Driver, I will give you a reward of two hundred rupees if you can take us to Haridwar before 03.00 A.M."

The driver looked at Yogesh with a look of glee in his eyes. "I can take you there even before that provided your partner closes his leaking tap."

"I will ask him to exercise better control," said Yogesh.

"In that case, you keep two hundred rupees ready," said the driver as he pressed the accelerator hard.

Yogesh returned to his seat. He had no way of knowing that Nikhilesh had already left New Delhi in his Scorpio with three of his cronies. They had adequate quantity of arms and ammunition with them.

12.00 P.M.

General Surinder Pal was not happy when he got the message that the Home Minister wanted to see him immediately. Given his way, he would have put a bullet through the head of Sukhraj Malik. But he remembered the advice given by the Defence Minister. He must keep his cool till next morning. Since Sukhraj Malik was the seniormost minister present in New Delhi in the absence of the Prime Minister, the COAS decided to obey his orders and reached the Control Room as desired by him. The Police Commissioner and the Home Secretary were present there with the Home Minister.

"Good evening minister!" said the army chief. He did not feel like addressing him as 'sir'.

"Good evening General and welcome," said Sukhraj Malik as he got up from his chair and shook hands with him. General Surinder Pal shook hands with the two officers as well and took his seat.

"General," began the Home Minister, "you are aware of the day's developments. One young man tried to kill our Defence Minister and we have not been able to nab him yet. The Honourable Prime Minister spoke to me from Haridwar. He is annoyed that we have allowed the culprit to escape and has ordered me to take all steps to apprehend him. We have received information that this young man Yogesh Naqvi is trying to leave Delhi. We have directed the police on all roads leaving the capital to carry out a thorough check of all the vehicles leaving from here. We hope that they will be able to catch him soon."

General Surinder Pal kept a stoic silence. He was amazed at the cool performance being put forth by Sukhraj Malik. It was the case of Devil advocating the cause of Angel Gabriel, he thought. He was angry within but kept a straight face.

The Home Minister continued, "But I have just received reports that there is some movement of army troops on the streets of Delhi?"

So there it was! He was getting scared of being exposed. The General had ordered the troops deployed along the Pakistan border as well those stationed in Delhi to be in a state of readiness. He had calculated that he might receive orders from the President of India for Army help if and when Pakistan invaded India. He did not want to be seen failing in his duty.

"Yes," replied the General.

"But that is unauthorized move, General." said the Home Minister. "Besides, it is unnecessary. I agree that the attacker has escaped the police net on a couple of occasions but we are sure to get him soon. I do not think we require the assistance from the army in this simple case. You must withdraw the troops and order them back to the barracks. Any movement of the troops on the streets of Delhi might cause panic among the citizens of the city."

The General wanted to compliment Sukhraj Malik for putting up a very convincing reasoning. Coming from a man who had very nearly been cornered, it was indeed praiseworthy, he thought.

"I'll have to speak to the Defence Minister," said the army chief.

"Why Defence Minister?" asked Sukhraj Malik in surprise. "He is an injured man and needs complete rest."

The army chief gave a quick thought to what the Home Minister was telling him. 'It was already past midnight. Sukhraj Malik's game will be over within a few hours. So let him continue to weave a web around himself for some more time. Ultimately he would get entangled in the web of his own making and would not be able to come out of it.'

"Right minister," said the army chief as he got up to leave. "I will order the troops to confine themselves to the barracks for the time being."

00.30 A.M.

The bus reached Muzaffarnagar Bus Stand, still more than ninety kilometres short of Haridwar. Many passengers got down there to have refreshments. The driver appeared to have given up the race to Haridwar. After they left Meerut, the frequency of checking of passengers by the police increased many times. The bus was stopped by the police every ten kilometres or so and a search was made. Yogesh knew that they were looking for him. But the leaking tap of his friend in the adjoining seat came as a big help in keeping his identity hidden from the police. Whenever the police stopped the bus for checking, Yogesh would dutifully take his friend down and help him ease himself. The old man appreciated the care that his new found friend took of him. The police hardly gave a second look to the two old men so intimately attached to each other. The frequent search, however, resulted in slowing down the effective speed of the bus.

Yogesh also got down from the bus and looked around. He saw a family having refreshments inside their Maruti Esteem. One middle-aged man occupied the driver's seat. Next to him on the other seat was a middle-aged lady, obviously, his wife. On the rear seat were two young girls. One of them was about fifteen years old and the other about ten. Yogesh approached the car.

"Excuse me son!" he said.

"Yes grandpa!" responded the man affectionately.

"Son, where are you going?"

"We are going to Roorkee to attend a wedding there."

"Could you please give me lift up to Roorkee?" asked Yogesh. The mention of Roorkee reminded him of his uncle, Colonel Sanjay Sarang. The man in the car looked at his wife. "I have to see my uncle there, you see! He is very sick. I received the news in Delhi this evening. I am travelling in that bus. But it is moving too slow. I must see my uncle soon. I may not see him alive again, you see!"

"How old are you?" asked the younger girl in the back seat.

"Twenty-four," said Yogesh. All the members looked at each other in surprise. Yogesh again bit his lip. "I mean I was born in nineteen twenty four."

"That means you will be hundred years old a few years from now," said the older girl.

"That is right dear," said Yogesh with relief.

"And how old is your uncle?" asked the younger one.

"He is already a centenarian. He is hundred years plus," replied Yogesh. He had no other option but to lie.

"Hundred years plus? Incredible!" said the younger one again. "Papa please take him along. I have never seen a hundred years old man. I want to see his uncle, please! Won't you too, Kanu?"

"Yes papa," said the older girl. "Lipi is right. I would also love to see this hundred years old man."

Their father gave a laugh. "OK my sweet angels, if you so desire. So grandpa, please bring your baggage and hop into the back seat with the girls."

"I don't have any baggage son," replied Yogesh. "You see, I rushed to catch the bus when I got the message of my uncle's illness. It simply did not occur to me that I should carry some baggage with me."

"That is even better," said the man. "But you must promise to show your uncle to my daughters!"

"Sure! Sure! Why not?" said Yogesh, as he sat in the car. He began to worry about what he would do when they reached Roorkee. But he decided to take things as they came and not be unduly worried about the ensuing meeting of the girls with his uncle in Roorkee.

The car left Muzaffarnagar even as the passengers of the bus were still busy having refreshments. Yogesh felt sorry for his friend in the bus but had to leave him to his fate so that he could attend to the most important job of his life.

00.50 A.M.

"Yes, General Sehgal here," said the DGMI as he answered the phone.

"Good morning, sir! I am Major Chahal, Duty Officer from Sena Bhavan."

"Is it already morning Major?" asked General Sehgal as he blinked his eyes and looked at his watch. He had hardly slept for an hour.

"It is 0050 hours sir," came the reply.

"Yes Major Chahal. What is the emergency?"

"Sir sorry to disturb you at this odd hour. But I couldn't help it."

"Go on."

"Sir, I am on duty here since 2200 hours. When I reported for duty I was told by the relieved Duty Officer that one lady wife had reported that her husband had not reached home from Sena Bhavan in the evening. That lady wife has been giving me a ring every fifteen minutes or so ever since I joined duty. I have tried to pacify her saying that the officer might have been held up somewhere but she is becoming frantic and has threatened to come to Sena Bhavan if the whereabouts of the officer are not made known to her. I have checked up with the police already. But they have no information on his whereabouts, sir."

"What is the name of the officer?"

"Sir, he is Colonel S K Bali." The reference to Colonel Bali made the DGMI sit up. Major Chahal continued, "Sir, he works in your branch in the Army Headquarters. You must be knowing him?"

"Of course I know him. He is my 'Colonel Intelligence'. Have you checked up his room?"

"No sir, not yet. All the doors in Sena Bhavan are locked."

"The keys must be in the Duty Room?"

"Yes sir. But as per the SOP, I need your permission to open the rooms of the Int Branch."

"Permission granted," said the General. "Please keep me informed, whatever the hour."

"Thank you sir, I will do that."

01.10 A.M.

The police continued their search of all vehicles on all routes leaving Delhi for other towns. The car, in which Yogesh was travelling, had been stopped by police at four places so far. He had, however, hit upon a new trick to hoodwink the police. He began telling interesting stories and anecdotes to the two girls who seemed to enjoy them thoroughly. Yogesh was not aware of his talent to manufacture stories. The sombre atmosphere at home had curbed his natural ability to express himself in words. Whenever the policeman stopped the car, Yogesh would start telling the kids some new story. A perfect family, the policemen thought! A well to do man, a happy wife, two sweet children and an affectionate grandfather! The police waved the car to move on after carrying out a perfunctory eye check.

In between the stoppages, the car maintained a good speed. Yogesh began to hope that with luck, they might reach Roorkee by 2.15 A.M. and he and his uncle might make the remaining thirty kilometres to Haridwar before the Prime Minister arrived at Har Ki Pauri to offer his prayers. But at the fifth police checkpoint, he was in for a shock.

"Where are you coming from?" enquired an old police constable, with years of service behind him.

"Meerut," replied the man at the steering wheel.

"Where are you going?"

"Roorkee."

"Can I see your driving license?"

"Sure!" the man took out his purse, opened it and brought out his driving license. He handed it over to the police. The old constable returned the same after examining it carefully. He, then, peeped inside the car.

"Is she your wife?" he asked.

"Yes and these two girls at the back are my daughters," the man volunteered the additional information, anticipating the next question.

"And who is this old man, your father?"

"Oh no," replied the man. "He is just a co-passenger. He has taken a lift with us from Muzaffarnagar."

"You are coming from Muzaffarnagar?" the policeman addressed Yogesh.

"Uh.......... from Delhi actually," replied Yogesh with slight hesitation. He was tempted to say yes, but he soon remembered that the family in the car knew that he was coming from Delhi.

"Why have you taken lift in the car?" the policeman probed.

"I have to reach Roorkee you see, to see my old uncle. I was travelling in a bus but the bus moved too slowly. So at Muzaffarnagar I happened to meet this kind family and they agreed to give me lift in their car." Yogesh was beginning to feel a little jittery at the old policeman's insistence on thorough investigation.

The policeman viewed him suspiciously and asked, "You have some identification papers with you?"

"I don't think so," said Yogesh with difficulty. His heart began to sink. He knew that given another two minutes of questioning by the old policeman, he would find himself in police custody.

"You must be having your purse with you?"

"Not really." said Yogesh. "I don't carry a purse with me these days."

"You mind coming out of the car for a minute?"

There he was! Yogesh's brow began to sweat heavily. He knew that his disguise as an old man will not stand close scrutiny. He closed his eyes for a moment and felt like crying.

"What are you still doing there, you lazy old cop?" Yogesh heard a voice outside the car. He opened his eyes and saw a young Inspector hurrying towards the car.

"Sir I am questioning this old man here," replied the policeman.

The Inspector gave a quick look to Yogesh and turned to the old policeman. "Ram Kishan! You will never improve. That is why you have remained a constable all your life. You think Yogesh Naqvi has grown that old in one night? You have become senile now."

Constable Ram Kishan was used to the scolding. He did not say anything.

"I apologise to you sir on behalf of Ram Kishan and UP police," the Inspector addressed Yogesh, the old man. "He is getting old you know? Sorry to hold you up. You may please go."

"It is alright son," said a highly relieved Yogesh. "He is merely doing his duty. In old age we all tend to be a little fussy. Goodbye Inspector and good luck Ram Kishan!"

The old policeman continued to look wistfully at the speeding car.

01.15 A.M.

The phone rang again. General Sehgal picked up the phone. "General Sehgal here!"

"Excuse me sir, I am Major Chahal, the Duty Officer again."

"Yes Major! Could you check Colonel Bali's room?

"No sir. We have tried all the keys of the Int Branch but none of the keys is fitting the lock. I am sure the key is missing."

"That means the officer has taken the key with him?"

"Could be sir, but I suspect something wrong."

"Why?"

"Sir, I spotted some dried up blood just below the door of Colonel Bali's room."

"Are you sure?"

"I think it is blood sir, though I may be wrong."

"Major! You arrange some men to break open the door. I am coming to Sena Bhavan myself right away."

01.30 A.M.

The Home Minister continued to be present in the Control Room. He received reports on the search being carried out of all the vehicles leaving Delhi. Yogesh Naqvi had not been sighted by anybody.

"It is quite likely that he is still in Delhi," said the Police Commissioner.

"I also think so," said Ramachandran, the Home Secretary. "Otherwise he would have been found out by now. May be he changed his plans after being separated from that woman in police custody. What is her name?"

"Natasha!" The Police Commissioner gave the name.

"I think you are right Ramachandran," said Sukhraj Malik. "Most probably, Yogesh Naqvi is hiding somewhere in Delhi only."

"Precisely sir," said Ramachandran. He was not in the habit of staying awake late at night. He wanted to get back home soon and catch up with the lost sleep. But he dared not leave the control room as the Home Minister was still there.

"OK, then, gentlemen!" said the Home Minister finally. "I think there is no use of staying up here any more. Let some duty officer man the control room. The rest of us can call it a day."

"Right sir," said a relieved Home Secretary. "Good night sir!"

"It is good day Ramachandran," said the Home Minister with a smile and left.

The Home Secretary did not like the joke but kept quiet. He left the room hurriedly as soon as Sukhraj Malik left.

The Police Commissioner stayed on to give some parting instructions to his officers before leaving for home.

01.45 A.M.

Major Chahal was waiting for General Sehgal at gate number two of the Sena Bhavan. That gate was closer to the Duty Room on the ground floor.

"Could you arrange some men?" asked the General as he got down from his car.

"Yes sir," replied Major Chahal. "We have six jawans with us with some iron rods and a heck-saw."

"That is good. Let us go."

They took the lift to the eighth floor. General Sehgal hurried towards room number 818. Others followed him a few steps behind. He stopped in front of the door of Colonel Bali's room and looked below. He saw a dark spot.

"This was the spot I was referring to sir," said major Chahal. "It looks like dried up blood."

General Sehgal bent down and rubbed the spot with the thumb of his right hand. The spot was dry and it indeed looked like a bloodstain. He tried to look into the room through the keyhole. He could not see anything. The room was dark inside.

"Alright boys," said the DGMI. "On the job! Please break open the door as quickly as possible."

The six men went about their work in an orderly manner. They first tried to break the lock. But the inbuilt locking system was not easy to break. They tried to cut free the portion of the door that held the lock. They could not succeed in their attempt. Finally, they decided to break the door with the help of the iron rods. It took them some time but they succeeded in the end. Major Chahal entered the room first. He searched for the switchboard and switched on the light as soon as he found the switchboard. What he saw left him aghast. He stepped aside. General Sehgal entered the room and saw with a shocking disbelief the dead body of his colleague, slumped in the chair. A stream of dried up blood ran from the chair to the door.

General Sehgal moved slowly forward. He touched the face of Colonel Bali with both hands. The face was ice cold. He took his head in his hands and planted a warm kiss on his forehead. "Bali," he spoke with tears in his eyes. "Bali my friend! Your death will not go unavenged."

General Sehgal straightened himself and took out a handkerchief from his pocket. He wiped his tears and said, "I want to speak to Gyan Mehta, the Personal Secretary to the Defence Minister immediately." He trooped out of the room followed by a bewildered Major Chahal.

02.00 A.M.

The huge clock on top of the two-storeyed clock tower on the bathing ghat of Har Ki Pauri at Haridwar struck two. The assassin looked around from the parapet on the first storey balcony of the tower where he had taken position as planned. There was very little movement on the Har Ki Pauri. He looked at his rifle and adjusted its silencer. It was ready to shoot. He kept it aside.

There was one more hour to go.

02.15 A.M.

The car finally reached Roorkee. Yogesh looked at his watch. There was still enough time to reach Haridwar by 3 A.M, provided, his uncle was at home.

"Please stop here," said Yogesh. "This is the bungalow."

"This is an army bungalow," said the man at the steering wheel. "Does he live here?"

"Yes, he lives here," said Yogesh as he got down from the car. "My nephew, my uncle's grandson, is in the army. My uncle lives with him"

Yogesh opened the gate of the bungalow and briskly walked in, not knowing how he would handle the situation. But he felt relieved that he had made it to Roorkee very much in time and did not care much about what would happen in the meeting of his uncle with the kind family that gave him lift in their car. He pressed the doorbell.

"Who is there?" came a gruff voice from inside.

Yogesh thanked God that his uncle was at home. "Yogesh," he replied. He looked at the gate and saw the two girls running towards the house.

"Yogesh!" yelled his uncle when he opened the door and saw him standing in disguise outside. He did not need any explanation for his strange behaviour. He had seen it all on the T.V. "Please come inside."

Yogesh entered the room quickly, leaving his uncle to face the situation.

"Where is he?" shouted the younger girl when she saw Colonel Sanjay Sarang.

"Who?"

"That man's uncle?"

"I am his uncle."

"No, you are his nephew."

"Don't be silly. He is my nephew," said Colonel Sanjay Sarang with a straight face.

Just then the parents of the two girls also came there. Their father intervened, "Excuse me sir. My daughters want to see the hundred years old uncle of the man who came with us in the car."

"There is no hundred years old man living in this house," said Colonel Sanjay Sarang sternly. "I am his uncle and I am not hundred years old yet. God willing I will be hundred years old one day but for that you will have to wait for another fifty years. Now if you excuse me, I have to be with my nephew." He shut the door.

The two girls felt thoroughly disappointed as they walked back to the car.

The man and his wife wondered whether it was the old man who had taken a ride from them or it was they who were taken for a ride by the old man.

"Jaanu!" The wife suddenly called her husband as soon she sat in the car with her husband.

"Yes honey!"

"This old man had become a bit fidgety when that policeman was questioning him about his identity."

"So what?"

"Could he be the militant that the police is looking for?"

The man gave a quick thought to what his wife said. "Listen dear, whether he is a militant or a military man, I do not wish to see him again and I do not want to get involved in any police matter either. It is too much trouble. Let us just forget him."

02.20 A.M.

When Police Commissioner Bedi reached home, he looked quite fresh for a man who had spent the whole day in tension. He was not surprised when he saw the Chief Postmaster General waiting for him at his house.

"Hello Mathur!"

"Hello Bedi!"

"I believe you tried to contact me during the day also?"

"Yes I did. You know this boy Yogesh Naqvi. He is my son-in-law."

"Yeah, I know. I am sorry for you and your daughter. Didn't you verify his antecedents before marriage?"

"Bedi, Yogesh is innocent. He is such a nice boy, he can't hurt anybody. And now he is accused of trying to kill the Defence Minister of India?"

"You are mistaken my friend. Yogesh has had a troubled childhood. His father died when he was a kid. His mother couldn't give him proper care. He was a deprived child, you know! No wonder he grew up to be a jihadi and an ace criminal. An educated, sophisticated and respectable criminal. A new breed of criminals coming from respectable Muslim families. My officers have drawn his real profile."

"It is all wrong Bedi, it is all wrong," protested Mathur. "He is the son of an army officer who gave his life for the country. He is the son of a proud mother who gave him the love and affection of both parents."

"I am sorry if I hurt your feelings Mathur," said Bedi. "But I can't help you in this matter. It is beyond my control. The Prime Minister is taking lot of interest in this case and the Home Minister is personally monitoring the progress. I really can't do anything to save him, even if what you say is true.'

"Bedi, I have not come here to ask you to save Yogesh," said Mathur. "I have come here merely to request you to kindly spare a few minutes for my daughter, Sunita. She says that she knows some state secret of highly classified nature, which she must bring to the notice of the Home Minister very urgently. For that we need your help. You must listen to her for five minutes. I wanted to bring her with me but your chaps in my house won't let her move out. They are expecting that Yogesh will give her another call sometime soon."

"Can't it wait till tomorrow?" asked the Police Commissioner.

"Bedi, for old times sake my friend!" pleaded the Chief PMG. "Sunita says it is one meeting that you won't regret granting ever in your life. But it has to be now. Tomorrow may be too late. In fact it is already very late. I have been waiting for you more than two hours."

Bedi relented and said, "Alright Mathur, if you insist. Bring Sunita here and I will change in the meantime. Don't worry about the policemen on duty. I will convey to them my orders through the control room."

Mathur left his house without wasting any more time. He was with Sunita in less than five minutes. There was a distinct change in the behaviour of the police officers on duty. They stood up when they saw him coming. The lady police officer gave a helping hand to Sunita who walked with a limp because of the bandaged foot.

02.25 A.M.

General Surinder Pal looked at the two gentlemen in surprise when he met them at his house where they had arrived only minutes ago.

"General Sehgal, Mr. Mehta, what brings you here at this odd hour?" he asked, "I hope everything is alright?"

"Everything is not alright, sir," said General Sehgal "That is why we have come here."

"Why? What happened," asked the army chief as he settled down.

"Sir, Colonel S K Bali, my Colonel Int, who had received the message from Yogesh Naqvi, has been murdered," said the DGMI.

"Good God! When? How? Who did it?"

"He was shot dead in the evening," said Mehta. "Three bullets in his chest."

"Who shot him?" asked the army chief.

"Nikhilesh, the nephew of our Defence Minister," said Mehta.

"Good God, why should he kill him?" asked the army chief in bewilderment.

"He killed him because he suspected him to have helped Yogesh escape from Sena Bhavan," replied Mehta.

"But did Bali really help him escape?" asked the Chief.

"Yes sir," replied General Sehgal. "He helped him and I helped him too."

"Sehgal, what the hell are you talking about?" the army chief was about to lose his head.

"Sir, kindly permit me to tell you everything in detail," said General Sehgal.

02.30 A.M.

Bedi came out from his room wearing a nightgown when Sunita and her father entered the drawing room of his house.

"Namaste uncle!" said Sunita.

"Namaste Sunita," said Bedi. "How is your leg now?"

"It is alright uncle," Sunita replied as she sat down. "Uncle, I know that you and other people think that my husband is a terrorist. I won't ask you to change your views simply because he is my husband. I know that he is innocent but I have not come here to request you to save the life of my husband. Truth is with him and God will save him. But what I certainly want you to do is to take action to save this country. You do not know that the country is sitting on a time bomb, which is ready to explode within the next half an hour or so. I'll request you to kindly read this letter that my husband has somehow managed to send to me this evening. It will make clear to you why he has been branded a terrorist by the Defence Minister. We must bring its contents to the notice of the Home Minister immediately."

Sunita gave the letter to the Police Commissioner. She had taken it out of her bra when she was in car with her father. Bedi gave her a look of surprise and began to read the letter.

Sunita looked nervously at the wall clock.

02.35 A.M.

"Yogesh, I must carry a gun from the unit and take some ammunition as well," said Colonel Sanjay Sarang, as he started the Gypsy.

"You think it is required?" asked Yogesh trying to adjust the army cap on his head. He had removed the disguise and had put an army uniform as per the advice of his uncle.

"You never know," replied his uncle. "From what you have told me, it is clear that Raman Kumar is a dangerous adversary. He will go to any length to realize his ambition. We must go fully prepared. There might be some explanations tomorrow for unauthorized drawl of arms and ammunition. But to hell with it! Who has seen tomorrow?"

They went to the unit and Colonel Sanjay Sarang took one machine gun, about hundred rounds of ammunition and a bundle of jute rope. He signed the register for having collected the items.

"Why this rope uncle?" Yogesh asked.

"Standard battle equipment my boy," replied the Colonel as and Yogesh sat in the Gypsy. "You never know which item you may need."

Just when Yogesh and his uncle left Roorkee town in the army Gypsy, Nikhilesh and his gang entered it in their white Scorpio.

Nikhilesh looked at his watch and then pressed the accelerator even harder. He didn't want to be late for his date with destiny.

02.40 A.M.

"Sunita, from what you have told me and from what I have read in Yogesh's letter, it indeed appears that Raman Kumar is playing a dangerous game," said the Police Commissioner thoughtfully. "But it is a serious charge against a senior minister of our government. Before I speak to anybody else about it, I must verify the facts from at least one more source. So let me speak to General Sehgal, the DGMI, and hear what he has got to say on the subject."

"By all means uncle," said Sunita. "I am sure that General Sehgal would vouch for Yogesh's statement. But please do it fast. We are running out of time."

02.45 A.M.

"I had seen Nikhilesh and Mr. Mehta going to Colonel Bali's room and return empty handed," General Sehgal continued his explanation. "I thought Colonel Bali too had managed to get out of Sena Bhavan. But when I saw his dead body, I knew that he was killed by Nikhilesh. So I called Mr. Mehta and urged him to tell me the truth."

"Nikhilesh asked me to keep silent about Colonel Bali's fate for the time being," said Mehta. "At that time I believed that Yogesh was indeed a terrorist who had shot my minister and Colonel Bali had helped him escape. Out of loyalty towards the Raksha Mantri, I decided to keep my lips sealed. I was not aware of any message about the assassination plot. When General Sehgal told me about it, everything became crystal clear."

"So what do you make out of the whole affair?" asked General Surinder Pal, still trying to recover from the shock of the explosive information.

"It all fits in," said Mehta. "Yesterday when Yogesh Naqvi came to see the minister, he was not in his chamber. I asked him to wait there. The minister came in after ten minutes along with Nikhilesh. He asked me not to disturb him for some time. I thought that the two of them wanted to have some confidential conversation with Yogesh Naqvi. But after half an hour when the minister spoke to me, he was not even aware of Yogesh Naqvi's presence in his room. As Yogesh told Colonel Bali, he had hidden himself in the toilet and overheard their conversation. They decided to finish him off to silence him forever. That is how they embarked on this shootout mission. I tend to believe what Yogesh Naqvi told Colonel Bali. It must be Nikhilesh who shot the Defence Minister with his consent so that they could put the blame on Yogesh Naqvi and brand him a terrorist. Colonel Bali also had to pay the price for knowing too much."

"Good God," said the army chief. "How deceptive indeed the appearances are! All along I have been thinking that

Yogesh was a terrorist hired by the jihadis. But why didn't you tell me about it before, Sehgal?"

"Sir, now I realize that it was my mistake," replied the DGMI. "But nobody would have believed Colonel Bali at that time. By reasoning I too did not believe him, though, by instinct I did."

General Surinder Pal looked at his watch and said, "My God! The time is running out. We must do something fast."

Just then the phone rang. The army chief picked up the phone to answer.

"Yes, General Surinder Pal here."

"Good morning sir! I am Major Chahal, the Duty Officer from Sena Bhavan."

"Yes Chahal!"

"Sir! Sorry to disturb you. But is the DGMI with you sir?"

"Yes, he is here."

"Sir, Mr. Bedi, the Police Commissioner of Delhi wants to speak to him. He says it is national emergency."

"Yes, I know about it Chahal. Where is the Police Commissioner?"

"Sir, he is at his residence. His phone number is 2301-7800."

"Right Chahal. We will speak to him." General Surinder Pal dialled the Police Commissioner's number himself.

"Police Commissioner Bedi here," came the response.

"Commissioner! I am General Surinder Pal, Chief of the Army Staff this side."

"Yes, General! Any news?"

"Yes. My DGMI, General Sehgal, Mr. Mehta, PS to the Defence Minister, and I have been trying to put the various pieces together. It appears that Yogesh Naqvi is not the man, we should be after."

"It is Raman Kumar, the Defence Minister," the Police Commissioner cut him short.

"Good God! How do you know?"

"I have with me Mrs. Yogesh Naqvi and her father who is an old friend. They have with them a letter from Yogesh that makes it clear that rather than him, it is Raman Kumar and his nephew Nikhilesh who should be the fugitives, if at all."

"That is what we believe too," said the army chief, "But right now our first priority is to contact the right people in Haridwar and inform them of the danger to the Prime Minister's life."

"The right man to pass the instructions is the Home Minister," said the Police Commissioner. "You reach his residence and we'll reach there soon too. Meanwhile I will try to get in touch with the DG of Uttranchal Police in Dehradun."

"Right Commissioner," said the General. "See you at the Home Minister's residence and please make it in double quick time."

The Police commissioner dialled the Police Control Room from his mobile phone even as he called for his car and signalled Sunita and her father to move to the car.

"Hello! Control room! Please call DG Police Uttranchal and SP Haridwar and ask them to call me urgently on my mobile. Tell them that it is national emergency."

Having given his directions to the Control Room, Bedi dialled a local number as he sat in the car and asked the driver to take them to the Home Minister's residence.

"Hello! Is it the security officer?"

"Yes!" came response from the other side.

"Officer, this is the Police Commissioner here. I am coming to see the Home Minister at his residence. Please wake him up. National emergency!"

02.50 A.M.

The security officer at the residence of the Home Minister was taken by surprise when he saw the Police Commissioner Bedi getting out of his car, wearing a nightgown.

"He is Mathur the Chief PMG and she is Sunita, his daughter," said the Commissioner to the security officer. "They are with me." He hurried inside the house. Sunita followed him with assistance from her father.

The security officer was further taken aback when he saw General Surinder Pal get down from his car in a night suit. He recognized Mehta and General Sehgal and let them get into the house without questioning. He followed them into the house.

"Have you woken up the Home Minister?" The Police Commissioner asked the security officer.

"No sir," replied the officer. "The Home Minister does not like to be disturbed once he goes to sleep"

"You fool!" Bedi lost his cool. "I told you it was a national emergency! And a grave national emergency at that! Please go and wake him up now!"

The security officer could now make out that only a grave national emergency could make two senior officers to come dressed in that manner to the residence of the Home Minister at such an odd hour. He rushed to his bedroom and gave a knock.

Sukhraj Malik took his own time to open the door.

02.52 A.M.

Prime Minister Prabhat Rai and Swami Suryananda left the Circuit House by car to offer prayers at Har Ki Pauri. Two smart commandos occupied the front seat alongside the driver. Prabhat Rai and the Swami sat in the rear seat. The car was followed by a Gypsy in which sat a radio operator with his radio set through which he was on direct communication with Director SPG, who remained at the

Circuit House.

"Please drive slowly," said Swami Suryananda to the driver. "We have sufficient time with us."

02.54 A.M.

The assassin looked at the clock above. Prabhat Rai will be here in another five minutes or so, he calculated. He was sure of his shot. He believed that Prabhat Rai did not have more than ten minutes to live. He showed no sign of nervousness. For him, it was just another job.

02.55 A.M.

Sukhraj Malik entered the drawing room, still yawning. He looked at Sunita and the five gentlemen in surprise and asked, "What is this emergency?"

"Sir, we don't have much time left," said the Police Commissioner. "Kindly let me tell you in brief."

"No, not brief," said the Home Minister. He took another yawn and said, "Tell me in detail, whatever you have to tell."

"Right sir," said the Police Commissioner. "But sir do you have the PM's mobile number with you? His life is in danger."

"What?" shouted Sukhraj Malik.

Bedi began to tell the Home Minister the full details.

03.00 A.M.

Yogesh thought that their Gypsy was going at a breakneck speed and no other vehicle could overtake them. He was surprised, however, when a white Scorpio overtook them about ten kilometres short of Haridwar. The rear glass of the Scorpio was covered with a dark film and as a result, he could not see anyone inside the vehicle. On backside of the glass screen was a sticker showing a white horse in running stance. Below the horse was a caption that read, "Catch me, if you can."

Yogesh felt as if he had seen the sticker before. He scratched his head and soon remembered the white Scorpio that tried to run over him and Sunita.

"Uncle," he shouted. Colonel Sanjay Sarang looked at him in surprise. "Uncle, Nikhilesh, Raman Kumar's nephew."

"Where is he?" asked Colonel Sanjay Sarang.

"He is in that Scorpio."

"Are you sure?"

"I am positive. It is his Scorpio. Only he could drive a vehicle that fast on this night. He is following me. He might harm the Prime Minister. We must stop him."

Colonel Sarang did not take long to decide. "Give me my gun," he said. Yogesh picked up the gun from the rear seat.

"Load the magazine!"

"Where is the magazine?"

"It is lying on the rear seat."

Yogesh saw two black coloured steel objects, each about nine inches long and two inches wide. They must be the magazines, he guessed. He picked up one of them. It was open from one side and he could see some bullets stacked in it.

"Load it," said Colonel Sanjay Sarang.

"How?" asked Yogesh."

"You have not done NCC in college or school?" asked Colonel Sarang, trying to control his irritation.

"No uncle," replied Yogesh, feeling guilty. His uncle continued to concentrate on the Scorpio and followed it about twenty meters behind.

"You see that opening near the trigger?" he asked. "Put the mouth of the magazine there and push it in with a jerk"

Yogesh did as told. The magazine fitted nicely.

"Now cock it," said the colonel. "Just pull that knob near your right hand and then release it."

Yogesh cocked the gun and gave it to his uncle. Colonel Sarang took the gun in his right hand and controlled the steering wheel with his left hand. He moved the gun out of the window of the Gypsy and took aim at the Scorpio. Then he released the safety catch and pulled the trigger. The shot hit the rear glass screen of the Scorpio and made a shattering sound. The Scorpio swerved sideways for a short distance and then came to a halt. Colonel Sarang overtook the Scorpio and stopped the Gypsy about hundred meters ahead. He hurriedly collected the rope, the remaining ammunition and the second magazine from the rear seat and asked Yogesh, "You know driving?"

"Yes, uncle. But I have driving license only for a motorcycle."

"Never mind. You proceed to Har Ki Pauri and do your job. I have got people in the Scorpio to give me company." Just then a few shots from the Scorpio hit the rear of the Gypsy.

"Hurry up," said Colonel Sarang as he ran to take position by the side of a culvert.

Yogesh put the vehicle in gear and sped off.

03.03 A.M.

"My God Bedi!" said Sukhraj Malik as the Commissioner finished speaking. "No one ever told me that the Honourable Prime Minister was to visit Har Ki Pauri to offer his prayers. What is the time?"

"It is past 3 A.M. already, sir," said Sunita, getting impatient.

"But why the PM is not answering his mobile?" Sukhraj Malik had tried the Prime Minister's mobile few times but there was no response. He did not know that the Prime Minister had left his cell phone at the Circuit House. He did not want to be disturbed when he would be performing the yagna.

"Unfortunately we have not been able to contact even Uttranchal Police yet," said the Police Commissioner. "There are far too many drawbacks in our security drill."

"Balwant," shouted Malik when he saw his son-in-law enter the room. "Do you have Director SPG's number at Haridwar?"

"I think I have," replied Balwant.

"Please connect me to the Director SPG at Haridwar without delay? National emergency!"

03.05 A.M.

The assassin was happy with the vantage position that he had chosen. He had a clear view of the entire stretch of Har Ki Pauri and the area of car parking beyond it. There was hardly a soul at Har Ki Pauri at that unearthly hour. Most of the pilgrims were expected only after 4.00 A.M.

All of a sudden three Gypsies drove into the parking area. About a dozen men in safari suits got out of the three vehicles, holding walkie-talkie sets in their hands. The men, obviously body guards of the Prime Minister, soon dispersed along the Har Ki Pauri and took positions. The assassin knew that Prabhat Rai would be arriving any moment. He adjusted his rifle on the parapet of the balcony. He kept an eye on the parking area where the Prime Minister was likely to get down from his car.

Soon afterwards the assassin saw a white Ambassador car, with red beacon light on its top, pulling into the parking lot, followed by a Gypsy. The vehicles came to a halt.

The assassin took aim at the rear left door of the car.

The driver opened his door and came out of the car. He looked around but did not open any of the rear doors.

The assassin was confused. He looked at the Gypsy. There was no movement near the Gypsy either. He looked towards the main entrance of Har Ki Pauri. He saw Prabhat Rai and Swami Suryananda walk briskly towards the Laxmi Narayan

Temple that stood on the southern bank of the river Ganges.

The assassin did not know that they had decided to get down from the car a short distance behind so that they could enter Har Ki Pauri quietly, without being noticed. He took aim again but before he could take the shot, Prabhat Rai and Swami Suryananda had already gone inside the temple.

"Damn it!" the assassin muttered to himself. He would have to wait till Prabhat Rai finished his prayers in the temple and came out in the open to have dip in the holy water.

03.10 A.M.

Yogesh drove into the parking and saw the Ambassador car with the red beacon light on its top. He left the army Gypsy and ran towards the car.

"Has the Prime Minister arrived?" he asked the driver.

"It is not the Prime Minister's car," said the driver. He was under instructions to tell the curious onlookers that it was the car of some State Minister.

"Damn you!" said Yogesh as he ran towards Har Ki Pauri.

03.11 A.M

The Home Minister was finally able to get the Director of the SPG on the line.

"Dhillon, where the hell have you been?"

"Sir, I was here only."

"Has the Prime Minister left for Har Ki Pauri?"

Dhillon remained silent.

"Dammit, I know that he has to go there to offer his prayers, though you did not tell me anything about it."

"Sir those were my instructions." pleaded Dhillon.

"Has he left already?

"Yes sir. He has"

"Does he have adequate security with him?"

"Only two personal bodyguards, as desired by the PM."

"Can you contact them on top urgent basis? The life of the PM is in danger."

"What?" asked a shocked Dhillon. "Life of the PM in danger? Sir, please give me the details. I am through to the commandos on the radio in the Gypsy."

03.15 A.M.

Yogesh had reached the stairs of Har Ki Pauri and was running up and down the stairs looking for the Prime Minister who was nowhere to be seen.

"Listen soldier," a tall, smart looking man in Safari suit called Yogesh.

"Me?" asked Yogesh.

"Yes, you," said the man. "I have been watching you running here and there on the ghat for the last several minutes. What is your problem?"

"I am looking for the Prime Minister," said Yogesh.

The man pulled out a gun from under his shirt in a quick reflex action. "Who are you? Show me your Identity card," he asked and pointed the gun towards Yogesh from hip position.

Yogesh looked at him in surprise. "Sir, are you from the PM's security?" he asked with hope in his eyes.

"Yes," replied the man after a pause.

"Sir, I am not a soldier. My name is Yogesh. I have come all the way from Delhi to inform you that the life of the Prime Minister is in danger. I have information that there is someone hiding somewhere here who wants to assassinate him."

The commando looked inquisitively at the innocent looking young man. He knew from his experience that the young man was not pulling any prank. "Partner!" he called his colleagues over the walkie-talkie in a low but clear voice. "Enemy in range! Position unknown."

The other commandos also pulled out their guns. They all began eye search of all the vantage points along the ghat.

"Sir, where is our PM?" asked Yogesh.

"I can't tell you." replied the first commando.

Just then the radio operator from the Gypsy came running and shouted, "Enemy in range, position unknown."

"I know," said the first commando. "Give security cover to the Prime Minister."

The radio operator looked at him in surprise.

"Go!" shouted the commando.

The radio operator ran towards the temple. The commando gave a hard look to Yogesh.

"Sir, please trust me," pleaded Yogesh. "I love my country and I love our Prime Minister. I am ready to lay down my own life to save his."

"OK!" The commando relented. "You may go to the temple. Join the commandos there."

"Thank you!" said Yogesh as he began to move.

"Wait a minute!" shouted the first commando. He carried out a quick body search on Yogesh and found nothing. "Are you the man who is accused of shooting the Defence Minister?"

"Yes officer," replied Yogesh. "I have been implicated by Raman Kumar because I had found out that he had hatched a plot to assassinate the Prime Minister here at Haridwar tonight. Only God knows how I have managed to hoodwink the Police and my enemies to reach here. But please make sure that my efforts do not go waste. Let us save the life of the Prime Minister first. I will give you the full details later."

"OK. You go ahead. Don't let the Prime Minister come out of the temple till I give you a green signal. By the way, I am Major Chauhan."

"Right Major Chauhan," said Yogesh as he ran towards the Laxmi Narain Temple.

03.18 A.M.

The assassin was getting desperate. He kept looking at the temple door. He steadied himself when he saw the Swami coming out of the temple followed by Prabhat Rai just one step behind.

Major Chauhan noticed some movement behind the parapet of the first storey of the clock tower. He stood motionless and fixed his gaze at the spot where he had noticed the movement.

The assassin took aim but was distracted when a cop and an army man came in his line of fire. The two of them were persuading Prabhat Rai and Swami Suryananda to get back inside the temple.

The assassin watched all that with utter disbelief. 'The bastards have found out,' he said to himself. He could not afford to wait a second longer. He took aim at the door of the temple and pulled the trigger.

He did not have time to know that his bullet fell on the bed of the river Ganges because the fire burst from the gun of Major Chauhan had hit him on his head, microseconds before he pulled the trigger of his rifle, thus deflecting his shot.

"You be near the Prime Minister," shouted Major Chauhan to his colleagues as he ran across the bridge towards the clock tower. He opened the door of the clock tower and ran upstairs. When he reached the balcony on the first floor, he saw a frail looking young man lying dead in a pool of blood with rifle still held in his hand. He looked at his colleagues who were near the dazed Prime Minister and waived his hands in the air.

"Please have your holy bath sir," said one of commandos to the Prime Minister. Prabhat Rai said nothing. He rushed to the water and took a quick dip. He hurriedly walked back towards his car, followed by Swami Suryananda. Just when he sat in the car, the Prime Minister saw Major Chauhan who had rushed from the clock tower.

"What is all this Chauhan?" asked Prime Minister Prabhat Rai from his senior commando. "Who did you shoot and why?"

"Sir I think there has been an attempt on your life but you are safe because of that young man in military fatigues," replied the officer. "He is Yogesh Naqvi and it appears that he has been falsely implicated in shooting of the Defence Minster because he had found out the truth behind the plot of this attempt on your life."

Yogesh had left Har Ki Pauri and was walking back to the Gypsy. He thanked God for having saved the life of the Prime Minister.

"Can you call him here?" The Prime Minister asked the commando.

"Yes sir," replied Chauhan. "Mr. Yogesh! Please come here for a minute."

Yogesh reached the Prime Minster's car. "Good morning sir!"

"Good morning young man!" replied the Prime Minister. "You mind sitting with me in the car? I want to know the full details."

"I'll certainly tell you the full details sir but first I have to rush back to the Roorkee Road. My uncle, who is a Colonel in the army, is fighting a lonely battle with Nikhilesh who has been following me from Delhi so that he could stop me from reaching here and save your life."

"You sit with the Prime Minister, Yogesh," said Chauhan. "Leave the fighting to us. I will request the director through the radio to send help to your uncle. I assure you that the help will reach him before you reach there."

Yogesh sat with the Prime Minister in the car.

"Chauhan!" the Prime Minister called. "Keep me informed about the happenings on Roorkee Road."

"Yes sir," replied the Commando and ran to the Gypsy with the radio and sped off.

Not long thereafter the Prime Minister's car reached the Circuit House. The Prime Minister heard Yogesh in silence.

"Never before in my life have I been this wrong in judging a man," lamented Prabhat Rai after he had heard Yogesh. "I treated and trusted Raman Kumar like my own son. What a bloody fool I have been!"

03:25 AM

S. S. Dhillon entered the lounge of the Circuit House where the Prime Minister was sitting with Yogesh and Swami Suryananda.

"I am so sorry sir," Dhillon remonstrated with the Prime Minister. "I have failed in my duty."

"Not your fault Dhillon," Prabhat Rai consoled him. "The responsibility for the lapse in security lies squarely with me."

"But I still feel I should have been more assertive. Anyway! Sir, there is a message from Chauhan. Mr. Yogesh may proceed to Roorkee Road. It is safe now."

"He won't go alone Dhillon," said Prabhat Rai. "I will take him to his uncle."

They reached the site within ten minutes. About a dozen commandos were already there surrounding the Scorpio. Colonel Sarang was standing near the rear door of the Scorpio with gun in his hand and pride in his eyes.

Yogesh rushed out of the car. He saw his uncle and shouted, "Uncle, you got them?"

"Yes my boy," said Colonel Sanjay Sarang. "I got them. What about your side? Is the Prime Minister safe?"

"Yes, uncle," he replied.

"Mission accomplished. I am glad," said the Colonel. "Good morning Prime Minister, sir!" said Colonel Sarang when he saw Prabhat Rai and Swami Suryananda appraoach the Scorpio.

"Good morning officer," said the Prime Minister. "I hope you are alright!"

"Absolutely fine sir," said Colonel Sarang. "Couldn't be better. Just see, I have finished three of them, sir. They are lying dead there. The fourth one is here in the back of the Scorpio. Bloody traitors! They did not know that one fauji is good enough for many more like them."

Two commandos moved to the back of the Scorpio and opened the rear door. "Sir, he is here!" They told the Prime Minister.

Prime Minister Prabhat Rai and Swami Suryananda moved to the back of the Scorpio. They saw Nikhilesh lying on the floor of the Scorpio with his hand and feet tied with a rope.

"Sir, I ask for your forgiveness," Nikhilesh started pleading. "Whatever I did, I did it on behalf of Raman uncle."

"That does not lessen your crime," responded the Prime Minister. "Dhillon! Please take him into custody for full investigation." The Prime Minister gave his directions to the Director SPG.

"Just a minute sir!" Yogesh moved forward. "I want to ask him why he implicated me!"

"I didn't implicate you," replied Nikhilesh. "You were implicated by Neena, my girlfriend. She wanted to avenge herself for some slight you inflicted upon her in college."

"Neena? You mean, Neena Singh? My classmate from the KM College?"

"Yes. It was her planning."

"Oh my God!" sighed Yogesh as the realization hit him 'Hell hath no fury like a woman scorned', Yogesh remembered the old adage.

"I am amazed at your planning Nikhilesh!" Swami Suryananda joined the group. "But you do not know the power of yagna. My yagna had made sure that no harm would come to the Prime Minister."

Most of the bystanders were not so sure whether the Prime Minister was alive because of the yagna or whether it was the yagna that had very nearly cost him his life.

07.20 A.M.

Raman Kumar was getting desperate. He had not slept the whole night. He expected the call from Nikhilesh latest by 5 A.M. But the expected call did not come. He tuned in to various TV news channels, All India Radio, BBC and Radio Pakistan in turns. There was no news of any assassination at Haridwar. He was confined to his bedroom and had no means to know what exactly had happened at Haridwar. The anxiety, caused by the lack of information coupled with the shoulder pain and resultant sleeplessness, made him fell miserable. His bloodshot eyes and a day's stubble on his face made him look like a person who had returned from hell.

There was a knock on the door of his room. He rushed to open it, hoping that he would find Nikhilesh at the door. To his dismay, he found two commandos standing there. Before he could ask any question, they moved forward and began a body search on him.

"Can we come in Raman Kumar?" queried a voice from outside the door.

Raman Kumar looked up and was horrified to see Prime Minister Prabhat Rai and Home Minister Sukhraj Malik standing there. The commandos finished their search and moved aside. Raman Kumar kept looking at the Prime

Minister with disbelief. Prabhat Rai and Sukhraj Malik moved inside the room and proceeded to occupy the sofa lying in one corner.

"Let us have some talk Kumar!" said the Prime Minister.

Raman Kumar remained speechless. Slowly he moved forward and occupied one seat, his head bent down.

"Why did you do it Kumar?" asked the Prime Minister. Raman Kumar remained silent. "You thought MalikJi and I were adversaries and you could pit us against each other and finish both of us with the help of some enemy countries?"

"You did not realise that difference of opinion is an integral part of a democratic set up," said Sukhraj Malik. "We may have political differences but our loyalty to the nation, to the government and to the party is unquestionable. Rai Sahib was democratically elected the leader of the party and I accept him as my leader without any reservation. If I have to fight him, I will do so purely on a political platform. But you sold your soul to the enemy and launched a bloody and dangerous operation whereby you could have killed both Rai Sahib and me and usurped all power for yourself!"

"Individuals do not matter that much Raman Kumar," said Prabhat Rai. "Heavens are not going to fall if Prabhat Rai dies. But you tried to kill more than a few individuals. You tried to kill democracy in India. It has taken us all these decades to nourish and develop democratic ethos in this country and you attempted to destroy it with one stroke. I admit that there are still many shortcomings in our body politic. But democracy is not responsible for those maladies. A system is only as good or as bad as the people who run it. In any case, a system gets stabilised with the passage of time, provided one shows patience. Over the years, people of this country have achieved considerable maturity in grasping the essence of democracy. In the years to come they will become more mature and strengthen the roots of democracy. But you tried to uproot a plant that is still young and trying to establish its roots firmly in the minds of the people. For your misadventure and for your act of treason, you will have to face a public trial and undergo the punishment as ordered by law."

Raman Kumar raised his head and spoke in a feeble voice. "For the sake of the services rendered to the nation by me, can't I be forgiven and given a second chance?"

"No," said the Prime Minister firmly. "Your crime is too heinous to be even considered for mercy. You had very nearly succeeded in realising your dangerous ambition. The country would have been in turmoil by now but for the sincerity, dedication and doggedness shown by a young man, Yogesh Naqvi, who barely escaped with his life from your murderous plot. Salute to his courage!"

Raman Kumar looked at Prabhat Rai inquisitively.

"Your nephew Nikhilesh is in police custody at Haridwar," the Prime Minister continued. "He has told me everything about you and your plan to replace our system of government with a Chinese type system. He is singing like a bird."

Raman Kumar heaved a sigh and said, "What I attempted to do was only for the sake of this country. I wanted to bring a political system in India that suits us the best."

"You think the Chinese system of government is better than our system?" questioned Prabhat Rai. "I feel ashamed that I allowed myself to be fooled by the media to induct you into my council of ministers. You don't even have the wisdom to judge that democracy, with all its shortcomings remains the best political system anywhere in the world. Your elevation to the cabinet rank itself is a proof of my statement. What you see in China is what they want to show you. You do not know how many skeletons they have in their cupboards. That is why they cannot afford to be transparent. It is only democracy that can afford to give a transparent government. But more than that, the thing to remember is that China views us as their biggest rival in their global ambitions. They will do everything to destroy us and can never accept us as their equals. With gullible people like you, they might even succeed one day. But people like you will realise their folly only when everything has been destroyed."

"I thought I could use my capabilities in the service of the nation, though I may have been wrong in selecting my path," said Raman Kumar.

Prabhat Rai gave a faint smile and said, "Unbounded brilliance and unbridled ambition make a lethal combination. You, Raman Kumar, have this combination. It is dangerous. It is dangerous for you, it is dangerous for the government and, most importantly, it is dangerous for the country. This danger must go."

Raman Kumar remained silent for a few minutes. Prabhat Rai and Sukhraj Malik also kept silent. Finally, Raman Kumar took a deep breath and spoke, "Sir, a public trial will be very humiliating. Can't there be some other way out?"

"You suggest?" the Prime Minister queried.

"The other day," replied Raman Kumar, "I was reading a book on General Rommel. I was impressed by his life history."

Prabhat Rai looked at Sukhraj Malik. Both got up from their seats and began walking to the door. "Raman Kumar," said the Prime Minister, "the police will reach here in about ten minutes time. Be ready to go with them. Goodbye."

"Goodbye sir! And goodbye MalikJi," said Raman Kumar. "Wish you all the best!" Sukhraj Malik gave him a disdainful glance but said nothing. He followed the Prime Minister out of the room.

07.50 A.M.

T. Joseph came running out of his residential office when he saw the Prime Minister's car enter the driveway through the gate.

"Sir!" he shouted as he opened the door of the car. "I have just received a phone call from the Defence Minister's house that he has shot himself in his head."

"Really!" said the Prime Minister coolly and walked into the house.

07.55 A.M.

Police Commissioner Bedi decided to head the arrest party himself. He asked the police personnel to surround Badri Prasad's bungalow. There was no need to do so because when he entered the house of the DCP, he had already hanged himself from the ceiling fan in his bedroom.

08.00 A.M.

The news had spread like wildfire. Pronnoy Roy, the doyen of the TV journalism in India, was coordinating the coverage on his TV channel from the studio.

"Hello viewers! I wish I could say a very good morning to all of you as usual. But I am afraid; it is not a usual morning today. There has been an attempt on the life of Prime Minister Prabhat Rai at Haridwar in the early hours of this morning. Fortunately, he is safe. But the Defence Minister Raman Kumar has not been so fortunate. He is dead. What is even more shocking is the news that Raman Kumar has not died of yesterday's alleged attack on his life, nor has he been killed by anyone. He has committed suicide. He has committed suicide because it was found out that it was he who had hatched the plot to assassinate Prime Minister Prabhat Rai.

"Yesterday, an announcement was made on the television that a reward of fifty thousand rupees would be given to the person who gave any clue that would lead to the arrest of a young man named Yogesh Naqvi whose photo you are seeing now. The Police Commissioner of Delhi has informed that

Mr. Yogesh Naqvi has been exonerated of the charges of making attempt on the life of the Defence Minister and yesterday's announcement of reward for his capture stands withdrawn. A spokesman of the Prime Minister's office has stated that far from making any attempt on the Defence

Minister's life, Mr. Yogesh Naqvi showed an exemplary courage in unearthing and smashing a grave political conspiracy launched by some foreign countries with the help of Defence Minister Raman Kumar to destabilize the country. We will continue our coverage of this really big news during the day."

11:30 A.M. Islamabad

The chief of the ISI entered the office of the President of Pakistan. He had been called by the President to meet him immediately. He had left his meeting with S-6 and rushed to the office of the President, not knowing why he had been called. When he was in the corridor, he saw Malay Mishra leaving the President's chamber. Mishra was the India's Ambassador to Pakistan. The ISI chief was surprised to see the Indian Ambassador there. When he entered the chamber, he saw the President sitting with the Prime Minister and Foreign Minister of Pakistan.

"Salam-a-lekum," he wished the President and also gave a bow to the Foreign Minister.

"Val-ekul-salam!" replied the President. "Please sit down." The Chief took a chair.

"Chief," began, the President. He always addressed him as chief. "I have called you today to inform you that our efforts to build bridges of friendship with our neighbour, India, have suffered a severe setback. As you are aware, after many years of living like bitter foes, the political leaders in both countries had realized that peace, progress and prosperity in the sub-continent was possible only if we removed the wall of mistrust that divided us. We realized that we must learn to respect each other's sovereignty and live like brothers. Accordingly, both governments have been trying for the last few years to bring the two countries together. There are some people, however, on both sides of the border whose loyalties are not questionable but whose judgments are clouded by unfounded fears. They are out to wreck any peace moves initiated by the two governments.

A few weeks ago I arranged to send a bouquet of red roses to Prabhat Rai on completion of three years of his government. He has sent a message that red roses sent by me remind him of blood. I do not know who has given my roses the colour of blood. I wish I could make them give an all pervasive look and fragrance of friendship, trust and peace."

The chief understood what his President was trying to convey. He kept quiet for some time and then said, "I am beginning to realize that I have been wrong all along. Perhaps the path that you have chosen is indeed the right path. But I am an old fashioned man. It is too late for me to change myself completely. You will have my resignation on your table within half an hour. I will advise my men in the ISI to work in future only within the policy framework given by the government of Pakistan." Having said so he got up from his chair but before leaving the room, he spoke again. "Sir, I will pray to the Almighty Allah to help you and Prabhat Rai achieve what you have set out to achieve. Goodbye, sir."

General Ginai looked up towards the sky when he came out of the building. The sun was coming out from behind the clouds. Despite it being a hot summer day, the sun appeared to be smiling benevolently at him. The chief found himself smiling back at him.

For the first time in thirty-six years of his service, he seemed to be at peace with himse

Chapter 28

25 May

The office of Sonyog had opened after a fortnight. Sunita's wound had almost completely healed. Yogesh's mother, Sunita's parents and brother and Shafi had come to accompany Yogesh, Sunita and Natasha on the reopening of Sonyog. Natasha had come out of the shock of having to spend one night at the police station. Yogesh's feeling of sorrow for the loss of his new friend Colonel Bali, was overcome by the pride that his martyrdom gave him. The newspapers, magazines, radio and television had made him famous overnight. They extolled his act of bravery against heavy odds. They also said words of praise for Sunita, Natasha, Shafi and the two brave soldiers-Bali and Sarang.

"Back to work," said Natasha. "Remember we have to give a presentation to the M.D. of Sweet Drinks."

"We'll have to think of some brave new ideas to promote Cool Kit," said Yogesh.

"Brave new ideas gives me an idea," said Sunita. "Why not make use of Yogesh's celebrity status? Something like Cool Kit for Yogesh, Cool Kit for the brave."

"That is an excellent idea!" gushed Natasha.

"But why only me?" said Yogesh. "Why not you two as well? Something like Cool Kit for Sunita, Cool Kit for Etiquette."

"Uh! How cute?" Sunita chukled.

"Or Cool Kit for Natasha, Cool Kit for a fresh up."

"I like that!" Natasha giggled.

"What about me?" Shafi also got interested. "Make some slogan for me too!"

"Yes Shafi bhai." It was Sunita. "What do you say to ....What is there in coffee. Cool kit for Shafi!"

They all burst out laughing. Their laughter was interrupted when the door opened and two gentlemen walked in. One of them was in a Safari suit and the other in khadi kurta pyjama. Yogesh immediately recognized the man in the Safari suit. He was the commando whom he had met at Haridwar.

"Hello sir!" Yogesh said. "Welcome to Sonyog."

"Thank you," said the commando. "Meet Mr. Balwant Naik. He is the son-in-law of ...."

"Of the Home Minister," interjected Sunita laughingly. "We'll never forget him. We had misunderstood him completely."

"Never mind," said Balwant.

"Let me introduce," said Yogesh. "She is Sunita, my wife and this is Natasha, our dear friend, he is Shafi, another dear friend, my mother, Sunita's parents and her brother. And folks he is ....."

"Major Chauhan, hello everyone", the commando introduced himself.

"What would you like to have?" Yogesh asked his guests when they all sat down.

"A grand party," replied Major Chauhan.

"Why?" asked surprised Yogesh.

"Because I have got some great news for you," said Major Chauhan. "The Prime Minister has directed me to personally inform you that the Government of India has decided to confer some awards for the acts of bravery shown by you people. The awards are - Yogesh Naqvi-Ashok Chakra; Colonel Sanjay Sarang-Ashok Chakra; Mrs. Sunita Naqvi-Kirti Chakra; Colonel S.K. Bali-Kirti Chakra awarded posthumously and special commendation for Natasha and Shafi Rehman."

"That is great!" exclaimed Yogesh as he got up and hugged Sunita. He looked at Natasha and Shafi who were left speechless with surprise and happiness. Yogesh and Sunita put arms around their friends. Sunita's parents, brother and Yogesh's mother too joined them in their moment of pride.

"And I have come to make a deal with you on behalf of my party," said Balwant.

"What is it?" asked Yogesh.

"The elections to seven state assemblies are being held next month. Our party has decided to entrust its publicity campaign to Sonyog. Here is a cheque of twenty lakh rupees as an advance payment. Please get on the job right away!"

"I can't believe it!" exulted Yogesh.

"I can't believe it either!" shouted Sunita.

"Absolutely marvelous beginning to Sonyog," said Natasha with a soft smile. "With people like Sunita and Yogesh at the helm of its affairs, it deserved a dream beginning like that."

"And the Prime Minister has sent a special present for you," said Balwant. He opened the door and a man holding a bouquet of flowers walked in. Balwant took the bouquet from him and gave it to Sunita. She looked at the flowers.

It had about two dozen roses, half of them bright red and the other half sombre black.

"Oh, how thoughtful for him!" commented Sunita. "Red roses are beautiful."

"But to me black roses are more beautiful," said Yogesh.

They all burst out laughing.

Index